Documentation, libraries and archives: studies and research   4

Titles in the series *Unesco manuals for libraries*:

Titles in this series:

Planning national infrastructures for documentation, libraries and archives

Outline of a general policy

by J. H. d'Olier
and B. Delmas

The Unesco Press   Paris 1975

Published by the Unesco Press,
7 Place de Fontenoy, 75700 Paris
Printed by Imprimerie des Presses Universitaires de France,
Vendôme

ISBN 92–3–101144–8
French edition: 92–3–201144–1
Spanish edition: 92–3–301144–5

Preface

For some years past the governments of industrially developed countries and of developing countries alike have recognized the need for integrating plans for the development of documentation, libraries and archives services with the planning of economic and social development so as to enable all the groups in the community to have access to the information and documentation which are essential for decision-making, research work, studies and even for recreational reading.

To help identify and solve the problems involved in such planning, Unesco organized regional meetings of experts on the subject in Latin America (1966), Asia (1967), Africa (1970) and the Arab States (1974). It also included in its programme for 1973-74 the organization of an intergovernmental conference with the task of drawing conclusions of a general character from the recommendations of the regional meetings. In addition, Unesco had two studies made with a view to formulating a general policy of national planning of infrastructures for documentation, libraries and archives, taking into account the conclusions and recommendations of the regional meetings and the experience of countries at different levels of development.

These two studies have been brought together in the present volume, which consists of two parts. The first, prepared by J. H. d'Olier, Deputy Director of the Documentation Centre of the Centre National de la Recherche Scientifique (France), deals with the planning of infrastructures for documentation and libraries. The second, prepared by B. Delmas, Keeper of the Archives Nationales de France, for the International Council on Archives, relates to the planning of infrastructures for archives and is based partly on the findings of a group of experts which met in Paris in December 1972.

This volume is intended for governmental authorities responsible for national planning programmes, planning experts and documentalists, librarians and archivists who have the twofold task of giving opinions and advice on the planning of their respective services and of participating in the implementation of such plans.

The authors of these studies are responsible for the selection of the facts presented and for their interpretation. The opinions expressed are those of the authors and not necessarily those of Unesco. The designations employed and the presentation of the material in this volume do not imply the expression of any opinion whatsoever on the part of the Unesco Secretariat concerning the legal status of any country or territory, or of its authorities, or concerning the delimitations of its frontiers.

Contents

Appendixes

Documentation and libraries

by J. H. d'Olier

Deputy Director, Documentation Centre
of the Centre National
de la Recherche Scientifique (France)

Purpose of the study

1. Infrastructures for documentation and libraries must include institutions and services for documentation and libraries.
   The planning of a national infrastructure includes the planning of the following: (a) services; (b) organizational structure of the infrastructure; (c) interrelations between institutions; (d) international relations and co-operation; (e) manpower, equipment, supplies, methods, financial resources required for the functioning of the infrastructure.
2. The study should establish the general principles of planning policy and explain in detail the methodology of planning.
3. The study should take into account the experience of countries at different levels of development and provide material for the working papers which were submitted to the Intergovernmental Conference on the Planning of National Infrastructures for Documentation, Libraries and Archives, held in 1974.
4. The study should take into consideration the recommendations of the regional meetings of experts on planning which took place in Latin America (1966), Asia (1967) and in Africa (1970). It is desirable to point out, however, that these meetings did not deal systematically with problems relating to the planning of documentation services; special attention should therefore be given to the latter.

I   Information and development

Exchanges of scientific and technical information have played
a leading part in the historical development of the industrial
societies, by making possible discoveries, the application of techniques, the criticism of scientific findings and the gradual working
out of new theories. Advances in knowledge are the result of the
two-way flow of information between scientists, or between scientists and engineers, or again between the latter and all those who
are potentially capable of benefiting from such advances or of
putting them to use.

1.1   Information circuits according to the various stages of development

Thus three major information circuits become apparent, the relative importance of which naturally varies according to the stage of
development and the cultural level of those between whom the
information is conveyed.

1.1.1   EXCHANGES BETWEEN RESEARCHERS

At the top are the exchanges between scientists who constitute the
spearhead of research. Here the information is highly specialized,
divided up between a large number of very detailed documents
or elements, often very precise in their content but strictly confined

to the specific field covered. This information, which is essential to specialists in the field concerned, is in the main only really used and sought by a limited group of scientists. When advances in knowledge are swift, which is often the case, or when the situation with regard to research changes rapidly, the urgency of documentation becomes particularly marked. For there is a sort of rivalry between the various research teams working on the subjects in question and at the same time a need to avoid avenues already too thoroughly explored, so as not to do again what has already been done elsewhere, except with a view to criticizing or checking it. Obviously, this kind of information, the essence of which is exchanged at congresses through direct contacts between researchers, chiefly concerns countries which have reached a very high level of development and possess well-equipped research laboratories. In most cases fundamental research is costly and, at the present stage of industrial societies, applications are remote. While it is true that the lapse of time required before a particular finding of basic research can be applied is becoming shorter and shorter, the means which must be brought into play in every respect are much greater than they were in the past and, consequently, are only within the reach of those possessing a considerable human and material capital.

I.I.2   NEEDS OF EDUCATION (LECTURES, BOOKS, JOURNALS OFFERING A CONSPECTUS OF GIVEN SUBJECTS)

However, this type of research is often connected with the teaching of science because the persons concerned are in many cases university teachers, those who are in fact capable of preparing the members of the younger generation for new ways of thinking and introducing them to the scientific world of the future. Teaching must bear on the future, and the future of technology and development is the present of fundamental research.

So a second circuit in the distribution of information comes into view: exchanges between teachers and students. Not all students will become researchers or teachers. It is even desirable that only a very small minority should do so. But they all need to receive a basic training which will enable them subsequently to assimilate

new techniques when they attend courses for the updating of
their knowledge or as they advance in their careers. Among the
necessary tools, three main ones are evident:

Lectures (available in France in mimeographed form), which are
the result of a rather special dialogue between a group of
students and its teachers. Such lectures are as a rule of a very
localized interest, being designed for a particular group of
students at a certain stage in their education and corresponding
to this or that teacher's particular method of teaching.

Scientific books, much more elaborated and much more general
in scope, designed for a body of students and teachers as a
reliable and methodical teaching tool. A good book gives a
comprehensive account of what has been done in a particular
branch and so becomes a first-rate work of reference. These
books are published and sold commercially. Unfortunately their
high cost limits their distribution. Books have always been
regarded as essential in secondary education, and there the cost
can be offset by large printings. Today the number of students,
on the increase in all countries, is of about the same size as was
the number of secondary-school pupils only fifty years ago.
Specialization has been taken further, of course, and the subjects
are more varied than the traditional secondary-school subjects,
but a rational policy with regard to scientific and technical
books could lead to a considerable development of this kind of
document. Hitherto, only the United States of America and the
Union of Soviet Socialist Republics have been in a position to
publish these works systematically in an economic fashion. The
way is now open to many other countries.

Lastly, journals offering a conspectus of given subjects are very
much read by advanced students in some countries at the stage
where individual creative work begins to supersede the accumulation of knowledge and the training of the intellect.

This form of documentation is also necessary in all countries,
irrespective of their degree of development, but it is designed solely
for that part of the population which has reached a high level of
education. Here, then, the principal parameter is the number of
students and teachers in each special branch of learning. If this
community is too small, an independent effort will not be warranted; it will be necessary to join with others in groups, according
to geographical region or linguistic area. A book cannot be sold

cheaply if fewer than 5,000 copies are printed; the same applies to a journal. Below this figure, distribution is confined to libraries and collective bodies such as readers' clubs, faculties, laboratories. The price then goes up and this restricts printings still further.

Moreover, the subjects dealt with in these documents should be very directly related to the preoccupations peculiar to the country or group of countries for which they are intended. Here it is not the stage of development which matters, but the nature of the national or regional resources, the particular aptitudes of the populations, their traditions, the geographical situation, etc.

1.1.3   INTERSECTORAL AND TECHNICAL INFORMATION

So far we have considered exchanges of information within a specific sector, but one of the essential components of development derives, as is well known, from the bringing into play of intersectoral relations: knowledge of scientific information by scientists in other branches, use of fundamental research findings by engineers and technologists and, conversely, use of recent technological innovations by researchers or by engineers in other special branches. By engineers and technologists we mean here not only those working in the traditional sectors, such as chemistry, transport, electricity or building, but also medical practitioners and hospital physicians, farmers, data processing specialists, linguists, social-welfare workers, management consultants, planners, economists, etc.

This information circuit is understandably one of the most fundamental for development. It is also the most difficult to plan, because the information comprised in it is intermingled in a highly complex way. It comes from very diverse sources, through very diverse channels. As an example we might mention the commercial/technical documents and the instructions for use or maintenance which suppliers of technical equipment or chemical products distribute among their customers.[1] This channel is very

1. James Brian Quinn, 'Scientific and technical strategy at the national and major enterprise level', *The role of science and technology in economic development*, Paris, Unesco, 1970, 216 p. (Science policy studies and documents, 18.)

different from the means by which documentation centres try to give engineers access to research findings. Its importance should not, however, be underestimated, for it contributes in no small way to enabling technologists to keep up to date and through it a considerable proportion of important information is conveyed. Unfortunately, this is always more or less biased and is designed to associate the customer with the products of this or that supplier.

Compared with this channel, that of scientific journals and technological journals is much less suited to the manifest needs of engineers in all countries, but more particularly in the developing countries; for, although containing valuable information, this documentation is not usually adapted to the needs of users. It is presented in bulk and does not seek to impose a particular point of view. But for this very reason the documentation is difficult to assimilate in its original form. It must first be processed if what is relevant to a particular subject or centre of interest is to be correctly selected from the mass of documentation. That is the job of libraries and documentation centres.

However, this is still not enough; there must be teams of researchers working in the field concerned and interested in identifying the essential points which should be brought to the knowledge of the authorities or of production engineers. Failing this, or to supplement it, the need arises to have information-analysis centres able to form a link between the documentation presented in bulk which is going around the world and the specific needs of the group or groups of users for which it is intended.

We thus have three levels: (a) the libraries holding the documents; (b) the documentation centres equipped to sort them and prepare for their channelling and selection; (c) the information-analysis centres, sometimes an integral part of the laboratories, capable of carrying out the necessary selection and giving the right emphasis.

It is by means of these that a specialist can be kept informed of what is of interest to him in other special branches. It is also by means of these that engineers and technicians can be kept informed of advances made in other technologies and of the latest findings of research. Naturally, these three levels have always existed and they are still in many cases more or less implicit; but, with the proliferation of documents which complicates the task of the information specialist, it becomes increasingly desirable to draw attention to them, even if institutions patterned on them are not contemplated.

Reverting to the example of the information conveyed from supplier to customer, we note that these levels are to be found in the technical and commercial activities of big firms, whose research departments and technical services collect and stock the documents after making an initial selection and adaptation in the light of the firm's needs. The material is then processed and a second selection is made with the customer in view, and the information is finally presented for his use in readily assimilable form.

We have already said that such information is too partial, even if it comes from a number of different suppliers, but it must be admitted that any channel of information is partial: exhaustiveness is very costly. Moreover, scientific and technical journals do not contain everything, as we know, for certain information is protected by patents or by secrets of manufacture. In so far as technology is concerned, patents have to be included in any documentation network. Secrets of manufacture are obviously not accessible, but some aspects of them filter through the technical/commercial documents published by firms, so that it is often worth while to take this literature into account, if only as background material.

According to the various stages of development, the difficulty is clearly to estimate the profitability of circuits of this type, especially as linguistic problems arise in a much more acute form here than in connexion with pure science. In all the countries of the world distinguished scientists are highly cultured and are familiar with one or two foreign languages. In practice, this solves three-quarters of the difficulties of communication due to the use of different languages.

The same does not apply in the case of engineers and technicians; the latter seem to be somewhat shaky when it comes to expressing themselves properly even in their mother tongue. So we are faced with the problem of documents written in a variety of languages, and also with that of a public which undoubtedly has difficulty in reading anything which is not presented in an easily understandable form.

The major developed countries possess vast libraries, documentation centres and information-analysis centres. In fact, this applies almost solely to the United States and the U.S.S.R., which have reached an advanced stage of development and have to inform a very large population of users.

The problem already arises in the case of the medium-sized developed countries. To what extent can they take advantage of what has been done in the United States and the U.S.S.R.? What part or parts of these information circuits ought they to possess themselves? How should this be organized at national level? Is it worth while for some of them to combine so as to reach a wider public of readers and users, even at the risk of being inconvenienced by linguistic problems? These are, of course, the questions which countries belonging to institutions such as the Council for Mutual Economic Assistance (COMECON) or the Common Market are pondering.

At international level, after a costly experiment in the nuclear sector, the UNISIST conference did not find it reasonable to set up a central body for the dissemination of information. On the other hand, UNISIST aims to unite the efforts of all the countries and, through continuing co-operation, to give them the means of turning to account a world information network as well organized as possible.

The place of each of the developing countries within such a network deserves careful study, as also the advantages which might result from regional grouping or from grouping according to the principal language areas. As this task is too vast to be undertaken all at once, priorities will have to be recommended, depending on various parameters, some of which are as follows: population of the country; population of the neighbouring countries and existence of any agreements for cultural or economic co-operation; literacy and school enrolment percentages; number of students; number of researchers, engineers and technicians; principal economic and cultural activities; development prospects; natural resources; situation of small business, of arts and crafts and trades, and of agriculture; relations between the universities and economic activity; situation in regard to adult education and lifelong education.

For, while it is true that exchanges of information constitute a powerful factor in development, they are really profitable only in a technical and cultural context that is already evolved. However, the setting up of information and library networks or systems can only be a gradual process, and while they are being set up the situation will change considerably. Thousands of students will have become engineers or researchers with an imperative need to keep abreast of current developments in technology to enable them to successfully carry out any constructive work. Others will themselves have become teachers able to train staff while introducing them to the latest discoveries. An even larger proportion of secondary-school pupils will go on to higher education.

All these changes, which will no doubt have considerable consequences, are going to occur in the space of a few years in most of the developing countries. It would be advisable not to wait until they have happened and until the need has become desperate before beginning to set up the requisite information networks and libraries.

1.1.4   PUBLIC INFORMATION. LIBRARIES

Progress, which we too often tend to attribute to the achievements of a few brilliant teams, derives in fact from the resolve and competence of a whole population. Culture and science must therefore be distributed universally. It is only an educated people kept properly informed of new advances which will produce the architects of development. What is more, the latter will be powerless without the help of very large sectors of the population able to understand the mechanisms of development and to take an active part in it. The two instruments which supplement the work of education to this end are, on the one hand, libraries with the resultant dissemination of books and, on the other, information designed for the popularization of knowledge, which is provided through books, journals and the audio-visual media.

While literary culture is capable of improving the quality of life, it is at the same time the most powerful medium of lifelong education. It is through reading and writing that we become able to express ourselves, and if reading is not a pleasure we read very little. If we are not in the habit of reading a great deal, we write very little. Unfortunately books in themselves do not attract us *a priori* unless we have been given some idea of their contents, enough to incite us to read them, and unless, too, they are readily accessible. In Europe and North America, libraries have historically played a prominent part in this respect, but many other factors—political, social and religious—have contributed to the rapid development of literature and to the quality of the expression of thought. Today circumstances have changed. In the developed countries, a very strong cultural tradition underlies a powerful book and newspaper industry, which has at its disposal considerable resources for advertising and can put into circulation vast quantities of cheap books (one volume costing less than the hourly wage of an unskilled worker). In addition, readers' clubs and circulating libraries have been organized everywhere, on the initiative of private or semi-public bodies. Not only are books read and exchanged but their contents are discussed.

Municipal and national libraries play an active part in this movement (open to the public, bookmobiles, etc.). They also serve as depositaries where all written works are preserved and where consequently what is not available in the bookshops can be consulted. It was thought at one time that, with the advent of audio-visual techniques, reading would decline and these techniques would compete with the printing trade. This has not happened: the consumption of paper has broken all records and, among the various branches of the economy, this sector has one of the highest rates of expansion. Contrary to expectation, television is abundantly used to introduce books and to make known newspapers and periodicals.

In the developing countries there is, unfortunately, no such deep-rooted tradition of book culture, so that reading will have to be encouraged by energetic governmental measures and appropriate publicity. In the libraries, the role of conservation and reference, so necessary in Europe, will have increasingly to give way to a supremely important endeavour for book promotion. Reading associations based on municipal or local libraries might well deserve careful consideration in the light of the country's organization and way of life.

The size of the funds to be devoted to libraries is very directly dependent on the setting up of these associations, for, as books and periodicals are costly to acquire, full use must be made of them. Lending libraries may give rise to certain problems, however, due to the fact that the books borrowed are not always returned. The literacy rate is of course a primary factor in deciding whether such libraries are worth while and in selecting books to be acquired. However, it is not the present literacy rate which should be taken into account, but the expected rate five years hence, since any library programme will, as we shall see, require about that length of time to become effective.

Popularization is another aspect of culture for the masses. It depends partly on libraries holding scientific or technical books and periodicals and partly on films and television. It has a great deal in common with lifelong education, but a distinction should be made according to the level of development and the type of activity.

In the highly developed countries, for many technicians and engineers working on very specific subjects, often difficult or tedious, popularization is a form of relaxation. It brings them relief from their everyday cares while stimulating their intellectual curiosity. It is a pastime indulged in for no other purpose than the satisfaction of cultivating the mind and maintaining a sound balance. In point of fact, readers almost unwittingly gain in this way a great deal of knowledge which is of use to the future of their profession. The principal motivation remains none the less leisure-time enjoyment, and so the means employed are in keeping with this aim: periodicals of this type are as attractively presented as possible, with excellent photographs or art engravings designed to appeal to the mind or awaken the imagination.

In contrast, there are the needs of persons who seek to use all their spare time for the rapid improvement of their social position or for the development of their professional activity. Naturally, cases of this kind are met with not only in the developing countries but also in the most advanced countries, among farmers, fishermen, craftsmen, tradesmen, and increasingly among industrial workers. The means required to meet these needs are as a rule more specialized and consequently more varied. While television and films play a prominent part in drawing attention to and disseminating certain basic information, they soon prove unfit to play the part of educator or popularizer for the purposes of direct professional application. On the other hand, they may constitute an incitement, an introduction calculated to produce a motivation.

By far the most widely used medium for the achievement of the principal aim mentioned above is still the printed work, whether in the form of books, periodicals or other documents. For instance, many ordinary newspapers intended for rural communities include a considerable amount of material of occupational interest. The same applies to periodicals for groups or associations which strive to keep their members up to date on their profession and its techniques. A great many users of such documents have little money to spend and require more and more specialized information as they progress. Libraries therefore constitute the chief, if not the only, source of information capable of meeting their needs.

Although in a number of developed countries a fairly large fraction of the population begins frequenting libraries in childhood, it is well to note that, faced with an ill-defined and poorly stated technical or occupational problem, the potential reader is induced to consult a library only following a fairly long and laborious psychological process.

The earlier stages, in which his mind should be stimulated and his enthusiasm aroused for learning more about a fairly specific subject, are essential; these are: general popularization (for example, by means of television), a trade paper, a journal treating a subject in popular form, an introductory work in which he finds useful information, discussions with colleagues, etc. A potential reader, plunged straight away into the atmosphere of a library, even if he is pleasantly guided by competent staff, is liable not to find what he wants and not to be strongly enough motivated to keep up for long the effort required for turning his visits to account.

Furthermore, to assist understanding and sustain interest, libraries will be led to have more and more documents in audio-visual form for individual or group use. A specialized film is often a more effective teaching tool than a book during the phase of initiation, which may be long.

Here we come upon the idea of the learning society mentioned in the report[1] of the commission presided over by Edgar Faure. Irrespective of the level of development, continuous training is imperative in the modern world. Libraries have an essential contribution to make in this respect and they must prepare for it. The socio-cultural environment, the socio-professional climate, the mass-media of communication will imperceptibly lead a growing number of people towards reading and study, and consequently towards libraries. The latter, for their part, are rapidly organizing themselves to meet the new demand as it should be met, to welcome the visitor, to present their store of knowledge attractively, effectively and completely, while at the same time seeking to provide

1. Edgar Faure *et al.*, *Learning to be*, Paris, Unesco; London, Harrap, 1972, 313 p.

a service of true merit at minimal cost. They are already and will become still more so, the principal centres for the dissemination of knowledge and culture.

1.2   The essential supports for the communication of information

1.2.1   MEANS OF PRINTING

Not much is said about typography in librarianship or documentation. It is thought of as an art which has long since reached its peak, and the production of printed matter is regarded as no longer posing any problem. It is true that for a long time books were read mainly by an élite. It is also true that since the invention of printing book prices have come down so far that they scarcely affect the market of potential readers, representing in all cases a very small item in the reader's budget. As more and more people became literate, book prices naturally decreased with the increase in the number of copies per printing.

Around the middle of the last century the penny newspaper appeared, and around the middle of our own century the pocketbook won an unprecedented success simply by applying existing printing techniques to the needs of new markets. So the situation appears in a very favourable light when there is a large reading public or when readers have a high enough purchasing power. This latter point is worth mentioning, for it plays an important part in the dissemination of culture.

The cost of printing is almost independent of the number of copies printed, amounting to a sum in the region of U.S.$0.004 per character, so the cost of a book totalling 1 million characters (or one or more numbers of a periodical of the same length) is as shown in Table 1.

These prices are not selling prices, for up to two-thirds of the costs of periodicals and newspapers are defrayed by advertising. On the other hand, the following costs have to be included for all kinds of printed material: (a) the cost of printing, in proportion to the

TABLE 1. Price of printing a book with 1 million characters
(figures are approximate)

Kind of document	Number of copies	Unit cost of impression per volume (U.S.$)
Thesis, report	100	40
Specialized document, scientific or technical book	1,000	4
Dictionary, technical review	10,000	0.4
Popular science magazine, best seller, pocket book, weekly newspaper, daily newspaper	100,000 over	The cost of printing becomes small by comparison with the other costs

number of copies, which depends mainly on the quality of the paper and the standard of workmanship; (b) copyright; (c) transport and distribution costs.

In many cases, the latter double the costs of printing and circulation. Taxes must also be added in some cases. Furthermore, even a best seller will have to bear considerable distribution and transport costs, which may double or treble the normal price, if it has to be dispatched for distribution to a region where only a small number of copies can be sold.

If we compare the figures (see Table 2) for the consumption of printed paper, leaving aside for this very rough approximation the exchange of books and newspapers, we shall see the situation as regards the production of printed matter per inhabitant according to the various levels of development. We have tried to establish a relationship between the number of printed characters and the weight of the paper, assuming that a kilogram of paper contains 3 million characters (double that number in the case of newsprint). For each of the paper consumption figures we have added an adjustment coefficient to allow for advertising (unread), wastage and paper used for other purposes (typing, etc.).

In the case of the poorest countries the coefficient 1 allows for the fact that many publications will be read several times, which compensates for the other grounds on which figures are reduced.

Let us take as a minimal basis the figure of 1 million characters per educated inhabitant. If we want to keep the cost of printing down to a level permitting of mass distribution, we must reach a

TABLE 2

Type of country GNP *per capita*	Consumption of printed paper *per capita*			Consumption of newsprint *per capita*			Number of television sets per 100 inhabitants
	kg	coef-ficient	charac-ters (millions)	kg	coef-ficient	charac-ters (millions)	
Very high (North America)	30–50	0.2	20–30	30–50	0.2	30–50	40–50
High (Western Europe, Australia, New Zealand)	15–30	0.2	10–20	15–20	0.3	35–40	15–30
Average (certain Mediterranean countries, Eastern Europe, U.S.S.R., Latin America)	3–7	0.5	5–10	3–5	1	10–25	5–15
Average (countries developing rapidly, Japan, Israel)	10–30	0.2	10–20	10–15	1	15–30	10–25
Low (Asia, Africa, Latin America)	0.5–5	0.5–1	1–10	1–4	1	3–10	1–10
Low (Africa, Asia)	0.1–1	0.5–1	0.1–1	0.1–1	1	0.3–3	0.1–1

circulation of about 100,000 copies. It is evident, then, that the size of the cultural area in which the books or periodicals can be distributed is of fundamental importance.

By 'title' we mean a current periodical, a textbook or a pocket-book, etc. In Table 3 we have assumed that the smaller the number of potential readers, the less diversified the culture would be. This means that in relatively small cultural areas where people read little, all that can be offered at a reasonable price is books or periodicals for which the maximum distribution is sought. Works with only average printings and specialized works, on the contrary, will be few and far between.

In highly developed countries, however, cultural areas with populations of 10 million and even less can be offered a much wider variety of reading matter. Here works with a large cir-

TABLE 3

Size of the population of cultural area (millions of inhabitants)	Average number of characters per inhabitant per year	Number of characters read per year in the cultural area (thousands of millions)	Proportion constituted by widely distributed books or periodicals (%)	Number of titles of works each consisting of 300,000 characters and reaching a printing of 100,000 copies
5	0.2	1,000	50	15
50	0.2	10,000	50	150
5	1	5,000	50	75
200	0.5	100,000	50	1,500
50	1	50,000	50	750
10	20	200,000	10	600
50	20	1,000,000	5	1,500

culation account for only 10 per cent of the total, that is, much less than 10 per cent of the number of titles published.

Despite this concentration it seems highly desirable to reach the point where at least sixty titles of widely distributed works are published annually, or several widely distributed periodicals continue to appear, in each cultural area (having regard to economic and educational requirements).

It is apparent, therefore, that in theory the traditional methods of printing suffice to meet the need for best sellers—that is, the minimum required if people are to remain literate and make progress in speaking and writing for general purposes. Achieving this, however, presupposes that the developing countries establish priorities and resolutely apply the policies which follow therefrom:

In the case of States with small populations, this is of course facilitated if they can combine with others to form a larger cultural area.

Each country or group of countries should possess its own equipment for printing in order to avoid the additional cost of transport and distribution, which would soon become prohibitive.

Priority should be given to a fairly small number of carefully selected titles, which should be distributed as widely as possible. If this is to be done, the whole venture will have to be concerted: first, publishing and sales; second, systematic deposit in all libraries, even municipal libraries; and third, promotion by radio, television, the press and other suitable media.

If a score of titles are published annually in the poorer or more thinly populated countries and if 100 or 200 will shortly be published in the larger or more affluent countries, we should, in a few years' time, build up a universal stock of books for the general public, which is essential if basic education is to be taken a step further. The books selected and the contents of the periodicals must above all be attractive to readers. Periodicals included in this stock could print articles contributing to vocational training generally.

As soon as we get on to specialized literature, difficulties arise. In highly developed or extensive cultural areas (the European countries, U.S.S.R., China, etc.), a circulation ranging between 10,000 and 100,000 copies is acceptable for good educational books or good technical reviews. Elsewhere, the circulation is much too small to be economic, and in any case selling prices which could offset the costs would place the works out of the reach of all but a small élite.

A distinction should be made between two cases. The first is that of a work of potential interest to a wide public and connected with some important government project affecting agricultural development, land reclamation, the introduction of mechanization on a large scale, electrification, etc. This is really a matter of general knowledge, and it should be possible to deal with it in the same way and by the same methods. In such a case, the works, though less numerous, will be acquired by most libraries.

In the second case—that of needs amounting to a few hundred copies in a particular place—the usual methods of printing are obviously inappropriate, and it will be necessary as a rule to import the books. Importing is seldom possible for the individual, but it is feasible for libraries of a certain size. If collections are to be used, however, people must know about them. One of the most important aspects of library promotion policy, as we shall see, is informing the potential public concerning the library's holdings.

Apart from the question of purchasing abroad, new technical advances have made it possible to reproduce typed documents by offset. Even for large numbers of copies the offset process has many advantages as compared with letterpress printing. The main one is that the plates are easy to keep, and a second impression can be made without any further expense. With typesetting, on the contrary, either the type has to be kept a long time and valuable stock immobilized, or else the whole job has to be set again for each successive edition. Apart from industrial uses for very large printings, the price of the offset process is very competitive for small numbers of copies, especially if typed documents are accepted as a basis. It is often convenient to reduce the size of the page by about 20 per cent. This improves its sharpness and reduces the amount of paper employed, without making the text difficult to read. With this process the right-hand margin is not perfectly even, but can be accepted in view of the price.

The process consists merely of using a typed text (which may be aligned on the right-hand margin to improve its appearance), making an aluminium plate (if the number of copies is to be in the region of 1,000) or even a cardboard or paper one (if the number of copies is to be less than 100). This costs no more than a tenth, or even less, of the cost of typesetting, which is 2 centimes per character. It is true that the price of producing each copy by this process is considerable. Yet it serves very well for the circulation of research findings of interest to specialists in a whole region or of surveys or textbooks necessary for research, study or other purposes in medium-sized communities.

A similar method derived from electrostatic photocopying consists of making an electrostatic positive photograph on an appropriate machine from which dozens or even hundreds of copies of the same document can easily be reproduced.

Not only are methods of printing being modernized, but methods of text composition are rapidly evolving. Some works, such as directories and bibliographies, lend themselves particularly well to the use of new methods.

For instance, in order to find out what the various libraries contain and make this information available to the public it is necessary to compile and keep up-to-date union catalogues in which the information can be found under several heads (author, subject, title of periodical, etc.). This arrangement necessitates considerable sorting.

Then again, documentation centres usually circulate biblio-graphical lists, current awareness lists or abstracts bulletins which can be consulted from as many different indexes as possible (subject, author, etc.).

Finally, in order to make contacts easier, directories have to be published listing laboratories, current research subjects, research workers, activities of libraries or documentation centres, etc. These publications also involve considerable sorting, which is uneconomical except with a computer, but computer listings do not lend themselves very well to direct publication, for they give documents which are difficult to read. Various forms of photo composition are therefore preferred. Another advantage of photo-composition machines is that they can generate complex new characters at little cost. This is particularly valuable in the sciences or when different systems of writing must be employed. For instance there are photo-composers with some founts of Roman type and others of Cyrillic or Arabic type. Greek type is quite commonly available. It is also very easy to add another letter to the Roman alphabet in order to render a particular sound in a language or a number of languages not widely spoken (local languages, for instance). The process is as follows: a team of keyboard operators punch a text with specially adapted keyboards. The punched tape so obtained may appear with different codes according to the type of material used. It is almost always an eight-track tape, but it may also be a magnetic tape. Corrections are made by mixing in the computer. For this purpose a correction tape is punched with each of the signs to be changed situated in relation to the original text.

Before giving instructions to the photo-composition machine, the computer can do all the sorting required and generate the indexes and tables decided upon without there being any need for further punching. The corresponding orders will have been transmitted along with the ordinary type when the punching was done in the first place.

In this way the photo-composition machine produces a fuller text than the one originally punched, according to the number of tables and indexes. This process is also very useful for commercial directories, directories of the *Who's who* type, administrative charts, etc. The cost of photo-composing the same number of characters is slightly higher than it would be if hot metal were used. It is about the same or even less if one considers the number of characters actually printed.

The number of users of a directory of this kind is nearer 1,000 than 10,000 (if we exclude commercial or telephone directories), so the selling price is rather high. This equipment is well worth possessing either for important operations decided on by governments and largely financed by them, or if specialized bibliographical bulletins or widely used directories are to be published. So here again we find the two factors, size and level of development. However, photo-composition seems to be an excellent process if it is used on an international scale. It should make it possible to take into account at a reasonable cost the variety of forms which should be made available to users.

I.2.2   REPROGRAPHY
         AND MICRODOCUMENTATION

The techniques used in reprography apply only in exceptional cases to widely distributed documents and seldom to books. These techniques are expensive. In such cases the usual cost of reprography—between 0.50 franc and 1 franc (between 10 and 20 cents) per page—would be quite prohibitive, for it would mean that the cost per copy of a book which can be produced for between $2 and $4 would be as much as $20 or $40.

However, this process is invaluable to the librarian when a careless borrower loses an issue of a periodical or a book which is out of print and the collection has to be completed regardless of the cost, so that it will correspond to the catalogues available to users. The librarian may borrow the missing item from another library for a short period, but it would often involve a lot of time to complete the collection by the usual methods, and the outcome would be uncertain.

Reprography is also invaluable to the research worker, teacher or engineer interested in a specific subject and anxious to get together a number of documents to which he has found references. Instead of having to enter into correspondence with a score of different bookshops without any certainty of obtaining satisfaction, he can ask the nearest library for the reproductions he requires.

This process is bound to develop still further as libraries acquire the necessary equipment, which is not very costly. Prices are going to drop slightly, too, for the principal patent protecting electrostatic photocopying recently expired. However, it does not seem likely that this process will be an economic substitute for purchasing an additional copy of a book or of an issue of a periodical when the circulation is a large or medium-sized one.

Even in the case of a small circulation, offset processes are still much more economic. It is true that the two processes can be combined, an electrostatic reproduction being used as the basis for an offset plate. There is certainly a future for this in the circulation of documents when requirements are not known beforehand, but it is even more promising if it is associated with microdocumentation.

Several microdocumentation processes are being used at present, and others are being tested. In the case of both microfilms and microfiches, reduction rates in the region of 15–30 : 1 are current. They allow a reduction of more than 95 per cent in the volume of archives. However, some archivists think this is inadequate. Possibly, too, in big centres for storing documents, a slight saving can be effected by reducing the total volume of archives by the ratio 30 : 1. Two processes are now making their appearance: the ultrafiche (900 pages on a fiche 21 by 29.7 mm) and holograph processes which lead to an equivalent reduction in volume. Microdocumentation has two advantages: in addition to the reduction in volume it allows automatic or semi-automatic access to any document in the collection.

For this purpose, microfilms are provided with a strip of black and white squares against each frame, and the way they are arranged characterizes it by representing a number in binary languages. In order to find the page required, the whole film goes through an appropriate reader, which reads the numbers in the margin and stops the film when it reaches the number designated. Microfilms come in cassettes or strip form which are very easy to handle.

Microfiches, the most common format of which at present—the A6—corresponds to one-quarter of an ordinary page (i.e. 105 by 150 mm), may contain either a few frames for plans and diagrams or 49, 60, 64 or 128 frames for the text. It will be seen that the latter are grouped in two reduction ratios—14–16 : 1 on the one hand and 20–23 : 1 on the other, according to the format of the original and according as the document is photographed one page or two pages at a time. There are devices for automatic or semiautomatic access which can contain something like 700 to 1,000 microfiches—i.e. approximately 1,000 million characters, or a library of 3,000 volumes, to which one can have direct and immediate access page by page. Access is semi-automatic if it is necessary to know beforehand the number of the fiche and the number of the page on the fiche and to obtain it by manipulating the apparatus. It is entirely automatic if page and fiche numbers come out of a computer in which they have been worked out following a request expressed in a natural language.

Although these files are not very expensive, it is naturally not worth while using them to stock the contents of library books, for it is of no great importance that readers of library books should be able to have direct access to a previously designated page. The situation is quite different with scientific and technical documents or with dictionaries, tables, directories, bibliographical bulletins, laws, decrees and regulations, or even patents, etc., in other words with what is acquired not for reading in its entirety but for reference.

The purchasing price of the above apparatus is between $10,000 and $20,000, so it is within the means of libraries and documentation centres of a certain size. The materials needed to constitute the stock are slightly more expensive, but for files of moderate size (less than 1 million pages to be microfilmed annually) it is generally worth while to farm the work out, either to commercial specialists or to a national or regional centre which serves all the libraries and centres in the country or the region. The advantage of the latter solution is the certainty that the distribution (number of pages per microfiche) and arrangement of the microdocuments will be the same in all the centres.

Finally we might mention aperture cards. These are based on both computer techniques and microdocumentation, since they can be sorted and filed in the ordinary apparatus and they contain a microdocument in the centre window.

Against the advantages of microdocumentation—the small amount of space taken up and the ease of access to any point in the collection—must be weighed two disadvantages: the cost of setting up in microform and the necessity of special reading apparatus.

First let us consider the former. It is a serious disadvantage, because taking the photo necessitates unavoidably a certain amount of handling and of working time. At best it means an expenditure of a least 20 centimes a page. This is a prohibitive cost for documents which may not all be very frequently consulted. However, the situation would be quite different if, instead of each library setting up its archives in microform, several libraries were to club together to obtain duplicates, very cheaply, from a master microfiche.

Similarly, publishers of scientific and technical journals and of directories, bulletins and other reference material are beginning to issue microeditions as well as their paper editions.

One of the technical advantages of a microedition is the facility with which it can be duplicated cheaply. However, this is a disadvantage to publishers, for it is difficult to keep check of the number of reproductions made in this way and to fix the amount to charge for permission to duplicate. Nevertheless, it is such a useful practice that it is bound to become established in the long run. Microdocuments are not legible, of course, but readers can be coupled with systems for restitution by electrostatic or rapid silver photocopying at little cost. Reproduction on paper from a microfiche library is more economic than reproduction from an ordinary library, since it obviates all the costs involved in searching and refiling. It also takes less time.

One can even make a sort of offset printing with little trouble from a photocopy obtained in this way.

Now if we take ultrafiches or holograph processes we have basically the same possibilities as with the processes described above. The storage capacity is much greater than it is with microfiches or microfilms: from 10,000 million to 100,000 million characters can be introduced into a single apparatus. This represents more than all the directories of whatever type and all the bibliographical bulletins and dictionaries published annually, or again more than all the laws and decrees and administrative decisions promulgated in several countries, or more than a library of 100,000 volumes. No doubt the price of the equipment required to do this is relatively high, but if we bear in mind the amount of documentation processed in this way and the facility with which it can be used as a result of such processes we shall very probably decide in its favour whenever the size of the documentation centre or library warrants it. The adoption of these methods will incline planners and specialists towards centralization even more than the adoption of ordinary microdocumentation did. A limited number of libraries in different parts of the world will finally assemble the whole sum of human knowledge in this dynamic form, making it rapidly accessible. Of course the archives on paper will not be destroyed; they will be conserved for safety's sake. However, these processes are developing fairly slowly, not so much for technical as for economic reasons, the market for equipment with such a great capacity being of necessity relatively limited. It would be different if standard equipment able to compete with traditional microcopying equipment could be produced by the same methods. It would only have to give a slightly better performance and as a result of this basic market the few hundred extremely powerful appliances could be produced at a reasonable price.

It will be realized from the foregoing that the techniques of reprography will have a decisive influence on the planning of the development of libraries and documentation centres. Existing institutions that have long been established will gradually have to modernize. As for the new libraries or new centres being set up, they will perhaps be in the best position to take advantage of the latest technical advances and offer the highest standard of service at the lowest cost.

1.2.3   FILMS AND AUDIO-VISUAL METHODS

It is not our intention here to deal with audio-visual documentation *per se*, although it is likely to assume paramount importance in years to come. Books, periodicals and most written documents have long been systematically catalogued, but cataloguing is still in its infancy when it comes to films and television sequences. We do not doubt that these will finally be catalogued, but it is still impossible to estimate how long it will be before art films and cultural films are catalogued on a large scale. The effort being made in this direction, however, by the Italian Radio and Television Corporation is worth mentioning. As a result of the method of documentation employed, this institution can easily find any film or sequence dealing with a given subject.

Educational films and more especially educational television sequences are the most important to catalogue first. While we know that such a distinction is artificial, we may look at two sample cases. One is that of the countries, or regions, where almost the whole population is not only literate but can obtain a broad general education through television at all events and also through reading. The other is that of regions where educational and cultural promotion on a mass scale is essential to development.

In the former, audio-visual programmes are chiefly for recreation, and what people seek above all in them, as in all forms of recreation, is variety and entertainment. This does not preclude some treatment of science and technology, but it must be attractively presented and if possible stirring. Science is all the better for being seen as an art or a passion, a competition or even a struggle. Documentary films and some excellent television programmes are beginning to meet this need for an introduction to science, but most of the time they go no further. Scientists and technologists are frequently introduced to the public. The latter, however, is rarely given a chance to learn more about their work, or even to make some small contribution to their efforts.

Authors are called upon to present their books which is an excellent introduction to reading and culture. Reference is similarly made to the works of authors of the past, and this arouses a desire to know more about what they wrote and the times they lived in, although little indication is given as to how this can be done. In so far as engineers or scientists are concerned, there is a missing link in the chain which should lead the keenest members of the audience to broaden their knowledge and so contribute to their lifelong education.

Obviously films or television programmes can hardly be planned; they are shown as they become available or topical. However, they are usually announced in advance. So it would be possible to combine with any such introduction a book exhibition (all those organized at present are a great success) and to have the relevant books and periodicals put on sale and even displayed in shop windows concurrently. Here, too, libraries and documentation centres can play a prominent part if they have the means of advertising their services, that is, if some of their services are available on a paying basis. In this context it is very important to be able to discover old documentary film or television sequences and to show them as part of the joint programme and also to indicate where additional information can be found.

True, there is a tendency to dwell on ambitious research which is within the reach of the very few (the moon, supersonic flight, the atom, etc.), whereas those in charge of production are increasingly aware that the public is just as much interested in achievements or research of a more humble nature in which everyone is directly involved and to which everyone can make a personal contribution. These may concern new agricultural techniques (selection, hybridization, etc.), the reclamation of a mountainous or coastal region, the life of a fishing community, the wonders of data-processing, the advances made in telecommunications, the conveyance of power, books, pollution, etc.

The learning society can do more than this: useful addresses and even some idea as to possible openings can be given in the course of programmes. The addresses of information centres equipped to tell people where to apply can be given—and more and more people will apply if they can be efficiently informed and above all advised. One of the functions of these 'relay' documentation centres will be to see that the requisite educational facilities are actually available when they are needed, and that they are of adequate standard and as attractive as they should be (first, books containing the rudiments, then specialized books and documents, on the one hand, and the guidance of specialists or facilities for further education or retraining, on the other).

The case of the less-fortunate regions, where the educational level is still low, is obviously very different. It would be uneconomic in these countries to leave audio-visual information of an educational nature to chance. In view of the small number of films or programmes on these subjects available as compared with the magnitude of the needs, the results would very likely be almost nil, or at all events problematical.

On the contrary, it seems preferable for them to concentrate their generally limited means on a few goals, carefully selected in the light of the needs and also of library and university facilities. For this purpose fairly careful planning is necessary. It should comprise:

Selecting a few goals, to be reviewed annually in the light of the development of needs and means.

Identifying introductory works and more advanced material on the subjects selected and ensuring that they are available in libraries.

Enlisting the help of experts, university teachers and competent persons for in-service training.

Organizing exhibitions, including books, and if possible displaying other items as well.

Influencing public opinion through the press, radio and television.

So far as possible, selecting relevant sequences from films being shown in cinemas, with a view to associating them with the goal or goals pursued.

Bearing in mind the need to supply useful addresses and essential factual information needed to help people obtain the education they desire with the minimum of difficulty.

I.2.4   COMPUTERS AND THEIR CONTRIBUTION
         TO DOCUMENTATION CIRCUITS

With each generation, as those who build computers say, the storage capacity of such equipment is multiplied at least tenfold, if not one-hundredfold and more. It is hard to foresee just how far we can go in the matter of speed of calculation of the central units—we are perhaps approaching the highest point we can reach—but, in the opinion of documentalists, the calculations to be effected are simple and the present speeds have not yet been exploited to the full. They are limited for the time being by storage capacities, speed of transfer from one storage to another and means of access to this or that point in auxiliary storage. In this connexion the use of medium- or large-capacity discs is found very helpful.

They are also limited for economic reasons, that is, the cost, which is still high, of subsidiary equipment (printers, data channels, mass storage, arrangements for storing and loading magnetic tapes). Furthermore, some parts of this equipment, such as printers, are generally not suited to the needs of documentation. Finally, document processing, which is comparable with management processing, has a number of special features. So it is advisable, although not essential, to use computers of a form suitable for such processing. Software too, if it is to be efficient, is often written in assembly language not readily transposed from one type of computer to another.

In scientific, technical and cultural information computers are used for the following purposes:

For keeping directories of the activities of libraries and documentation centres up to date and directing users to the centre or library best able to meet their requirements (guidance or reference centres).

For library house-keeping (book orders, subscriptions to periodicals, lending service).

For union catalogues, that is, registers containing complete lists of the collections of all the institutions participating in the catalogue (the contents of union catalogues are arranged under various headings—subject, title of periodical or work, etc.).

The computer is indispensable for doing all the sorting according to the different criteria and also for periodically inserting additions and changes without recreating the whole catalogue. Complete editions are of course remade on the basis of material in which the additions and changes have been incorporated.

Queries can also be put to the computer, which is capable of answering them, thus avoiding the necessity to refer to the complete catalogue. Similarly, partial catalogues can be published by listing, for instance, only a few fields of knowledge or the collections of a limited group of libraries;

For locating documents on the basis of their contents.

These are some of the principal applications of the computer to documentation. A number of keywords are associated with each document, as also various other elements making up the bibliographical entry. All this is introduced into the computer with a reference number, the title of the document and in some cases a summary or a part of the text of the document itself.

As will be readily understood, this does not suffice for the computer to be able to arrange the documents so recorded in such a way as to produce on request all those concerning a particular subject. At present semi-mechanical methods are used which require human intervention at the input stage (before the facts concerning each document are recorded) and at the output stage; either the questions to be put to the computer are framed after careful study or the work is done afterwards on indexes of the KWIC[1] variety or other subject indexes.

Despite the doubts entertained a few years ago, it is clear that the procedure very briefly described above and usually alluded

---

1. Keyword in context.

to as 'mechanized documentation' is bound to prevail in the future. The reasons for this are as follows:

The help of the computer is essential if we are to find our way amidst the innumerable documents recounting, with varying success, past achievements in knowledge and culture.

It has been demonstrated that this help is useful already, inasmuch as, while scarcely being labour-saving, it makes it possible in many cases to arrive at a more complete result.

Thanks to the computer the tasks formerly performed in a number of different documentation centres can now be co-ordinated.

Considerable progress can be anticipated in the studies of applied linguistics now being carried out in a number of documentation centres. Their impact on the future of the transfer of knowledge warrants giving some idea of them.

In the first place, these studies involve working out 'documentary' languages and giving those languages a structure in the form of a thesaurus. Documentalists do not concern themselves solely with this semantic aspect of language; the potentialities of the computer lead them to concern themselves with the spelling and grammatical structure of words. Leaving on one side the possibility of automatic correction of the most frequent spelling mistakes, we should like to dwell for a moment on declensions and conjugations (feminine and plural forms, verb endings) which it is essential to eliminate more or less systematically if the brain work of preparing documents to be put into the computer is to be limited. Once this problem and the problem of vocabulary are solved, by means of well constructed thesauri including the desired synonymic relations, only a minimum of preparation is required for punching titles and abstracts of documents and even the introductions and conclusions of documents or, in the case of patents for instance, the list of claims.

What is more, the computer is made to divide words up letter by letter (KLIC)[1] so as to bring out the prefixes (to be deleted in some cases), the suffixes of interest for the sake of comparison (in chemistry, the suffixes 'ane', 'iene', 'ol', etc.) and roots to be compared with those of other words. So a whole series of tools is gradually being computerized in each of the languages in which documents are processed. In the future these tools will prove as

---

1. Key letters in context.

important for a language as alphabetical writing was in the past. It is therefore highly desirable that they be established, at least in the principal languages used for the exchange of information.

As all this involves the investment of considerable sums, here too a certain concentration or pooling of resources is advisable, with a view to making effective use of the appreciable assistance which computers can give in documentation.

1.2.5 TELECOMMUNICATIONS AND MAIL

A great fuss has been made about documentation obtained by turning a knob, that is, consulting files at a distance and receiving the answer to a question from the office of a senior official or engineer within a few minutes. It is certainly spectacular when demonstrated: a list of facts, which is easily made perfectly relevant for test purposes, appears on a console no larger or more complex than a television set. A more detailed study, which we shall resume later when considering the needs of users, will show that such apparatus can at best be employed a few hours daily and that several years will elapse before the services rendered warrant the expense incurred. This procedure is only economic for the consulting of files which are very frequently in demand, which are relatively small in size and which give a direct answer to the question put (for example, the files of customers of a car insurance company, in which each customer's file is referred to at least once a month).

In the case of documentation, the information required is generally a bibliography, and it is then necessary to ask for the original documents in order to study them, so an immediate answer is of rather limited value. Reducing the time required to a minimum is nevertheless an essential factor worth considering from all angles. The chief means of forwarding replies is still by post, that is, having books or documents dispatched to an address marked on each packet.

In many countries mail travels quickly (taking about a day) and postage is cheap. So no better means could be found for dispatching periodicals, reproductions, books, documents or any other kind of information in written form. This applies particularly to Europe, where distances are not great and there is so much correspondence that a powerful postal infrastructure is a paying proposition. In regions where the population is more scattered and postal facilities are not so much used, however, mail travels more slowly and the cost of postage is higher. It is unlikely that the volume of documentation dispatched will suffice to change the situation. Nevertheless, if such mail is grouped together on priority lines, it may be worth while paying the extra transport costs in keeping with its urgency (for example, organization of air freight for the exchange of periodicals and documents between Europe and North America or between North America and Japan), provided that quantities are great. Such grouping has another advantage: if a check can be made on departure and on arrival, it is at least a way of sending films and magnetic tapes without incurring the risk of damage by investigation on the part of the police or customs authorities.

In some countries too, even if the postal network as a whole is little developed as yet, the needs of the documentation network might serve as a starting point for improving a few lines where the traffic justifies a special effort or preferential treatment (the lines connecting a few big towns, with the mail entering and leaving certain postal boxes, rather on the same principle as the *courriers du roi* in eighteenth-century Europe). Users could go and fetch their mail from these central boxes or, if it is not urgent, ask for it to be forwarded to their address by the ordinary postal service. A similar system is in operation in several countries, where large quantities of newspapers are delivered in a very short time to a small number of agents.

There are always some occasions when, for reasons of urgency, telecommunications must be used. Telephone and telex are now inexpensive enough to be widely used (requests for information, formulation of questions, explanations, requests for reproductions or loans, and even in some cases dispatch of bibliographical references). In the latter case, the possibility of errors is to be feared rather than the cost of transmission. The same applies to the transmission of the results obtained on consultation of a data bank. When the number of queries does not warrant the installation of a terminal, the extra charge for sending the answer by telex is generally quite reasonable.

Direct communication by coupling on computers comes into its own in a number of cases, including the following:

A documentary stock on a computer is available at point A while a number of queries arise at point B, where there is no computer available in the vicinity for this work. It is worth while installing a terminal at point B rather than being dependent on the mail, a car link or someone who forwards everything by telex.

Two computers each hold documentary stocks, but these differ, being adapted to the needs of local users if they are situated in different places, or of specialists if their respective stocks cover different subjects. However, it often happens that one is questioned about material which belongs to the other's file. In this case it is worth while coupling the two computers by a link which, subject to compatibility, makes it possible for parts of a file to be temporarily transferred from one computer to the other or for one computer to consult the other at a distance.

As the telephone network is in many cases the most economic means of effecting such a link, the lines used for this purpose must have the necessary technical characteristics. Satellites will facilitate relations of this kind at great distances, enabling both specialists and laymen in different countries to discover new affinities and so establish a special kind of relationship which would otherwise not have been possible. For the time being there is no question of launching satellites for the exchange of documents, but it is probable that exchanges of information in general (political, cultural, scientific and technical information and news), which will increasingly take on the same features, although they are intended for different users, will soon justify operations of this kind.

1.3   Information and economic and social development

1.3.1   INFORMATION AND ECONOMIC PROGRESS[1]

Even now scientific, technical and cultural information plays a prominent part in economic progress, whether industry, commerce, agriculture or handicrafts and trades are involved, and it will be

1. M. S. Adiseshiah, *Let my country awake*, p. 131–4, Paris, Unesco, 1970.

even more important in the future. Its function is twofold, introducing and accompanying all economic activities, namely:

Constituting a fund of information on which all those who see the need for progress can draw. Here they find new ideas, ways of starting new activities. This is the pattern of the 'nucleus of development'.

Providing new information for existing economic activities, since those who sponsor them or who hold responsible positions in them (whether cadres, engineers, craftsmen or other) constantly need new information to keep abreast of knowledge in their particular sector, in an age when, in fact, the choice is between going on or going under. If the sector concerned is losing ground, it can only survive by diversifying production and services, and for this it is even more essential to be well informed.

In practice there are two kinds of relationship between information networks and the economy, a direct one and an indirect one, the latter having education, fundamental research and culture as connecting links.

Information networks play a direct part in the certain cases, as is shown below.

1.3.1.1 *In industry*

When somebody wishes to promote an invention (some idea which he has or an initial discovery which he wishes to apply) he wants to know where he is going before incurring heavy expenses for developing it. What obstacles stand in the way? What are the chances of success? What information is available on the question?

When deciding which direction research should take, selecting programmes, deciding on the best ways and means, it is necessary to be able to see constantly what has already been achieved and the failures or semi-failures which others have met with.

In order to diversify a firm's production, it is necessary to be informed as to what the techniques one has can produce and as to the means or the discoveries whereby they can best evolve.

Finally, industrialists must constantly keep up to date as to products and new methods which they can use in production and the conditions under which this is possible.

Much of this information is obtained from the market, from suppliers or financial groups with which the firm is in contact. It is essential for independent growth, however, that these sources should not be the only ones, for if they were the firm would become technically dependent on an important customer or supplier or on a banker. The sources of information should be outside the economic circuit, absolutely neutral and yet as complete, relevant and speedy as possible.

1.3.1.2   *In agriculture*

Today agriculture is becoming a veritable industry—an industry with its own particular constraints, inasmuch as it is carried on in an open, extensive environment, which must be regenerated at the same time as it is exploited. Information from very diverse sources is therefore essential, for example: chemistry and geology, for information on soils, fertilizers, the conservation of fertility, pesticides; biology, for information on cattle, cattle-feeding, cattle-raising, and also on parasites and the biological struggle; mechanical and civil engineering, for information on agricultural machinery, forestry, etc.; economics, so that production can be adapted to needs and to the market.

Here too a large part of the information is in many cases supplied by the buyers (greengrocers, *abattoirs*, food-packers, etc.), or by suppliers or their agents (companies handling food, chemicals and machinery) or by farmers' loan societies; but the farmers can only safeguard their freedom in so far as, individually or co-operatively, they can obtain impartial documentation collected and selected by organizations acting solely in the interests of the farmers or for the general economic development of the region.

1.3.1.3   *In the arts and crafts and in the trades*

A distinction is drawn between arts and crafts, on the one hand, and trades on the other. The former spring up spontaneously, but a network of social and cultural information can make a very useful contribution to their development. From the buyer's standpoint, trends in the demand are directly related to the social, cultural and economic situation of those who seek such products. The same is true of the artist or craftsman, especially if he lives at a distance from the buyers of his products, which is increasingly the case.

Some idea of what sells easily is of course conveyed by the

shopkeepers who act as intermediaries, but it is only a rough idea, governed by the desire for immediate profits and it takes no account of that element which, in the art lover, gives the artist new inspiration and which, coming from the artist, forms the art lover's taste.

This increasingly rewarding contact is maintained by reading documents on history, civilization, religion, tradition, and also on the state of culture today. It is through books that we understand a people; it is through day-to-day cultural information that we follow its development and maintain our regard for it. It is by this means that we appreciate its art; conversely, it is by this means that the artist or craftsman can produce works to which people will respond.

Of a more prosaic type is the information associated with the trades or which gives rise to new trades. While it is true that in Europe and in the east the cartwright, the blacksmith or the mason have always received their information by word of mouth, a number of such trades are vanishing, to be replaced by others, and the situation is different. With the advent of electricity and the internal combustion engine and the reduction in the price of electromechanical appliances, there is an urgent need for persons able to maintain and repair the wide range of equipment owned by every individual. This had led to the development of a large number of occupations such as the modern mason, the car mechanic, the specialist in timber, the electrician, the specialist in heating appliances, the electronics engineer, etc.

Documentation in these occupations at present consists of a heterogeneous collection of knowledge gained in carrying on one of the usual trades, together with the lists of spare parts and instructions for use which accompany the modern appliances that tradesmen are capable of repairing. Progress in these trades, which are essential to local life in the developing countries, is directly stimulated by suitable technical and economic information. Furthermore, they are in many cases starting points for new industries. Adequate information helps to bring about this transformation and therefore contributes to the industrialization of the country from ground level.

1.3.1.4   *In commerce*

When we refer to information designed for commerce, we mean principally economic documentation (nature of openings, trends therein, economic situation, manpower, etc.). Information is usually put in the form of figures (statistics on production, prices, etc.), accompanied by brief comments.

Documentation of this kind is certainly of primary importance to anyone engaged in commerce, and so is documentation on legal questions, taxation and customs, which governs his activities. However he also needs basic technical information whenever he considers the future of his business, its potential, its diversification or simply the way in which it should be developed.

Such medium-term planning depends largely upon technical information which has to be related to sociological or microeconomic information. The best market studies are in many cases based on such composite information. A study is made of how a new product is likely to be received in a given technical environment, which must be known, and in given social conditions, which must similarly be analysed.

Then again, no branch of the economic and industrial world can permanently satisfy a recognized need unless its position on the production market is satisfactory. Its competitiveness will be due partly to a favourable situation in regard to wages and employment and partly to the existence of suitable natural resources, easy to exploit, and a technical environment such that products of the requisite quality can be manufactured to meet the demand, while using methods and machinery that will reduce production costs to a minimum.

Finally, when the needs to be met are being evaluated, a commercial occurrence is never found in isolation. Whether it is due to a technical breakthrough (for example, the development of transistors and of computers), the crossing of an economic threshold (increase in *per capita* income and motor-car buying), or social or political phenomena (development of the employment of women and advances in the beauty-products industry), any commercial occurrence has consequences at different stages along the line—consequences which are chiefly scientific or technical in nature.

The above examples are obvious; the additional outlets made available in the three examples quoted are known in the main. However, there are a great many cases of commercial action of much lesser importance whose consequences cannot be foreseen without thorough analysis of scientific documentation.

Such documentation is not directly accessible to most dealers, nevertheless, or even to specialists in marketing, an intermediary with a technical and commercial training is required to select the appropriate material and, above all, to pinpoint what is important, in some cases to see it in relation to concomitant social facts, and on the basis of all this discuss the matter with the dealer, giving him in understandable language the objective information on which he can base his decisions. This intermediary, as we shall see, is to be found in specialized libraries (information-analysis centres, management and engineering consultants, research and vocational information centres, public information centres, etc.).

1.3.2   INFORMATION AND EDUCATION

In section 1.1.2 we examined the way in which information passed from teacher to pupil, and saw how the tools mentioned in this connexion (books, lectures, journals offering a conspectus of given subjects) were an invaluable and indeed indispensable aid to the teacher. The same applies to libraries, which acquire and conserve these documents and so make sources of information available to students and pupils. We have also seen how a network of libraries well supported by audio-visual publicity could play a prominent part in the learning society as conceived in the report of the commission chaired by Edgar Faure.[1]

An attempt will be made in the following pages to consider in more detail how the development of information circuits can accompany and promote the progress of education at the various levels: literacy training, secondary education, technical training, lifelong education, higher education.

1.3.2.1   *Literacy training*

In many countries literacy training is still a difficult problem to solve, both because there are not enough teachers and because, social conditions being what they are, it is difficult to obtain a basic education over a certain age. At all events, libraries will always be a marginal factor in countries with high illiteracy rates. It can be hoped, however, that 10 or even 15 per cent of illiterates will be reached. No doubt this proportion represents only from 5 to 10 per cent of the total population of a country, but it is enough to increase

1. Faure, *op. cit.*

the reading public by almost 25 per cent. So it is a big step forward. Whether established in a rural or an urban area, a library is a centre for literacy training provided it is physically accessible to a sufficient number of readers in this category—and of course provided it contains suitable works.

Literacy training for such people is designed essentially for adults or adolescents who need reading materials that are very simply expressed and carefully graduated, but by no means childish in content. These readers seek stories suitable for their level of social and emotional development, which is much higher than that of illiterates in developed countries.

Here, as in many other cases, libraries serve as an adjunct or an introduction; they would be ineffective on their own. Beginners in reading seldom go to libraries individually. They usually make the best progress as members of a cultural group, its work being associated with individual work and one of the members of the group acting as leader. For this purpose, libraries should of course have several copies of the same work for lending. If, as is desirable, literacy training is developed as part of a wider programme, television commentaries or even television courses being given in conjunction with it, pupils will have a number of copies of the same book, and a special edition adapted as closely as possible to the purpose might be warranted. Comic strips are an excellent tool if their cost price is sufficiently low, for in them verbal expression is the indispensable complement for satisfying the curiosity first awakened by the pictures.

This basic function of libraries in the developing countries has its counterpart, in slightly different form, in the industrialized countries, where libraries contribute to primary education—for children, of course, in this case.

Even when the school has its own library, the children sometimes prefer the different atmosphere of a municipal library. Many such libraries have long since set up special children's sections or reading clubs which are very popular and work satisfactorily in numerous countries in Europe and America.

1.3.2.2   *Documentation and secondary education*

The knowledge expected of secondary-school pupils is no doubt the hardest to acquire other than in a specialized institution. They must

47

master a basic language and mathematics, along with various other branches of knowledge (foreign languages, physics, history, etc.). They must practise if they are to master these subjects. Hence the necessity of a place to practise, the secondary school, which is the centre of educational activities. Books and other printed matter are the raw materials on which the pupil practises (with which he plays in a sort of simulation game preparatory to adult life). That is why this kind of education almost exclusively concerns adolescents, seldom adults.

Reading and study requirements are therefore considerable, but they are usually amply met by the schools, either in the form of textbooks or in the form of school libraries where pupils can easily borrow books. A decentralized system whereby the pupils (or if necessary the teacher) run the library and are financially responsible is sometimes the best way of keeping down losses and deterioration. This is inadequate, however, once a certain educational level is reached.

Libraries and more especially documentation centres which can be consulted are at all events essential for the following purposes: restocking class libraries; providing the bibliographies required for selecting the most suitable books, booklets and periodicals; facilitating the selection of textbooks; documenting teachers who want to write textbooks or adapt their teaching to present-day events and pupils' interests; affording pupils opportunities for individual work (preparation of talks, studies with a view to participating in group sessions, group research, etc.).

1.3.2.3   *Documentation and technical training*

Until recently it was customary for technical training to be acquired essentially on the job. As a result, a large part of the technological knowledge and practical skills on which modern civilization rests has never been the subject of a publication; in some cases it has not even been set down in writing. The precariousness of this situation has been realized. Furthermore, young people now have to be trained in schools and institutes of technology. Finally, industrial firms have had to acquire techniques foreign to them and conversely spread abroad a part of their accumulated knowledge.

So the number of technical books and textbooks (whether elementary or advanced) is on the increase, and technical periodicals are developing and flourishing. Other documents in increasing numbers are available to help technicians turn research findings to account and use the latest innovations (materials or processes).

In technical training today a distinction is made between the training given to young people (apprenticeship and technical schools) and the training provided for adults (evening courses, technical institutes, etc.), which is more often called 'lifelong education'. However, this distinction is not nearly so sharp in the developing countries. Where there are few technical institutes as yet, and a great many workers need initial training rather than further training or retraining. Schools, clubs, groups of persons engaged in the same occupation and groups working to promote development all need basic technical textbooks and also fuller documentation on certain special branches of knowledge.

It will be seen, therefore, that libraries are of primary importance; it is they which list and purchase technical textbooks, making them available, if need be, to the above-mentioned schools, centres or groups. In addition, technical documentation centres, which may be part of a library (in a small town) or separate entities (in big towns and capital cities), provide students in engineering with the bibliographical tools they require to carry out their studies (some project in a special branch, a technical thesis, or a *chef-d'œuvre*) and make available to practising engineers or teachers sources of information where they will find ideas for innovation, material for lectures or topics for group discussion.

1.3.9 4   *Lifelong education*

This leads us to the part played by documentation in lifelong education. In the case of retraining proper, the process is very much as described above in connexion with technical training. However, lifelong education more often than not assumes the semi-disguised form described in section 1.1.4, and working life, leisure, cultural development, technical training and in some cases even the social aspect of the occupation gradually merge in one educational activity. The farmer is learning as he seeks to improve his methods or increase yields, or as he thinks of the industrial firm which will buy his products or supply him at low cost with the tools he would like to have. The same applies to the workman, the technician and, *a fortiori*, the engineer or administrator.

All of these make increasing use of documentation networks, from which they expect the following services:

From time to time, basic information on the essentials of a subject, which is of use to them if they wish to change to another occupation or simply to find out about some new technique.

All the time, an opportunity to update their knowledge in their own particular branch, if possible without effort and as a distraction.

If need be, answers to specific technical questions on this or that subject.

Periodically, a recapitulation of the information previously obtained and, where necessary, its updating.

1.3.2.5 *Documentation*
in the service of universities

Universities are the ideal place for the dissemination of scientific, technical and cultural information. It is also in the universities as a rule that such information is produced. Every university has its own library, where students can find books which are not in general use or which are relatively expensive (they are encouraged to purchase for themselves the more commonly used basic works).

In many countries the public has wide access to university libraries, and the people regard them as a valuable source of information for the purpose of broadening their general education or vocational training. So the needs and budgets of university libraries have been related to student enrolments in the following paragraph merely for the sake of convenience.

For students reading for bachelors' or masters' degrees, libraries select manuals, conspectuses and courses written if possible in the students' mother tongue or, failing that, in the foreign language with which they are most familiar. As the numbers of such students are large, representing from 0.1 to 0.5 per cent of the total population even in developing countries, translations are warranted in many cases. Take, for example, a linguistic area comprising 30 million inhabitants of whom 0.3 per cent are students, first-year students representing a little less than 0.5 per cent. This means that there are some 15,000 students in the area studying in many different faculties (arts, law, medicine, physics, chemistry, civil engineering, mechanical engineering, etc.). Let us assume that 20 per cent of them will be studying the resistance of materials and that we want to provide enough copies of a book for it to be shared among three (which is reasonable for books in average use). This means that 1,000 copies will be needed, which justifies translating and publishing the work in the normal way if we can afford it ($20 a copy), or, if that is too much, producing it by an inexpensive offset process.

Teachers and persons working on a thesis need not only books which are more or less commonly used, but articles in journals, reports of congresses and specialized documents which are not in common use. To select them properly, bibliographies are used, and specialized knowledge is required. In certain universities the library has special units which are actually documentation centres dealing with a few branches of knowledge in which the university has achieved renown. They are usually led or supervised by a research worker or by a professor.

1.3.3   ROLE OF INFORMATION
           IN CULTURAL
           AND SOCIAL DEVELOPMENT

In section 1.3.1 above an attempt was made to show what part information could play in art, taking arts and crafts as an example. The process described is the same, with slight variations, in most branches of culture—books, films, architecture, music, tourism. Each has an economic aspect and a cultural aspect. The nature and the volume of exchanges naturally vary with the branch of culture, but also with the amount of interest taken in it by the country under consideration. Generally speaking, exchanges of documentation establish a flow of information parallel and complementary to the information transmitted by the commercial circuits (bookshops, film producers, building societies, tourist agencies, etc.). This flow has a favourable effect on exchanges and on all those commercial activities bound up with culture, helping to promote it and at the same time affording a means of curbing any excesses.

On the social side, documentation comes into the picture chiefly because it transmits research findings (sociology, medicine, town planning, hospital techniques). However, books contribute, along with newspapers and television, to the dissemination of information on hygiene, first aid, employment, social groups, etc.

1.3.4   INFORMATION AND SCIENTIFIC DEVELOPMENT

It is doubtless unnecessary to dwell on the role of information in scientific research. Some idea of it has been given in sections 1.1.1 and 1.1.3. Suffice it to recall that it was among research workers that the urgency of the need for exchanges of information was first realized and that it was also in research groups that the modern documentation techniques from which most human activities will increasingly benefit were developed.

2   Principles to be observed
     in building up a documentation
     and library infrastructure

2.1   Factors in the choices to be made

2.1.1   PRODUCTION OF LITERATURE

We have tried to estimate the amount of literature produced in
a few sample countries, basing our calculations on the survey
conducted by the International Federation for Documentation[1]
and the statistics published by Unesco.[2] The figures given are, of
course, approximations; they will be found in Appendix 1, together
with the very rough hypotheses which we were obliged to formulate
because we had to relate figures drawn from widely divergent
sources and concerning output which also varies from one country
to another.

By and large, it may be said that most printed literature is
consumed, i.e. read, or at least bought, otherwise publishing could
not continue and production would dwindle. Naturally, international trade must also be taken into account, since if this rough
method of calculating is used it pushes up the figures of countries
which export literature, whereas, in countries which import it,
much more reading may be done than is shown in the figures in
Appendix 1. Allowance being made for these hypotheses and
this limitation, it appears that in one year a Frenchman can
be expected, on average, to read the equivalent of fifty books

1. F.I.D. Committee for Developing Countries, *Study on national structures for documentation
   and library services in countries with different levels of development*, Paris, Unesco, 1973, 254 p.
   (Doc. COM/WS/301.)
2. *Unesco statistical yearbook, 1970*, Paris, Unesco, 1971, 786 p.

containing 1 million characters,[1] an American ten, a Russian thirty and a Hungarian thirty-five. These figures, almost two-thirds of which, admittedly, are accounted for by newspaper reading, correspond more or less to what intellectuals read in these countries, but are by no means representative of the average citizen (children included). The conclusion to be drawn is that a large proportion of what is written is not in fact read, or is only glanced at, or in many cases is merely filed away in public or private archives. This high proportion appears even more marked in contrast to some of the written material produced which is read by several people in succession. The report[2] recently submitted to the Organization for Economic Co-operation and Development (OECD) by Georges Anderla predicts that by 1985 the quantity of new scientific and technical material produced annually will be six or seven times its present size. By then, he estimates, the total number of scientific articles, books and reports in stock will exceed 100 million (which would require storage space of approximately 200 km of library bookshelves). Set against printed matter as a whole, these figures are certainly high, but not unreasonable if one considers that already some 300,000 new book titles are published every year, and if one takes a book to be the equivalent in bulk of nearly twenty scientific documents. By 1985 the total amount of new literature published may be expected to have doubled or trebled, which means that there will be 1 million new titles a year, comprising 1 billion characters. There will probably be 10 million scientific documents containing 500 thousand million characters; some of these will be new titles, in the case of new books or journals and others will appear in periodicals of long standing which are published year after year. It may be observed, nevertheless, that the proportion of scientific and technical literature, which at present amounts to scarcely more than 10–20 per cent of the total printed output other than newspapers, is showing a tendency to increase, and its bulk will soon rival that of literary and artistic works.

Since our task is to examine the problem of planning libraries and documentation networks and centres, it is wise to look several

1. France imports rather more books than it exports (26,000 tons as against 22,000 in 1968; these figures do not include newspapers).
2. G. Anderla, *Information in 1985*, Paris, OECD, 1973.

years ahead and to consider, if not the year 1985, then at least the decade up to 1980. Several observations spring to mind, which we will now discuss.

2.1.2   LARGE VOLUME
         OF PRINTED MATTER
         AND VARIETY OF DEMAND

We have mentioned that 200 km of shelves would be needed to store scientific and technical literature alone, and we have also seen that those who read a lot at present can scarcely be expected to read more. We are moving towards increasing diversification, which may already be seen in the most highly-developed countries in all kinds of literature. A great deal will be published, but each title published will have only a relatively limited number of readers. Thus, the needs of the general public, which are typically met by paperbacks, are contrasted with the growing needs of what in the past was an élite. But this élite is expanding, and now covers a very considerable proportion of the population; it is both increasing in numbers and becoming more diversified.

The readership rates of the 'documentary capital', therefore, will never be very high, since in a little-developed country the over-all number of readers will be limited, and, in a highly-developed area, a great variety—and hence a plentiful supply of material—will be required in order to satisfy the increased variety of needs. The exceptions to this rule, of course, are the few 'best sellers', which everyone reads. This is almost as true of technical material as it is of literary works.

2.1.3   OPTIMUM SIZE

In view of the above-mentioned facts, certain practical considerations must be borne in mind concerning the size of libraries and of documentation centres. On the one hand, as recommended in the report on the planning of library services in Asia,[1] reference

---

1. *Meeting of experts on the national planning of library services in Asia, Colombo, Ceylon. Final report*, Paris, Unesco, 1964, 34 p.

material should not be unduly split up, and, on the other, experience shows that if a library contains more than 10,000 m of
bookshelves its administration raises complex problems of organization. The same is true of a documentation centre which has to
cater for more than 1,000 research workers. It is, however, possible to make savings in larger units, but it seldom happens that
all the necessary conditions for doing this are fulfilled.

The optimum size therefore appears to be that of a library
or documentation unit designed to cater for between 1,000 and
10,000 students in the case of a university library, or between
100 and 1,000 research workers (in the case of a specialized
library or documentation centre) or, again, between 10,000 and
100,000 people in the case of a public library. However, this last
figure has been obtained from statistics for developed Western
countries, where people do not make much use of public libraries,
but prefer to join private reading circles (almost every association
and every company nowadays has its own library) or, in many
cases, to buy their own books. In France, for example, only
1 million volumes out of more than 100 million books of general
literature published were purchased by municipal libraries.[1] This
amounts to barely 1 per cent. Similarly, municipal libraries are
used by only 5 per cent of the population.[2] In the other European
countries (Denmark and the United Kingdom for example) public
libraries are used by more people (30 per cent of the population).
Nevertheless, reading of privately purchased books and membership of a private reading circle account for at least 80–90 per cent
of all books sold. In the Federal Republic of Germany,[3] for
instance, the standard objective of public libraries is to lend
4.5 volumes per inhabitant per year (as compared with 1.5 books
in stock in France). So German public libraries are certainly
much better stocked, but only about five times more so than
French public libraries. Similarly, the standard objective set in
the United Kingdom[4] is the acquisition of 250 volumes per year

1. General literature, as a rule, is taken to consist chiefly of novels and historical works
   but we have excluded the latter.
2. R. Pierrot, 'Les bibliothèques', *Le livre français hier, aujourd'hui et demain*, p. 199;
   M. Troubnikoff, 'Les données numériques', ibid., p. 113.
3. See also the percentage of the population who are members of public libraries, in
   F. N. Withers, *Standards for library service.* (Unesco, doc. COM/WS/151, rev. July 1971,
   p. 16–18.)
4. ibid., p. 51–4 and 101.

for 1,000 inhabitants. This amounts to approximately 13 million volumes altogether out of a total production which must be at least in the neighbourhood of that of France. It is true that in northern and eastern European countries purchases by libraries form a much greater proportion of the book trade. We have no definite figures, but the incomplete information at our disposal suggests that they represent 40 per cent or even 80 per cent in some cases for children's books.

At all events, in poorer areas, where books are expensive and where the reader often has very little space in which to keep books, the library is often the public's only opportunity for reading. For this reason, in places with less than 10,000 inhabitants the possibility of making simplified arrangements for libraries or running them on co-operative lines should be examined carefully.

2.1.4   COSTS

Let us call to mind the costs in terms of buildings and books, to which reference is usually made and which have been admirably summed up in the report of the Unesco experts on the planning of library services in Asia, and in the report made by F. N. Withers in February 1970.[1] However, these figures must be brought up to date, and this gives the following approximate costs:
Average price of a popular book (1 million characters): $2.
Price of a student's textbook: $10 20.
Price of a research worker's reference book: $20–50.
Subscription to an average periodical (monthly, with a hundred or so articles per year): $50.
Price per metre of shelving (multiplied by 1.5–2 for fittings): $20 minimum.
Quantity of books which can be stored per metre: 20 books or 20 million characters or 4 years' issues of periodicals.
Publication of typescript in microfiche form (3 or 4 microfiches are needed per million characters): $1 per microfiche (facsimile).
Cost of enlargement to original size: 1 copy, $50; further copies made by offset duplicator, $100 for 10.
On the requirement side we may reckon on one to two books per

1. Withers, op. cit., p. 16–18.

inhabitant, on average, and if possible an equivalent outlay on audio-visual material, which comes to approximately $5 per inhabitant. We shall see later how these books vary in kind according to the size of the libraries.

For students, the estimate is fifty books each, but this figure probably includes a certain amount of lecture notes and mimeographed material or their equivalents. In American universities, lectures are printed and put together in book form.

The prices arrived at are relatively high (buildings, book purchases, running costs). We shall try, as we go on, to find solutions which are not likely to restrict the dissemination of culture, even if they have to be less intellectually satisfying.

Let us nevertheless bear the following figures in mind:

Public libraries for 10,000 inhabitants: $120,000 in capital investments and $30,000 in annual running costs.

University libraries for 1,000 students: $725,000 in capital investments and $170,000 in annual running costs. In developing countries this last figure may be brought down to approximately $100,000.

Specialized libraries for 100 research workers: $250,000 in capital investments and $30,000 in annual running costs (not including documentary research). This last figure should be revised and increased to $90,000 to cover promotion and development.

2.2 Readership rates and standards of information

2.2.1 PUBLIC LIBRARIES

As we have seen in section 2.1.2, readership rates for libraries are low, as a rule. Public library readers represent only between 5 per cent and 30 per cent of the literate population, depending on which developed country and which age group is under consideration, but 50 per cent of the literate population read books at home and 80–90 per cent read newspapers and magazines. In fact, intellectual effort is actively sought after by an élite only, and the prevailing attitude is a somewhat passive one. Furthermore, readership rates for a library or a documentation service may vary considerably according to the attitude taken towards arousing interest among readers or potential users. The success of such ventures as travelling libraries—bookmobiles which travel around the countryside—is a good illustration of the kind of attitude needed. One must take the books to the reader.

On this supposition, the proportion of library subscribers in the developing countries should be in the region of 50 per cent of the literate population. The readership rate varies between one and ten loans per year for one volume in the library's stock (i.e. a rotation of one to ten loans a year on average for each book). This is suitable for wealthy countries, but could if necessary be doubled for the developing countries. One cannot go any higher than this, since to do so would mean that each book would have to be read in less than a fortnight.

2.2.2 UNIVERSITY LIBRARIES

Where students are concerned, a distinction should of course be drawn between the general library, which contains the same kind of books as the public library, although they are probably of a higher intellectual standard, and the university library proper. In a year, a student will read ten or so scientific books from cover to cover; he will study approximately twenty more in order to glean useful information from them. Similarly, he will read two periodicals regularly, and will look up information in a maximum of ten others. The generally accepted figure of fifty books (or their equivalent in periodicals) per student therefore corresponds to a readership rate which we shall attempt to express in figures as follows:

Reading material	Readership rate
First 10 books	$0.5 \times 10 = 5$
Next 20 books	$0.10 \times 20 = 2$
First 2 periodicals (equivalent of 5 books $\times$ 2 = 10 books)	$0.25 \times 10 = 2.5$
Next 10 periodicals (equivalent of 50 books)	$0.05 \times 50 = 2.5$
Total per student	12 books

It is not feasible to keep every volume or issue of a periodical permanently 'to hand'. If the rate of fifty books per student were adopted, three-quarters of the stock would remain in the library and only one-quarter would be in the hands of the students. It should also be noted that basic educational textbooks alone represent almost half the needs which have to be met.

Moreover, at this level the need for variety is already apparent; even if certain books and periodicals are very little used (for example for individual or collective final-year study), it is essential that the libraries should possess them and should keep them throughout the year, although they may be used for only a month or two.

If university libraries are open to the public for purposes of life-long education, the above figures should be increased by adding the considerable numbers of users whom, in this study, we have classified with the engineers and research workers who use documentation centres.

2.2.3   SPECIALIZED LIBRARIES
AND DOCUMENTATION CENTRES:
THE CONCEPT
OF AN EXCHANGE NETWORK

The above-mentioned tendency towards specialization is even more marked in the various fields of research. There is such a wide variety of needs that it is never possible to keep all the documents needed by research workers readily available in the library. Selections have to be made according to the means at one's disposal, the subjects the research workers are dealing with and the length of time they can be expected to wait while the information they have requested is being obtained from outside sources. The need for an exchange network, therefore, is obvious. University libraries and public libraries may exchange books or periodicals or even, indeed especially, tapes, films, records or video-cassettes. To a certain extent, these exchanges may be programmed.

University libraries will make their exchange arrangements according to the curriculum. Public libraries may be able to organize an almost systematic rota or planned exchanges of documents which are rare or of outstanding interest. These exchanges will operate in direct relation to the social or cultural development of the areas served. They can therefore be predicted or even planned systematically in some cases.

On the other hand, where research or technology is concerned, the need is always a specific one, and is usually difficult to foresee. This does not make it any easier to obtain the material requested. So a compromise should be sought by weighing up the number of documents to be kept in stock and the difficulty of obtaining those which one does not have. Bearing this point in mind, we shall attempt to interpret the figure given in the *Unesco bulletin*,[1] namely 25,000 volumes for 200 research workers. First, a great deal of this literature will in fact consist of periodicals; on the research front periodicals are far ahead of books, which contain knowledge that is already established. If we continue to reckon a year's run of periodicals as the equivalent of five books, we may have, for example: 5,000 books (of 1 million characters each); 2,000 periodicals (spread over three years at the time the library is established).

This is already a sizeable stock-in-trade for a group of specialists. It is worth noting that the Japan Information Centre for Science and Technology (JICST) receives only 8,000 periodicals, and the Centre National de Recherche Scientifique (CNRS) in France slightly more than 10,000, while Chemical Abstracts analyses only 12,000—and each of these organizations supplies several thousand research workers or engineers.

Owing to specialization and the very great variety of material needed, the number of books to be provided does not increase in proportion to the number of research workers. Whereas, in a public library, a book which is not borrowed by several people in a year should be an exception, in a specialized library an issue of a periodical which is consulted once or twice in a year is almost a 'best seller'. Of course, the existence of a library or a documentation centre does not preclude specialists from having their own individual libraries. They will also subscribe to a number of periodicals which are closely connected with their subject and which they will glance through and may either keep or throw away, but they should be able to find another copy in the library if necessary.

According to the budget allotted to him, the librarian must therefore decide on the system whereby research workers are to

1. *Unesco bulletin for libraries*, vol. XVIII, no. 2, 1964.

have access to useful documents, in accordance with criteria such as those suggested below for various types of use:

Regular use: several copies in the library for borrowing and, if required, further copies in the laboratories or personal libraries of the research workers; a microfiche for reference in the library.

Frequent use: one copy in the library; a microfiche for reference in the library.

Moderate use: one copy in the library.

Infrequent use (the most usual case): no copy immediately available, but one can be borrowed rapidly from another library, or a loan or a reproduction can be obtained from a national or regional library.

Very infrequent use (a fairly common case): recourse to a national or international network to obtain a microcopy (the only rapid solution which does not entail heavy transport expenses). This microcopy is then either consulted directly, or 'enlarged' to its original size, either wholly or in part, as required after consultation.

It is obviously desirable in most cases to adopt the last two solutions, always on the assumption that the exchange networks are functioning properly, namely:

That it is possible to find out exactly what material is available from other libraries and from the international network.

That communication is rapid. The cost of transport seems to be a minor consideration, in the case of a microcopy; on the other hand, it is of major importance when original documents or photocopies have to be conveyed from place to place.

2.2.4   TOOLS FOR LITERACY WORK.
COMPARISON WITH THE ESTIMATES
FOR PUBLIC LIBRARIES

It is as well to pay special attention to the public library section for the promotion of literacy, although we know that this is only a transitional stage, since anyway the illiteracy rate is rapidly going down, and will diminish still more when enough teachers are available to teach all children to read.

Expenditure on books is not heavy, since only a few editions are involved, and the number of copies, of course, varies with the intensity of the literacy drive in the adult age-group. However, audio-visual equipment is more necessary as an adjunct to formal teaching at this level than at others. The best kind of equipment seems to be magnetic audio-visual tape, which takes up little space, is easily transportable and can be selected, changed and regulated to suit the user and whenever he likes.

There is also a certain amount that must be spent on buildings and fixtures, as well as the salaries of staff to operate the library. Altogether, it seems that the ideal *per capita* outlay on illiterates should be in the region of the sum usually set aside for public libraries. But this amount will not be spent in the same way, either as regards materials or as regards premises and presentation. There is no doubt that the 'western European' type of library, with its aloof and forbidding appearance, does not hold any immediate attraction for people who are just awakening to cultural consciousness. It would probably be better to arrange things so that the individual can come in and out without complying with formalities.

One of the decisions to be made will be how many literacy centres are to be set up, and of what kind. We spoke earlier of one public library per 10,000–100,000 inhabitants. By 'inhabitants', we meant 'literate inhabitants'. In principle, a slightly smaller number of people should use literacy centres than public libraries. In section 1.3.2.1, we estimated this figure at 10–15 per cent of the illiterate population. Let us now recall the usage rate for the first of these.

Members (developed countries), 15–40 per cent of the literate population.

Potential members (countries where individuals buy few books), 50–70 per cent (rate corresponding to the total number of inhabitants who read books in the developed countries).

Number of books lent by libraries (developed countries) (books of 300,000 characters), five to twenty per member per year.

Number of books of general literature sold each year (books of 300,000 to 1 million characters) in the developed countries, four to eight per literate per year.

Clearly, it is difficult do deduce the usage rate for illiterates from these figures, but one may safely suppose that their desire for culture and for a better understanding of things is equally great. If, on average, 50 per cent of the literate population read one to two books per month, this represents something like two hours' reading per week. As a rough estimate, one may therefore take it that 15 per cent of the illiterate population will attend the centre or will read at home for one to two hours per week.

For a total population of 10,000–20,000 including 5,000 illiterates, this gives the following usage rate:

Members: $5,000 \times 0.15 = 750$.

Average: 1.4 times per week.

Being, per day: $\dfrac{750 \times 1.4}{7} = 150$ persons.

The figure is high if each person attends only a single meeting. This may be supplemented by reading at home, to an extent of two-thirds, for example, but nevertheless two one-hour sessions per day will be required.

In comparison, let us suppose that 30 per cent of the literate population are members of this library and that each person borrows five books per year (i.e. 0.4 per month). We thus arrive at the following figures:

Members $(5,000–10,000) \times 0.3 = 1,500–3,000$ readers.

Number of books: $(1,500–3,000) \times 0.4 = 600–1,200$.

Being a daily average turnover (ordinary working days)

of $\dfrac{600–1,200}{24} = 25–50$ books.

Of course, we find ourselves again working on the original hypothesis that a book is read in three or four hours on average, but, clearly, fewer staff are needed for improving reading ability than for teaching people to read from scratch. Starting with two roughly equivalent population samples, it may be observed that in one case it is necessary to organize one or two sessions per day, using audio-visual material, and while a large staff is not required for this nevertheless an up-to-date librarian is essential to operate the equipment, give explanations and supervise loans of books to be read at home.

In the other case, however, one need only record the lending of between 25 and 50 books and, of course, see to the shelving of books, deal with recalling of books on loan and, above all, note the cost of purchasing and renewing the book stock, which is an all-important factor in this case. Depending on the available resources, the wishes of the community and the most pressing needs, it will therefore be necessary to decide what must be done to provide literacy teaching for groups of adults and improve standards of literacy among the younger members of the community.

2.3 Selection and effective presentation of information. Specialized centres

2.3.1 OUTSTANDING IMPORTANCE OF SCIENTIFIC AND TECHNICAL INFORMATION

In this section we shall deal mainly with scientific and technical information. In point of fact, several of the ideas expressed in it are perfectly applicable to other sectors, but when the question of choices comes up and perhaps that of means, it is advisable to remember the prime importance of scientific and technical material as compared with all other kinds of literature, though of course the significance of the latter must not be overlooked, and it is unquestionably much greater in volume.

We have shown the importance of culture and have explained how it makes people want to read and to express their thoughts; and we have seen that it is indubitably a factor in development and progress. Nevertheless, life in modern society is based on the achievements of science and technology and their uses. Whatever criticisms one may level—sometimes justifiably—at technological societies, the fact remains that the machinery of social life and development is wholly geared to technology. All the means of controlling this machinery and putting it into action pass at some stage or other through the hands of scientists, engineers and technicians. So it is easy to appreciate the value of information on such matters, since the material success or failure of any given project depends ultimately on this information. In the great mass of libraries and documentation centres, the place occupied by science and technology is often only a small one, but it is all-important.

The question of selection arises primarily in this sector. Whether or not one decides upon a particular list of novels is of relatively marginal importance. But to have eliminated or overlooked certain technical documents may jeopardize an entire branch of the economy.

2.3.2   THE PROBLEM OF THE SELECTION
         OF INFORMATION

The documents available on a given subject at a particular time (assuming that one has unlimited access to them) are nearly always over-plentiful; it is not so much that they supply all possible information, which provides more answers to the problems than are necessary, but that they are over-plentiful in the sense that there is duplication, that many of them deal only with generalities and do not give detailed results, or that they are more or less irrelevant to the concerns of the user. Hence it is all the more necessary to make a selection, since most libraries do not have the facilities for stocking all the existing periodicals and documents in the field which it is their business to cover.

In making a choice one is assuming a serious responsibility. Yet research teams in both laboratory and industry are compelled to choose. Until a few years ago, it was possible to subscribe to several journals, which one scanned regularly and which gave the principal information. This was a very exacting, but relatively acceptable, means of selection. Nowadays it has become almost impossible to use it without running the risk of missing too many highly important discoveries.

Some people dream of an enormous library from which one could get whatever information one needed. Such libraries exist in certain well-equipped countries, but do not provide a satisfactory solution, since one has to divide one's time between information and action, so that choices are inescapable. There are in fact two criteria to be used in choosing, and they confirm each other. The first concerns the subject; one has to choose the relevant documents which provide the basis for an answer to a question. We know that it is possible nowadays to do this with a reasonable degree of success by the use of manual or computerized bibliographical methods. In addition, specialists may be asked to eliminate documents which are not relevant.

But the second criterion concerns the value or quality of the documents in question. Several research workers claim that, at least in some sectors, quite a small proportion of these (for example 20 per cent) is of genuine use to them. In any case, this second selection is made at the end of the documentary chain, by the user, who reads the documents and sees that many of them give him very little assistance.

At this point a question immediately springs to mind; rather than eliminate these secondary documents as a final step, might it not be possible to avoid cluttering up our library shelves with them, and remove them from our bibliographical bulletins? Despite numerous reservations, the current opinion is that such a pre-selection is possible, on certain conditions. First, the only persons qualified to make this choice are highly qualified specialists working on the research front or in close collaboration with those who are in the vanguard of progress. So there emerges the role of specialized documentation centres, in which certain research workers divide their time between research proper and documentation. They alone are capable of making a selection. Moreover, they are often obliged to do so, since the means at their disposal seldom allow them to acquire more than a somewhat limited number of documents.

No one, however, is infallible, and few people are fully informed about everything published. This scientific selection can be very risky if it is not backed up by clearing-houses which systematically collect and store everything that is printed and to which one should have systematic recourse.

These clearing-houses are, or should be, made up of the network of large scientific and technical libraries. One turns to them when one thinks that some aspect of one's special branch is developing rapidly, that new sources of information are being revealed, or that valuable work is being done in a given area of the world, hitherto neglected, or, lastly, when new discoveries or instruments (or fresh needs in other sectors) begin to affect the special branch in question.

But to do this is not enough, since often, when one becomes aware of such changes by this means, without previous warning, it is already too late. A policy of systematic investigation, through subscription to selected bibliographies on one or more subjects (bibliographies on specialized areas of knowledge), is indispensable if one is to keep up with and foresee this type of development, even if only a small part of these bibliographies is used. Most of the large world documentation centres provide the opportunity, either directly or indirectly, of subscribing to such selected bibliographies. No centre, however, is altogether satisfactory; for this reason, it is becoming more and more desirable to supplement these services by the libraries' contribution, in accordance with research and development needs in the country under consideration.

It will be seen that selection of itself is really a sort of processing of the raw material of information. This fining-down process results in a new product which is more readily usable, but which is closely adapted to the purpose for which it is intended. The same type of material will not meet the needs of a person engaged in pure research and one concerned with applied engineering, even if in both cases the material refers to the same subject, and even if all of it is relevant.

2.3.3 EFFECTIVE PRESENTATION OF INFORMATION

One must go even further. Earlier, we mentioned the need to suit the content of libraries to the requirements of the public, but also the need to take steps to attract the public. Even where scientific and technical information is concerned, this same necessity must still be borne in mind. Selection and pre-selection constitute a kind of adjustment of documentary stocks to meet certain categories of requirements; it is also necessary to prepare the user for the goods which will be placed at his disposal. One cannot overemphasize the importance of this educational task, which is sometimes called user training, but which we prefer to see from a different angle, namely, the effective presentation of information for the benefit of those who might need it. This would start, of course, with secondary education, but should be extended further and further, not only at the level of higher education but also in the form of constant communication, through systematic training and re-training, between those persons who are both the producers and the principal consumers.

Specialized documentation centres are prominent among the basic units in which this sustained work and unceasing communication take place; others include professional associations, certain administrative bodies, research centres, etc. Such training in fact takes place at two levels, the first of which is a sensitization of those who are known nowadays as decision makers, pointing out to them the advantages of being well-informed when making a decision, as well as the opportunity they have of gaining rapid access to information. Obviously, these decision makers will not be content with bibliographies, but as a rule they are surrounded by specialized advisers who are in a position to have the appropriate material sought out and put to use.

So these advisers and their assistants must not only be sensitized but also introduced to the new documentary methods. A series of lectures followed by visits to computerized documentation centres or modern libraries, together with practical work, will give them an idea of how an information network functions, and will enable them to appreciate the value and reliability of the methods used. A course in a specialized documentation centre will provide them with concrete examples of how to set about using the material which has thus been selected.

2.3.4 SPECIALIZED DOCUMENTATION CENTRES

As we have just seen, these centres play a leading role in most of the developed countries, and they are beginning to acquire importance in several developing nations.

They came into existence in response to the needs of both pure and applied research. Research workers, having spent a considerable amount of their time on acquiring information, entrusted documentalists with the task of collecting the most useful information on their behalf; then they realized that it would be more profitable to join forces and share part of the documentation facilities of their laboratories.

The specialized centre, which still conforms more or less to this original plan, is therefore the principal tool for acquiring information which the research worker has at his disposal—a tool which he has himself created. As an offshoot of this, one finds discipline-oriented centres in pure science sectors, while, for their part, applied research workers and engineers have set up mission-oriented centres.

The first category includes centres concerned with physics, chemistry, astronomy, mathematics and biology. In the second category, the most typical are documentation centres dealing with the environment, pollution, agronomy, tiles and bricks, and pottery, which have practical relevance to a great many scientific sectors according to the traditional classification.

Clearly, considerable overlapping between these centres may occur if one is not careful. Furthermore, the present trend of development in science and technology is tending to blur the distinction between mission-oriented and discipline-oriented sectors; as we have seen, biologists need information on precision mechanics, electronics and chemistry, while chemists are neither willing nor able to steer clear of the problems of pollution, the agricultural sciences , medicine, etc.

All these centres share characteristics which should be emphasized, although they are becoming less clear-cut in the oldest established centres. First, the research scientists for whom they work are always close at hand, with the direct consequence that the activity of the centres is aimed solely at satisfying their most immediate needs. The second is that the documentary tasks are carried out by specialists in the discipline or sector concerned, who are capable of communicating satisfactorily with the research workers and selecting the best of the information for them. This nearly always implies a certain amount of critical analysis of the written material, and at the same time an effort to glean information as soon as possible, by attending conferences, corresponding with various laboratories, etc.

In this respect, specialized documentation centres have strong affinities with information analysis centres, as described in OECD reports and listed for the United States in the COSATI booklet.[1] However, specialized centres were devised much earlier than information-analysis centres, and a number of them have diverged from their original purpose and have become documentation centres covering ever wider areas, even to the extent of turning into multi-sectoral documentation centres.

So in addition to the discipline-oriented/mission-oriented dis-

---

1. *Directory of federally supported information analysis centres.* Washington, D.C., Federal Council for Science and Technology, Committee on Scientific and Technical Information, April 1968.

tinction we must make a further distinction between broad-range specialized centres and narrow-range centres; the first category coincides in practice with that of large libraries or interdisciplinary documentation units, while the second is closely allied to information-analysis centres, and so becomes the basis of the network of services for users.

The work carried out in these centres varies considerably according to their size and according to the sector or sectors in which they specialize; it also depends on the level of development of their sector or sectors in the country to which they belong, as well as on the needs of the corresponding branch of technology. The documentation centre or centres will be adapted not only to the present state of this branch, but also to the country's ambitions in a given field.

They are also called 'specialized libraries' when, for example, they are attached to a university, or are situated in a country where scientific and technical libraries are highly developed. When first established, they usually perform the following functions:

They provide access to original documents in their special subject. For this purpose, they receive and stock those journals which are most often consulted, and get into touch with multidisciplinary libraries or centres in order to obtain rapidly any documents which they do not consider it necessary to keep permanently to hand. The category in which the documents are placed (those which are kept in stock and those which are accessible thanks to the co-operation of other bodies) is of course determined by frequency and variety of need, but it is also determined by the facilities available in the area. Why should a library burden itself with a large number of documents if a system exists providing virtually immediate and reliable access to them? Indeed, over and above the fact that to purchase and store a large quantity of material is expensive, it slows down retrieval operations considerably.

On the other hand, when external supplies are slow or unreliable, reserve stocks are inevitably built up, despite the resulting extra cost and other disadvantages.

Specialized centres always carry out bibliographical work so as to be able undertake documentary research by subject and to select the most valuable information for their users.

Over the years, this work has varied according to the quantity of existing literature and also according to what was being done elsewhere. In the early stages, most centres listed, catalogued and classified everything they considered useful; they also made abstracts of most of the documents which were analysed in this way. Nowadays, such a task is both impossible and unnecessary. Impossible, because one cannot keep pace with the vast output of information, and because it has become unrealistic to attempt to maintain a satisfactory classification system. Unnecessary, because the large multidisciplinary centres or the large libraries have already fed most of the useful material into a computer; inexpensive automatic pre-selections, which simplify the task considerably, are therefore feasible. These pre-selections still have a number of shortcomings: they are slow; some documents are not available, because certain sources are not processed by any of the large libraries or centres in question; the presentation does not always meet one's requirements, so that additional material operations are necessary: one is nearly always obliged to use several of these systems, with the result that the same document may be processed several times; furthermore these systems are not, for the time being, compatible with one another; the working language is not that used in the country, or it may not even be a language which one knows, and so on.

Nevertheless, these general services provide a basis which the specialized centres will use to an increasing extent. The most favourable situation is one where a large computerized documentation centre exists in the country itself, in a neighbouring country or in a regional organization. There is then close co-operation between the specialized centre and the computerized centre. The former can give the latter the benefit of its skills in its special field, take part in the development of cataloguing and especially indexing methods, and help with the operations of input, analysis, indexing, filing, etc.

In return, the computerized documentation centre provides the specialized centre with computer facilities which are usually high-powered, and which make it possible to sift a large quantity of information for the benefit of the latter and to select a maximum of useful items. This makes the task of the specialists very much easier, and being relieved of the tedious job of searching for information, they are able to devote themselves to the scientific work of selection, analysis in depth and synthesis so as to meet the needs of their research workers.

One of the major roles of specialized centres is to be prepared to give rapid answers not only to bibliographical queries but also to queries of a more scientific or technical nature. It will become increasingly feasible to obtain bibliographies by automated processes; but it is almost true to say that the real work begins when one has all the documents thought to be relevant in hand—the work of compilation, criticism, comparison, the search for additional documents traced through citations, etc., and discussion with the research workers of the results obtained, in order to reach satisfactory conclusions.

One may wonder why the process has grown so complex, and why there should not be a dozen specialized centres in each country, which would share all the scientific and technical documentation while, of course, remaining in contact with one another. This idea is theoretically attractive, but in fact leads to an impossible state of affairs, since a fair number of specialized centres are still, and to an increasing extent, mission-oriented. This is quite simply due to the fact that they have to meet requirements, and the requirements nearly always arise from research objectives, whether these objectives are chosen by the research workers themselves, as in the case of pure research, or whether they spring from economic circumstances or are imposed from outside by the needs of industry or the need for practical application.

Now, it is altogether impossible to divide up the field of knowledge according to objectives, of whatever kind. Even the theoretical division based on traditional classification is not easy to handle, but thanks to work such as the Universal Decimal Classification (UDC) (or the classification of patents) it is still possible to get a clear view of the situation provided one remains at the level of the broad major divisions. One can, for example, distinguish the life sciences from the earth sciences and physical sciences. But one can never distinguish between the needs of the petroleum engineer and those of the microbiologist, the oceanographer or the nutrition specialist.

Only the keyword method, used on a large scale, will gradually make it possible to arrive at increasingly satisfactory solutions. The necessary specialized glossaries and thesauri will be drawn up by progressive stages and will be developed through constant co-operation between specialized and multidisciplinary centres; and one of the more important tasks of the specialized centres is to identify and discuss the terms used by the research workers and so decide which to use in indexing documents, while keeping up with the evolution which is inherent in the progress of research.

It is apparent that the form assumed by specialized documentation centres will vary somewhat according to the environment in which they are situated. So we shall not go into the question of the large sectoral centres which are only to be found in one or two of the world's most highly developed countries, and we shall turn our attention more especially to more modest units, working in close contact with a group of users, units which, to avoid confusion, we shall call 'documentation and analysis centres'; these centres, according to their users' needs, may be concerned with more than one branch of knowledge, for example mechanical engineering and civil engineering, or forestry and the timber industry, or fats and nutrition, and so on. Perhaps the best examples of these are the specialized centres of Europe which work for technical research centres.

Some of the information analysis centres in the United States could also serve as models, although they are so numerous and their activities are so various that it would perhaps be difficult to draw universally applicable conclusions from a study of the way in which they work. Furthermore, in many cases they do less towards the setting up of documentary card indexes than European specialized centres. As a rule, the latter, which are controlled by an association, or work for a particular profession, consist of: (a) a research centre; (b) a testing laboratory; (c) a documentation centre.

The combination of these three means that the centre is constantly in touch with the research worker. If the centre is controlled by a professional association, all its activities will always be geared to short- or medium-term objectives, in application of a coherent, properly motivated general policy, in which there is a reasonable degree of continuity.

2.4 Need to build up an appropriate body of secondary or tertiary literature

2.4.1 EXCHANGES

Whether we are dealing with public libraries, literacy training, or, more especially, with documentation for students or research workers, the contents of each library, as we have seen, must necessarily be limited. In rich countries there may be a central library which stocks a wide range of collections, but in most cases such an establishment, although necessary, cannot fulfil this function completely. The number of exchanges within the large countries and between nations forming part of regional groups will increase. In the most simple cases, these exchanges can to a certain extent be planned or organized in advance. Apart from a limited number of titles which everyone clamours to read, the content of general literature is not usually of prime importance. No library can contain everything. It fills its shelves according to the tastes of its readers and the contacts made by its librarians, sometimes with second-hand books or with gifts.

But readers like variety, and not everyone will read the same kind of literature. After a time it will become indispensable to renew part of the stock, although it may not be absolutely necessary (or even possible) to acquire enough new books to satisfy this need. If the library takes no action, it will lose a number of avid readers. The way out of the difficulty is to exchange part of the stock with a neighbouring library.[1] In order to do this it is not necessary to have precise bibliographical details of other libraries' stocks. It is enough to know roughly what one has and to be able to compare the two. The simplest method of comparison is by author and title. Such a comparison is not made very often so that, as a rule, one need only tick off items on a list.

However, when stocks are very large (tens of thousands of books),

---

1. See in particular the 'Pioneer' system in the United States as well as the network of Canadian libraries in: F. M. Gardner, *Public library legislation: a comparative study*, Paris, Unesco, 1971.

this operation becomes very costly. It is perfectly easy for someone to keep a few hundred names in his head; it takes him at most one hour to check whether or not they are to be found in a list which also includes the two or three hundred titles offered in exchange. If 1,000 or more titles are to be taken in exchange, the task will take a day, but it is still feasible.

However, if two lists of 1,000 items must be compared, it will not be possible to learn the contents of one of them by heart; one must continually refer from one to the other, ticking off the items as one goes; much more time is needed, but the task can still be performed by a single operator if the work does not have to be done quickly. However, if we wish to compare two lists of 10,000 works, we can see that several people are needed and that they cannot share the work out in a rational manner, since one person cannot benefit from what the others have found. So the method has to be changed altogether, and the best way of proceeding is to use a computer.

2.4.2   UNION CATALOGUES

As we have just seen, it is still very easy for small libraries to make exchanges, since they have to catalogue only a small number of books or documents (less than 1,000 in practice). On the other hand, as soon as this figure is exceeded, it becomes indispensable for the library to belong to a system, in which (as in all operations involving a computer) there will be a number of restrictions as to format, presentation, etc., and which, having some claims to universality, will provide for a variety of cases which are not always of direct relevance to the problem in hand. Use of a computer also carries with it some very noteworthy advantages for the internal management of large libraries (interfiling of new works, orders, management of loans, recalls, etc.).

Theoretically, a system of union cataloguing may be extended to unlimited stocks. In practice, if the data are to be presented in a homogeneous manner and if the format is to be relatively uncomplicated, it is preferable to limit each system to a group of ten or so libraries, for example, and even this affords worth-while opportunities for exchange. In order to attract interest over a wider area, it is best to proceed in two stages, i.e. first of all to establish a cataloguing system for each group of libraries, and then to pool their resources by means of 'super-cataloguing'.

Union catalogues, which are useful for general literature, are becoming indispensable for university libraries and even more so for specialized libraries or scientific- and technical-documentation centres. Furthermore, remembering the role of the material housed in the latter (see section 1.3.1), one comes to the conclusion that it should be available, if not in each village, then at least in every urban or rural zone of approximately 10,000 inhabitants. Technical books are the promotional part of a public library. Now, this material, adapted to local needs, must keep abreast of progress, i.e. new information of benefit to the locality must be constantly added; otherwise the library may perhaps be a cultural centre, but it will certainly not be the nucleus of development which the country needs.

Even if the economy is still at a rural, craftwork stage, rapid changes are occurring, and in order to keep pace with and further this transformation there is a need for such a wide variety of information that it is impossible for each village to own all the necessary material. Moreover, the needs cannot be predicted—not, at least, by the librarian alone. On the other hand, within a network it will happen much more often that a fresh demand or a personal contact reveals a book's importance and induces one of the participating bodies to acquire it. If there are ten libraries instead of one, the chances of finding a particular title are much greater. If we take a group of titles whose topicality becomes apparent at a given moment, in relation to questions of interest, they will be greater still. Let us take an example. Suppose that in a centre one has one chance in five of finding a document. In a network of ten imaginary libraries, all the same size and with different stocks, in which this document is equally likely to be found, the probability of finding it will be 0.89, i.e. one has almost nine chances in ten of obtaining it. If we now consider five different and unrelated documents which must be found, in a single centre one will have only three chances in 10,000 in finding all five of them, whereas in the network of ten libraries mentioned above the probability will be 0.57, i.e. one will have more than one chance in two—an improvement of almost 2,000. Naturally, we are assuming that these libraries stock different documents. These results must therefore be qualified, but this significant example brings out the advantages to be gained

77

from large card indexes or, failing these, from operating in a network, provided one has access to union catalogues which are kept scrupulously up to date.

2.4.3   BIBLIOGRAPHIES

The preceding remarks about books in general are even more applicable to scientific and technical documents, in view of the numbers and the diversity of these. Fortunately, a large portion of them (between three-quarters and four-fifths) appear in journals published regularly, which barely exceed 10,000 to 20,000 in numbers. Moreover, there are several services whose purpose is to index all these documents, giving each one codes and characteristic key words for purposes of classification. Most of these services are provided in English. They exist, however, in French, Russian and Japanese; and for certain specialized sectors a few bibliographical services are also available in German and French.

In order to get a clear view of the role of scientific and technical documents other than books, one should bear in mind what section of the public consults them. Whether these documents be theses, reports on studies or research, articles in journals or reports of conferences, only a few persons have access to them, namely, specialized research workers and engineers, who wish to promote new techniques or develop their discoveries, and teachers and popularizers, who wish to keep up to date for the purposes of teaching, preparing a course, compiling a survey, writing a book, or informing public opinion. Even in the most highly developed countries, the proportion of such users is low: 50 per cent of the stocks of the British National Lending Library are never consulted, and 25 per cent are consulted only once a year. In France and the United States a similar state of affairs exists. Rare is the document which is requested more than once or twice a year—quite unlike the detective story or romance which is borrowed by several dozen readers.

Then again, it is certain that no research or independent progress is possible in a given country unless people have easy access to documents on the 'research front'. The choice to be made at this point is therefore a great responsibility. On the one hand, it is out of the question to burden libraries and documentation centres with

78

printed matter which will scarcely ever be taken out. On the other, unless arrangements are made for channels through which the necessary documents may be obtained easily and promptly as the need arises, the establishment is doomed to be starved out of existence. It should be noted that the very low readership rates mentioned above for the large European libraries nevertheless correspond to high absolute figures: every day the National Lending Library issues more than 3,000 copies of documents to its customers, and the documentation centre of the CNRS, in France, supplies nearly 2,000 per day. All the countries of the world may call upon the reprography services of the developed countries, and are given satisfactory service.

It nevertheless seems desirable that, on subjects which will be of the greatest use in its development, each country should possess at least one national scientific library which stocks a copy of all the leading journals relevant to the research and industry of the area.

If one wishes to have rapid access to these documents, a portion of them must also be indexed and described, the bibliographical system being geared to local needs.

However, this system should interlock as smoothly as possible with the international bibliographical network or with international systems such as Medlars, ISI, etc. True, this cannot easily be brought about for the time being, as these systems do not dovetail with one another. Depending upon the sector to which it belongs, the local library will tend to align itself with one of the existing systems rather than another. But care should be exercised not to take any action which is irreversible, and above all to conform to the standards put forward by UNISIST, which are being worked out by ISO. Even if our library has a computer for the automatic retrieval of documents, it will be well advised (unless this involves a serious loss of information) to use several magnetic tapes of foreign or international origin, and not to rely upon one source alone.

This is not the place to dwell on problems of co-ordination; let us merely recall that they occur at several levels:

Computer formats (changing formats is necessary, but this is not a very burdensome task, as a rule).

Homogeneity of bibliographical descriptions or cataloguing rules. This is no doubt the most important problem, since it is the bibliographical description which makes it possible to identify a document. Therefore, only if one has sufficiently detailed cataloguing rules can one recognize an article when one meets it the second time. It is also of great value to be able to recognize a document when one wishes to incorporate additional information about it into the system. For example, one may have a translation of it, or a more detailed indexing entry, or an abstract in a local language, or a review, and so on. It is obvious that if one uses properly standardized cataloguing rules one can enrich a system by adding the national or regional contribution to it.

Vocabulary. The retrieval strategy will vary, depending upon the thesauri used for indexing and the way in which the documents are indexed. It is very important, however, that the retrieval strategy used should be closely geared to the policy or policies followed in indexing and the writing of abstracts, where they are required. To this end, work is being done at international level to homogenize thesauri and to compile multilingual thesauri if they are needed. These tools are the keys to the computer processing of documentary material, and they will play an increasingly important part in the transfer of information and in communication in the scientific and technical fields.

Whole interconnected networks of computers are appearing in the most highly developed countries. These are coming into being because it is convenient to put questions to large computers at a distance while one's own materials are only on a modest scale. Furthermore, an overloaded computer may transfer part of the work to another unit in the network (especially when this network covers a range of longitudes so that there is a variation in time zones). In practice, documentary card indexes are among those that benefit from such interconnected networks, because they are bulky, difficult to stock all in one place and heavy to transfer, and, since they are widely scattered, only the network as a whole can supply a rapid answer to a query.

While bearing in mind the precautions mentioned in section 1.2.5, we may predict that such computerized bibliographical networks, combined with data banks of varying degrees of sophistication, will gradually be developed in all countries, and each country should be aware of the arrangements to be made in order to direct this development most effectively. These arrangements concern:

The choice of scientific and technical sectors on which the main work will be concentrated.

The appropriate way of processing the documents corresponding
to each of these sectors (selection of certain sources or certain
categories of documents; connexion with work done locally,
detailed indexing or analysis, or possibly reviews, etc.).

The practical task of setting up the network and the stages in its
development (one or more pilot centres, the possibility or otherwise of long-range interconnexions, etc.).

Foreign contacts, particularly with neighbouring countries, depending upon whether the country is in a geographical area
governed by formal agreements (Common Market, COMECON,
West Africa, Latin America, etc.).

2.4.4 SYNOPSES, LECTURE COURSES AND TRANSLATIONS

In every country which has reached a certain minimum level in
science or technology, technical research laboratories or units are to
be found. Even if these are on a very modest scale, they contribute
something to the growth of knowledge. Research workers and
engineers publish their work, and journals are started. This movement should be given as much encouragement as possible, since
a national journal has a much greater impact on progress than
even a brilliant publication in a remote provincial review. If a
country is too small to bear the expense of publishing a worth-while
journal by itself, it should join forces with neighbouring countries
or with teams working in the same cultural area, rather than allow
the fruits of its labours to be lost to view among the world output
of literature. This is the primary publication. But often, if this
publication is aiming at a sufficiently wide audience, it will also
contain synopses, sometimes translations, and even, in some cases,
select bibliographies. If they are well produced, such journals can
be of considerable assistance in teaching.

Obviously, in the most highly developed countries a distinction
can be drawn between the various kinds of journal; in theory,
primary reviews contain only original work, while synopses are
to be found in other publications appearing at irregular intervals
(pseudo-periodicals). Books and journals published in the country
itself constitute the national scientific and technical heritage; they
reflect the customary view of science and culture in the region

where they are produced. They thereby make an invaluable contribution to the intellectual wealth of mankind. For this reason their publication should be given every possible encouragement. In particular, the courses given in higher- and technical-educational establishments could well be published and disseminated.

As for translations, they are not used often enough to warrant publication; therefore, one should merely describe them and list them in bibliographies.

2.5   Priority sectors

The question of priority sectors does not arise in the same way at all levels of development. There are some countries in which all sectors are priority sectors, and where there is a need for the fullest possible information in all fields. At present, these are relatively few in number, since even the affluent nations are far from being universally competent. Many of them have an economy which complements that of other neighbouring or distant nations. However, the aim of research and, still more, that of information, is not only to strengthen and perfect known techniques, but also to encourage investigation of those which it is desirable to know. So choices should not be made solely with an eye to the present situation, but also in accordance with the state of affairs which will foreseeably exist five or ten years hence. At the same time, specialists capable of using the information which is thus accumulated will be needed. These choices are not unlike those which must be made in the field of research.[1]

In most wealthy countries, one will be well advised to have a supply of information on all sectors as soon as the population group concerned reaches 20 or 30 million inhabitants, and even this figure is being lowered, since activities are becoming more varied and the scientific and technical reserves needed by each of them are increasing. It is therefore very probable that by the end of the decade a great many population groups of 10 million inhabitants will have

---

1. H. de l'Estoile, 'Choice of criteria for a research and development strategy', *The role of science and technology in economic development*, Unesco, 1970, 216 p. (Science policy studies and documents, 18.)

to be equipped with virtually encyclopaedic libraries and documentation centres. Let us look, for example, at the evolution of some of the research and development centres established elsewhere than in capital cities, which initially focused on a few priority areas of knowledge, in accordance with the task of each region. We shall see that their original aims are becoming broader and broader, and the time is not far off when they will be all-embracing.

The case of the developing countries is similar, in that they are wise to start by concentrating on a number of key sectors, even if they confine themselves to background material for the remainder. Clearly, the first documents to be obtained are those which deal with the country and the geographical area and describe its natural resources and its potential. Unfortunately, it still happens far too often that anyone who requires documentation on a particular area of Africa or Asia is compelled to come and consult it in Europe or America. It is hard to see how a nation can emerge from the development stage if it knows less about itself than the outside world does. Even when a ministry gives orders for expert reports to be made on national resources, these are not always easy to obtain in the country itself. This holds good for geology, climate, hydrology and agronomy, including the study of forests and soils. Data about the people themselves, as well as about their traditional crafts, are also a starting point for development. It is true that information on these two subjects is, as a rule, readily available to the countries' leaders; some kinds of information have no need to be put in writing or expressed in figures in order to be brought home to the people whose daily life they reflect. Rather, what would seem to be lacking is a true appreciation of the value of this domestic potential as compared with techniques imported from abroad. Although there is no denying the technological gap to be closed, the problem is still rather one of language difference; this is an obstacle to any attempt to derive, from both internal resources and those imported from abroad, new applications and processes which the people could assimilate and which would be effective enough to bring about a material improvement, without doing violence to the rich heritage of earlier civilizations.

Of course, documentation cannot be divorced from the needs of research workers, and, broadly speaking, its function is to serve its users. There are cases, however, in which its purpose is to give encouragement, and this means that it must be well presented in order to be turned to good account; there is no need to be ashamed if, to achieve this, one has to resort to methods of semi-advertising. Thus, as regards the country's natural resources, it appears indispensable to acquaint engineers, craft workers and academics with the processing techniques whereby these resources may be used to the best advantage, for example mining techniques, agricultural sciences, mechanics, electrotechnics, building and rural development.

If the documentation centre has been properly thought out, it should promote not only basic lifelong education, but also the development of economic activities. It is sometimes said that mines must be run by big companies, because substantial funds are needed to work the subsoil, and such funds bring with them their own equipment and technology. This is true, no doubt, but one should not ignore the fact that the earliest European mines were small, locally run affairs, and that some African mines nowadays are better suited to semi-rustic management than to the importation of heavy plant, which is more rational in theory but sometimes more expensive. However, a knowledge of geology and mining techniques is needed in order to settle this point.

So in every instance one will have to select the type of documents best suited to potential needs, which can be discerned by a person with a sound knowledge of natural resources. The librarian should not be content to be a mere keeper of documents which he acquires more or less in response to current demand or book sellers' advertising; rather, he should acquire them on the basis of surveys of activities which ought to be encouraged in the area which he has to supply with information.

Something should be said about hygiene and health, since this is a human factor of the greatest importance. Nothing worth while can be accomplished if people are ill. Health is not a luxury for rich countries, but the necessary precondition for any really effective work. Information about hygiene and medicine is needed just as much as up-to-the-minute documentation on the latest research findings. In Europe, doctors keep abreast of current information by reading two or three important journals; there are audio-visual campaigns to educate the public, and the subject is also taught in schools (hygiene courses, etc.). Nursing and paramedical staff receive much of their information through the doctors in the hospital services. These channels of information are, of course, equally valid for the developing countries, but it should be noted that doctors are few and far between, and that hospitals, especially, are scarce, so that medical documentation at the technicians' level should rank proportionately much higher than in Europe. Moreover, there is no guarantee that the current European- or American-type documentation would be the kind best suited to their needs, even when it deals with tropical medicine. Health should therefore be singled out for priority treatment by all libraries. But the kind of documents and the way in which they are presented will vary considerably according to the type of library or documentary unit in question.

2.6 The documentation network in relation to population and level of development. Regional networks

One of the important points to be settled is how the documentation network should be organized. Obviously, it will not be organized in the same way in the United States as in Switzerland, or in India as in Japan. Three factors are of great importance:

Size of the country. A large country will have much more substantial national resources behind it than a country with a small population. Furthermore, a country's physical size will have effects which differ from those of the size of its population. On the other hand, it is difficult to organize a documentation network satisfactorily in a large country.

Level of development. This has a direct bearing on the number of users, the kind of documents to be acquired and processed and the funds which may be earmarked for the network.

Membership or otherwise of a regional network. In fact there are not many regional information networks as yet, but several are being formed. In some cases, the establishment of such networks is even strongly to be recommended. This has direct consequences for planning.

Let us go into these various points in greater detail.

2.6.1   SIZE OF THE COUNTRY

The recent International Federation for Documentation (FID) report[1] recommends that a national library and a national documentation centre be set up in each country. In addition, the UNISIST report advocates the setting up of a special institution to co-ordinate documentary activities. Such bodies will certainly take on very different forms according to the section of the population for which they cater. Theoretically, for public or school libraries, only the literate portion of the population should be taken into account, and for university libraries and documentation centres, only the numbers of students, engineers and research workers. However, let us not forget that the percentage of literates is rising rapidly, and consequently it would be unreasonable to plan long-term structures which do not cater for the whole population.

Moreover, we have seen in sections 2.1.3 and 2.2.1 above that the proportion of potential library users does not necessarily bear any direct relation to the level of development, provided that these libraries are well suited to their users' needs.[2]

We must also remember that the proportion of students is not really related to the country's wealth.

We saw earlier (section 2.5) that in order to justify multidisciplinarity, it is necessary to cater for a population of around 10 to 20 million. In turn, each population group of this size in the wealthy countries today and in the developing countries tomorrow, will very probably demand information on every subject under the sun. This is the case in the regions or in the regional metropolitan centres of the European countries. This figure is not, of course, invariable, but it is interesting to compare it with the estimates made in section 2.1.4. A population unit of 10 million inhabitants would require, in theory, 1,000 public reading units (at the rate of one per 10,000 inhabitants), and in fact we find that there are between 50 and 200 such reading units. If one takes the

1. FID Committee for Developing Countries, Budapest, *Study on national structures for documentation and library services in countries with different levels of development*, Unesco, Paris, 254 p.
2. In the developing countries, people read less, but they seldom have the wherewithal to buy many books. In the wealthy countries, people read a great deal, but, at least in some of these countries, they do not often use the libraries.

proportion of students to be between 0.1 and 0.5 per cent, which is an average percentage, but somewhat low, there would be 10,000 to 50,000 students, for whom ten university libraries or so would be needed (at a rate of one per 1,000 to 5,000 students). Lastly, assuming a well-balanced state of affairs, we can estimate the number of research engineers and research workers at one-thousandth of the total population (close to the number of students). Since no country has yet achieved this balanced state, we shall consider that the proportion of research workers in the population is somewhere between one per 1,000 (in a wealthy country) and one per 10,000 (in a developing country); twenty documentation units will be needed (at a rate of between one per 100 and one per 1,000 research workers).

Such a number of units—which has no doubt been over-estimated here, considering the resources of the poor countries—certainly needs careful co-ordination (union catalogues, arrangements for inter-library exchanges, task sharing between documentation centres, standardization of filing methods and indexing terminology, exchange of magnetic tapes, etc.). This still holds good for a smaller population (5 million inhabitants, for example).

Below this number, however, it seems preferable to seek to form an association with neighbouring countries. But it should be noted that the population of some countries is growing rapidly, and that when medium-term planning is being undertaken it is advisable to provide for the setting up of national co-ordination structures [1] On the other hand, they are not really justified in countries with less than 3 million inhabitants, since in this case there would be only one documentation centre, one university, and a large number of libraries located in the capital city. In this case it will be sufficient for the director of the documentation centre or of the national library—who should be one and the same person—to be in charge of all these units. This solution may be extended to cover a number of other instances, according to the level of development up to 10 million inhabitants, on condition that a fairly free rein is given to most public and school libraries as well as to university libraries when they have specific problems.

By way of contrast, if one considers large countries, when is it

1. P. H. Sewell, *The planning of library and documentation services*, p. 64–87. (Doc. IIEP/S.20/1 1969.)

advisable to share out responsibilities and subdivide the network? Three types of division are possible: by geographical area, by speciality and by function. It is extremely difficult to say which is the best solution for each specific case, all the more so since, very often, the structure of the national networks has been determined by a set of historical circumstances in which logic has played only a minor part. We shall nevertheless try, starting from four possible schemes (which do not exist in any country), to expound the arguments in favour of one or other of them:

Total centralization. A national body to which all libraries and documentation centres are subordinate.

Decentralization by function. For example: (a) a national public library handling widely-read books, to which all public libraries and, to some extent, school libraries are subordinate; (b) a national scientific and technical library handling primary books and documents, to which university libraries and regional or local scientific libraries, if there are any, are subordinate; (c) a national documentation centre responsible for the bibliographical description and indexing of books and documents as well as information retrieval by subject.

Decentralization by scientific sector. For each sector of science and technology there is a library and a documentation centre, which collect primary literature and also perform the task of bibliographical description. These two functions may be performed by a single body, or they may, alternatively, be split. Public and school libraries are treated separately in this scheme.

Regional decentralization. May, if necessary, be superimposed on one of the three patterns outlined above, each region then being treated as if it were a little State. But, owing to the smaller area covered, structures at the regional level will necessarily be more centralized than they would have been at the national level.

It would, of course, be possible to imagine more complex combinations and to adopt, for example, a pattern of centralization for libraries and one of decentralization by sector for documentation centres, or vice versa. Similarly, public reading facilities may be organized along lines different from those pertaining to technical documentation, etc.

Obviously, the first pattern is suitable for sparsely populated countries. Its suitability begins to appear questionable only when a nation possesses at least four or five major scientific or technical centres, i.e. depending upon the level of development and the geographical features of the country, when it has upward of 10 to 25 million inhabitants.

Even in large countries it offers distinct advantages. The organic dependence which binds libraries and documentation centres to their national management may permit: (a) adequate knowledge and updating of the content of libraries; (b) computerization of card indexes in a single system, which thus operates on a single programme in all libraries and centres; (c) organization of exchanges on the most rational basis possible; (d) computerization and full employment of documentary card indexes, thanks to the use of a single system. This does not rule out problems of external compatibility (if card indexes are received from outside which are incompatible with one another), but these are satisfactorily solved once and for all for the whole country. Furthermore, no problems of compatibility will arise within the country itself.

Needless to say, as with any centralized system, the advantages to be gained from it (at the level of costs, in particular) are liable to be outweighed by the disadvantages of the unwieldy structures to which it may give rise. As in any system, optimal size will be greater as the means of controlling it are more powerful.

In the public reading sector, clearly, most activities (loans, knowledge of readers' needs, etc.) tend to take place at the level of manual operations. Computerization will continue to be the exception. The overriding advantage of centralization is therefore that acquisitions may be grouped (with consequent savings) and, if necessary, union catalogues may be kept in a standard format and exchanges of books organized. A certain amount of centralization is also desirable for the purpose of investigating, defining and organizing the assistance which these libraries might be in a position to give to literacy training. Methods could be developed at national level, and the manufacture or acquisition of materials or tools would gain from being unified. This applies even to the largest countries, although alternatives would naturally have to be provided for population groups differing markedly from one another (different languages, traditions too remote from one another, or living conditions—town dwellers, country dwellers, or natives of mountainous or desert regions).

For scientific and technical literature (books and journals) there can be no doubt that it pays to plan acquisitions, but, at least in the affluent countries, there is no question, in a centralized system, of making a volume by volume check on what a library or a documentation centre purchases. We have seen, however, that a computerized union catalogue is essential. Taking the achievements in the United Kingdom and France as a starting point, it seems advisable to go further and to set up a central body which would act as a 'rear-guard' for the library network, and to which any query whatsoever might be addressed in the almost certain hope of obtaining a definite answer. The services rendered by this 'rear-guard' may, of course, be more costly and may sometimes even be a little slower than those which might be secured from the local library or university, but the certainty which it affords of finding an answer justifies the cost of centralization in this case. The British experiment furnishes ample proof of its value for human communities which enjoy a high technical standard and comprise more than 50 million inhabitants. This is not a ceiling. This figure may certainly be doubled, at least. Moreover, Japan also seems to be moving decisively in this direction. It should be noted, however, that the operation of a centralized library is very directly dependent on the infrastructure of the postal and telecommunications services. This system is certainly not ideal when communications by mail, telephone and telegraph are slow or unreliable. In addition, the rational organization which justifies it presupposes a fairly high basic educational standard, going beyond technical or scientific training. Those engaged in such an activity must be accustomed to working in a modern society, which implies a sense of technical and administrative relations and, at all levels, a sense of responsibility, without which a somewhat complex organization cannot hope to survive.

Where bibliography is concerned, centralization is even more profitable, since, if the documentation centres were autonomous, they would each find themselves repeating similar tasks on the same documents.[1] However, it is only as a result of the contribution of computer science in respect of automated bibliography that it is possible to ensure the efficient operation of large data banks of documentary references. There is at present a great deal of controversy in some countries on this subject, but it is due to situations

---

1. In France, certain journals are summarized as many as thirty or fifty times by different documentation centres.

inherited from the past which people are reluctant to amend, to the temporary inadequacy of certain national documentation centres, or to the fact that groups of users have decided to allocate more funds to documentation than others. The material and human investment needed to establish a satisfactory system is considerable and must be offset by attracting as much custom as possible. Furthermore, speed and quality are on the whole easier to obtain where centralization is the rule. The cost is in any case much lower. This holds good whatever the size of the country, but it does not mean that large nations adopt this solution, though it is probable that they will gradually come round to it.

We have just seen that the optimum degree of centralization varies according to functions. We may therefore be inclined to think that above a certain size it is preferable to have separate networks for the main information functions, these are: (a) public reading, culture and general education; (b) provision of scientific and technical books and documents; (c) bibliography; (d) network for direct information of technologists and specialists through analysis of everything the above-mentioned information sources can supply.

These are tasks of a somewhat different nature, which are carried on separately in several large countries. Public reading, in particular, is of a rather different nature in rich countries from technical documentation. It is bound up with the culture and education of the individual and his leisure time, whereas scientific and technical documentation is intended for groups of people (universities, industrial firms, research centres, agriculture) and accordingly is part of man's working life. The problems faced are different, and when it comes to communities numbering 10 to 20 million people some will think it preferable to have two distinct networks and maintain numerous links between them, for instance as regards cataloguing methods. The above range of 10 to 20 million inhabitants depends on the capability and drive of the bodies concerned and on the special conditions in which they operate.

In poor countries, the dividing line between working life and personal development is not nearly so clearly marked, with the result that this threshold should be raised considerably to some 50 million inhabitants at least. If poor nations are to develop properly, they need a forceful policy to promote literacy and individual culture. People acquire that culture in libraries and documentation centres, as well as in literacy centres, and there is no hard-and-fast boundary to be discerned between leisure and work.

If we now consider two other functions which are fairly different in themselves (particularly in the scientific and technical sectors)—first, bibliographical work and, second, work relating to research and the provision of books or source material (loans, reproduction facilities, microfilms, etc.)—we can see of course that they are quite different in nature, but by and large they serve the same public and concern the same documents. It would therefore theoretically be preferable not to separate them. The economic advantage of bringing them together, however, is not overwhelming. So it is very probable that in young countries where the logic of the planners prevails a single system, fulfilling both functions and coming under the authority of the same body, will be developed. The old nations, on the other hand, are most likely to maintain the present situation, in which two wholly or partly distinct networks function side by side.

We shall deal later with direct information services for users, which depend much more on the level of development than on the size of the country.

Another point to be settled in the organization of information networks was whether they should be decentralized by science sector. The advantage of decentralization becomes apparent whenever needs are felt in certain sectors which thereupon acquire a high degree of priority. It is noteworthy that expenditure on information is on an average very low in relation to the resources involved in economic activity. Total research budgets represent only 1–3 per cent of production budgets (at the most), and information budgets are measured in hundredths of research budgets, which means that they come to less than one-thousandth of production costs. This is the case so long as the need to be well informed, always regarded essentially as merely desirable, does not suddenly become imperative. If this happens in a particular sector, 0.5–1 per cent of turnover is readily spent on documentation requirements, and this has a considerable impact on information activities.

Organizing an information network by sector has no proper justification in logic and still less as regards costs. Indeed, it entails expensive overlapping of work and produces systems in which the various sectors are incompatible, but it is a situation that may have to be borne with, at least for a time. Doctors will obviously not be particularly interested in documentation on metallurgy or earth sciences, and conversely, but they will be prepared to pay a lot for a medical network that meets their needs. This holds good in the other technical fields, and one of the major concerns of specialists in information science is to curb the additional expenditure necessitated by this state of affairs.

To conclude, it is true that in most cases it is advisable to try to organize scientific and university libraries on as highly centralized a basis as possible, whatever the size of the country, but if this is done special attention should be paid to the services provided locally for users.

Centralized structures offer the following advantages:

They avoid situations in which there are two libraries with similar holdings situated close together (for example school library and public library, or documentation centre for development and university library).

They enable accessions to be planned for the whole system, while leaving libraries or local centres more or less free to acquire the books they need.

Truly compatible systems for bibliography and cataloguing can be used.

Exchanges can be organized.

However, all other decisions would of course be taken locally, such as: (a) hours of opening and closing, (b) organization of the library—number and recruitment of requisite staff (although conforming with general instructions); (c) material arrangements, which are a matter of local habits and needs; (d) accessions (though the general programme for the planning of accession must be taken into account); (e) all aspects of reproduction services, which must in part be organized locally; (f) computerized bibliographical services will perhaps in the future use terminals connected to a computer network, but the framing of questions and interrogation will nearly always be done locally, as will the interpretation of replies; (g) the fact that it is linked with general services will not prevent the library or the local centre from maintaining a bibliography on specifically local problems; (h) generally speaking, all relations with users, investigation of requirements and activities to publicize services are a matter for local decision; (i) under a general development programme, decisions to modify and improve services so as to meet local needs will also be taken locally.

Thus the size of the country, although not an entirely decisive factor, is of great importance in the organization of libraries and information services. Here, as in other cases, nations with a large population are theoretically at an advantage, but there are a good many factors against them. The sort of organization one is more or less obliged to work towards is often by no means the best or the least expensive. Their limitations depend as much on historical circumstances as on the stage of development reached, and on the material and moral infrastructure one may count upon.

2.6.2　THE DOCUMENTATION NETWORK
AND THE LEVEL OF DEVELOPMENT

We have considered the effect of the size of a nation on the form of its documentation and library network, and we shall see further on how to a certain extent this factor can be diminished in importance by means of associations or agreements within groups of countries. However, countries where libraries have been in existence for centuries may make quite different choices and have different preferences from young countries which have a much freer hand to choose the best possible structure.

In each case there is a different emphasis as regards the use of available resources. The concern of the latter countries is to draw up future operating budgets. In the former case, the requirement is to encourage the modernization, adaptation and transformation of the system, which, it is hoped, will at all events continue to maintain the quality of the service it offers. And the fact that old and young nations have different needs will affect the general structure.

In countries with a long-established tradition, the main task is to persuade existing bodies and those in charge of them to work together, to adopt common standards, to exchange their publications on a larger scale, and thereby to constitute a real information network rather than a number of isolated centres in juxtaposition. Two types of action must be taken in support of these ideas, and both will require financial resources.

The first consists in choosing an existing body (sometimes two) and developing it by modernizing its working methods and its services, so as to show both users and other libraries what can be achieved, and so draw attention to the advantages of the new information technologies.

The second type of action consists in subsidizing, from an assistance fund, first, work undertaken jointly by several centres to modernize their activities with a view to exchanging their publications and sharing their tasks and, second, isolated advanced-technology schemes serving as a kind of standard bearer for the network as a whole.

There is really no need to set up new bodies, except university libraries which will naturally be established as new universities are opened. What is needed instead is the formation of groups, but this can only be a very gradual process if it is not to come to grief for psychological and sociological reasons. This policy calls for a kind of national federating body acting through persuasion and subvention.

Countries with little experience in these matters are in a very different position.

We have just seen that for small nations (20 million inhabitants, for instance) it is preferable to keep down the proliferation of structures. The ideal would therefore be to have only one national body acting as the central library, the national documentation centre and the co-ordinating agency within the meaning of UNISIST Recommendations 15 and 20.[1] It is sometimes felt that the federating body is better able to fulfil its function if it has no executive or management duties. This is perfectly legitimate when what is being sought is a very much decentralized structure which will ensure the balance and development of several executive bodies (this is true in particular of research laboratories, where it is considered that if original thinking is to bear fruit a very great degree of independence is needed, and the desire is not to overlook any team, however unimportant it may seem).

This does not apply to the data and documentation banks of today, particularly in the developing countries, where the prime requirement is efficiency and utility, and the aim is to provide the most effective service at the lowest cost.

1. UNISIST. *Study report on the feasibility of a world science information system by the United Nations Educational, Scientific and Cultural Organization and the International Council of Scientific Unions*, Paris, Unesco, 1971, 161 p. See also the *Synopsis*.

We must not, however, overlook the initial training of specialists or the influence of the ministry responsible for them. The training of librarians and documentalists is a matter calling for the utmost attention. There are at present two schools, which no doubt stem from European traditions. The first is concerned mainly with the conservation and study of old books and artistic and literary documents; the second with the most up-to-date methods of analysing, indexing and computerizing modern scientific documents. Librarians of the former school usually come under a ministry concerned with culture, and those of the latter under a science or technical education department. University libraries may belong to one or the other of these two groups. Public libraries perhaps belong rather to the former, and documentation centres to the latter. It is most desirable to transcend this duality, for the most urgent needs of the developing countries cannot be exactly met by what either of these schools has to offer. Modern information methods are often too sophisticated to be used without modification to meet the needs of universities, of the public and even of technicians. Besides, the culture to be promoted in the developing countries is too different from European culture for the latter to serve as a model.

The qualities desirable in librarians and documentalists must therefore be determined simply by considering people who have already shown initiative and shouldered responsibilities, though the attributes of each of them should be blended into a single structure and constantly added to by bringing the local situation before them (attendance, figures, influence of libraries on the economy, handicrafts, literacy teaching, education, etc.), and care must be taken to keep a step-by-step check on its development and progress.

All this points to the desirability of having a central body, to which documentation centres in every branch of knowledge, as well as university libraries and public libraries, would be subordinated in a manner to be specified later in this report. Such a body would at the same time carry out research and planning, and would have resources commensurate which the policy it would assist in defining, in regard both to domestic matters and to foreign relations and exchanges.

This, we would recall, holds good for developing countries with populations of up to 20 or 30 million, according to the size and potential wealth of the country. Beyond that range, particularly in a region of some diversity, such a structure would no doubt be oversimplified, for adaptation to local needs will require decision-making centres that are much closer to the user than a central agency can be. Furthermore, communications will not generally enable exchanges to be made frequently enough for there to be real unity between the national library of the capital and this or that local library. A federal structure is an absolute necessity; but to avoid dispersion of effort it is essential to select a number of suitably experienced bodies and provide them with resources and funds so as to give them undisputed pre-eminence in the geographical or ethnic area entrusted to them. In order to maintain a balance between these regional centres and the national library of the capital, it is preferable for the federating agency responsible for policy and fund allocation to be separate from the national library and to be mainly concerned with research and the teaching of information science.

2.6.3   POSSIBILITY OF BELONGING
        TO A REGIONAL NETWORK

The existence of UNISIST and of various other bodies working in agriculture, atomic energy, and so forth serves as a reminder that information is a world-wide problem and that consequently any national policy is directly dependent on what is achieved in other countries, particularly those producing the bulk of original information. The centres where this scientific, technical and literary information is produced shift and vary ever more rapidly. For a very long time these sources were to be found in Western Europe, then they moved over to the United States, then in part to the Soviet Union, and nowadays the tendency is for them to be increasingly widely distributed throughout the world (Far East, South America, etc.) as an ever greater variety of people gain access to culture, science and technology.

There are affinities, however, between these various information-producing centres. Likewise there are political relations between various countries which induce them to co-operate more closely in the exchange of information. For instance, the Common Market countries have decided to embark on a series of joint activities in scientific documentation. So have the COMECON countries. So also have the French-speaking countries, which form a minority with common linguistic needs, the librarians of Arab universities and so on. There are also associations based upon geographical proximity (exchanges between certain Latin American countries, between certain African countries, etc.). An attempt has been made by UNISIST to determine what advantages a world system for the exchange of information could provide, as well as the difficulties it would entail.[1] We shall now describe very briefly the services that might be rendered by a regional network which would form the junction between the world system and the national groups. The multinational regional agencies, if any, will of course have only those responsibilities entrusted to them by the States in question, and those responsibilities will therefore be as varied as the particular situations with which they have to contend. We may tentatively suggest, however, what some of their duties ought to be. Broadly speaking, the main task of UNISIST is to establish conditions that will promote exchanges of information (standardization and harmonization of administrative methods and of structures, training, assistance to the Third World, etc.). On the other hand, the national centres should provide the direct services needed by the various categories of readers and users in their countries. In very large countries they can organize these services on a national basis, of course with the backing of the world system. But in small- or medium-sized nations certain tasks can be shared with other countries and a number of activities can be put on a regional footing, without impairing the quality and rapidity of the services rendered or lessening the responsibility of each country for important decisions.

2.6.3.1   *Cataloguing of books*

We have seen the considerable advantage of organizing exchanges of books and compiling union catalogues. The preparation of such catalogues is the job of the libraries, which incorporate in them lists of their holdings and of their accessions. A survey can be first

---

1. N. B. Arutjunov, 'The requirements to be met by national scientific and technical information systems', *Unesco bulletin for libraries*, vol. XXVII, no. 5, September-October 1973.

made on a national basis by computer. It is most advisable that a more general survey be carried out regionally, either by combining and collating the magnetic tapes produced nationally or, in the case of small nations, by introducing into a computer, with their assistance, the lists provided by their national libraries.

It is important that this should be done on a regional scale, but much less so on a world scale, for the distances are such that it is of little consequence to an Asian library, for instance, to know that a particular work is available in such and such a library in Central America. If such information is needed, which does happen fairly often in the case of rare documents, it is much more convenient to be able to apply to a regional authority which itself keeps the pooled union catalogues of libraries in Central America up to date. The same applies to Arab libraries, African libraries, libraries in the COMECON countries and so forth.

2.6.3.2 *Information retrieval*

Previous studies (section 1.2.2) have shown the importance of central reprography banks to which the user can confidently apply for a copy of any document he may require. At the national level these banks are an invaluable means of obtaining full information on a given subject. However, despite their efforts, they do not have everything. They make up for what they lack by means of exchanges among themselves and by regularly giving one another the fullest particulars of their holdings. In the case of periodicals this raises no problems, as there are only a certain number of titles, and the work will be further facilitated when the world register of periodicals (ISDS) comes out and they can be located by means of an international code number (ISSN). As regards books, mention has been made above of the regional pooling of national union catalogues. We are left, then, with the other documents, which are sometimes referred to as low-circulation literature.

It is undoubtedly for each country to organize the collection and cataloguing of its own low-circulation literature (theses, reports, studies, essays, etc.). But it should be noted, first, that some countries are too small to be able to make the best use of the results of this operation and, second, that even in medium-sized countries such a system will not be really worth while unless it is organized on the basis of a population of at least 200 million. This does not mean that each nation should not make an effort on its own, but there is an obvious advantage in pooling data concerning, for instance, the Senegal river or the Zambezi, the Nile, the Rhine, the Alps, the Andes, and so on. Furthermore, there are as it is fewer documents in Europe than in the United States, but in the developing countries there are far too few to warrant establishing independent national organizations. And yet documents do exist, but because they have not been properly indexed and conserved it sometimes happens that the same study is carried out twice.

The organization of regional co-operation in this respect will therefore differ according to whether the countries concerned possess a strong infrastructure or are poor and sparsely populated and possess as yet neither archives nor documentation centres. In both cases, nevertheless, the advantage of regional action is unquestionable, provided that it is regarded as an auxiliary and not as an administrative agent.

2.6.3.3   *Data banks*

In the most highly developed countries, data banks are now being set up besides libraries and documentation centres, and they are doing the work hitherto performed by tables of physical and chemical constants, or the technical tables that all engineers still use. With the aid of computers, these data banks store and disseminate a much wider variety of facts than mere tables of figures. They contain diagrams, relations between several variables taking the visual form of surfaces, or even corresponding to multidimensional geometrical sets, and so forth. They also contain properties to be located by qualifiers (colour, state, symptom, effects, composition, etc.). Plans for machinery, wiring diagrams and technological processes can nowadays be stored in this form.

Much of this information is still the property of industrial companies and is therefore kept secret. But a very considerable amount is already available to the public, and this will increase in the years ahead as technologists make greater use of computers and as we gain the ability to conserve inexpensively, on data carriers, collections of the calculations, plans, drawings, observations and so on produced daily by those professionally concerned.

The computer can be very useful, since it enables data from different sources to be brought together and compared and some

of the consequences of these comparisons to be brought to light
(this is especially true in the case of the observational sciences:
medicine, ecology, meteorology, soil science, etc.). The computer
can also be used to carry out interpolations and extrapolations, and
can even be interrogated on the conduct of tests that may be
carried out to complete or check the contents of the bank.

At the world level, the International Council of Scientific
Unions (ICSU) have established an association known as
CODATA which is responsible for supervising these banks all
over the world. CODATA is one of the non-governmental organizations that UNISIST intends to support, but for the time being
it is very difficult to work in this sector on a world scale. The
single-country scale, however, is generally unsatisfactory, as the
main work is the collection and input of existing data, which
must be compatible enough to keep down the cost of processing.
National data banks will nevertheless be established in the most
profitable sectors, but it is highly desirable that they should work
closely together and that there should also be data banks at the
regional level, where the necessary resources and facilities are
most readily available. Depending on the nature of each case,
services to users might be offered directly at that level (usually
through local documentation centres) or copies of magnetic tapes
could be distributed among the various member national libraries,
which would make the necessary arrangements for using them.
Arrangements must also be made to meet numerous demands from
abroad for all sorts of information about the region.

2.6.3.4   *Methodology and linguistic tools*

It is most desirable that the working methods used by the various
agencies in a country which belong to the information network
should be compatible, if not identical. This is difficult in the old
nations, but relatively easy to achieve in new countries where there
has been little previous investment. However, in view of the volume
of exchanges expected between neighbouring countries, or between
nations with close ties, it is essential to ensure that the methods
and tools to be used on either side of frontiers are co-ordinated (see
sections 1.2.4 and 2.4.3). Failing such precautions, communication will become very difficult or too expensive, and much of
the benefit of computerization will be lost.

The regional centre would accordingly have the following duties:

Permanent study of indexing and processing methods and maintenance of records relating to such methods.

Preparation and updating of linguistic tools (in some cases multilingual) used for indexing documents and books.

Study of classification systems and their relation to international systems (Universal Decimal Classification and others) and their special application to regional problems.

Dealing with all problems concerning transliteration (for the Arab countries and in general all countries using non-Latin alphabets or additional signs or special accentuation marks). These problems affect typewriters and printers as well as programming operations.

Maintenance of the regional library of software with, in each case, instructions for use, precautions to be taken so that they will be compatible with this or that category of file, conditions of use, necessary reformating, and so on.

2.6.3.5 *Work sharing*

Provided the above basic operations are performed, work can be shared among the various countries belonging to the regional organization. This can be done at the stage of data collection and storage, at that of processing and at that of dissemination. Allotment of these tasks, with specified dates and deadlines, can only be effected by the regional authority. In addition, it makes sense economically if the bulk of computer processing is also carried out by this authority with a computer of its choice. Its services may of course extend further than that, especially where there are small participating countries, but these are special cases which will vary according to the type of organization concerned.

2.6.3.6 *Training*

We shall see that the problem of training competent staff at all levels is one of the major concerns of all countries wishing to develop a satisfactory documentation and library network. It is not always easy to organize national training courses in the new techniques required by the establishment of modern documentation centres, for not only must there be teachers but it is also most important that pupils should be brought into contact with day-to-day reality and advanced techniques. If the regional co-operation mentioned in the foregoing paragraphs materializes, the regional authority will clearly possess the best tools for instruction and lifelong training. It is therefore desirable that the school for documentalists and librarians which students attend after taking the lower-level courses provided in other institutions comparable with ordinary universities should come under this authority.

Thus membership of a regional co-operation programme has many advantages for all medium-sized countries and even more for small nations. This holds good both for developing countries and for rich nations. Although theoretically having the same functions in both cases, the regional authority so constituted would concentrate, in the former, on development of the network of libraries, on promotion of reading and on technical training, while in the latter it would deal primarily with computerized information tools, the sharing of tasks and data banks.

The establishment of such regional authorities is of course the responsibility of governments. Where they already exist, they should be supervised by the bodies responsible for information and documentation policy at the national level. We have seen that in some countries the latter would be a national centre with the threefold role of national library, national documentation centre and co-ordinating agency, in others a co-ordinating agency alone, and in others again partly national library and partly national documentation centre (in the latter case it would be advisable to provide for two representatives for the country in question).

2.7 Role of staff training

In this chapter we have described the decisions all nations have to take with regard to information science and librarianship. Not the least of these concerns specialist training. The traditional training courses provided in the developed countries cannot readily be adapted to suit new requirements; and in the developing countries there are as yet too few schools and still fewer universities able to provide the requisite instruction. Furthermore, there is of course a shortage of human resources, money and equipment. The recent report submitted to OECD by Mr Anderla gives a very clear idea of the nature of these new needs. Noting that it will be difficult for each country to provide the requisite training for tomorrow's leaders, he concludes that an international college should be established. We, for our part, are not sure that this solution would benefit the small nations, for if they contributed personnel to such an institution they would lose a much greater proportion of their élite than in the case of large countries, since the latter possess far greater human resources. Moreover, this kind of institution in other spheres has proved an ideal channel for the brain drain, which the developing countries have great difficulty in stopping.

There are probably better ways of achieving the desired result. To begin with, there are several levels of training, and several aspects of the work to be studied at each level. It should be possible, for instance, for technical staff such as cataloguers, stack-attendants and reprographers to be trained locally, perhaps by specialists who have attended courses abroad in appropriate cases. Schools now operating in several developing countries take a great many pupils (owing in part to Unesco subventions) and provide excellent courses. More schools of this kind should prob-ably be established, but this is a step to be taken with care and in close co-ordination with the situation as regards employment openings. It would also no doubt be advisable for part at least of the instruction provided to deal with new information methods and procedures such as: (a) microdocumentation, applications of holography, up-to-date printers and microprinters, photocompo-sition, etc.; (b) use of the world register of periodicals, preparation of computer-based union catalogues, etc.

All this can perfectly well be done by developing existing schools, establishing new courses if necessary at the regional or multi-national levels mentioned in section 2.6.3.6 above, and from time to time sending pupils abroad on training courses (at least for the next few years) so long as the schools in question have no suitable examples to learn from.

Higher-level training, however, is a more difficult matter. There are very few high-level documentalists who are documentalists pure and simple and have no knowledge of the subjects covered by the documents they handle. Directors of public libraries are either literary men or technicians (depending on the type of educational material to be found in the libraries) before being librarians. Likewise, documentalists have generally had a basic training (as doctor, physicist, chemist, engineer, jurist, sociologist, etc.) before specializing in documentary techniques. The high-level courses are therefore of post-graduate standard. The situation is not critical in the developed countries, for they are now making the necessary effort to establish new courses of study or modernize library schools by adding courses on indexing methods, thesauri, applications of data processing, and so forth. In the developing countries such courses should also be organized either along with the less advanced courses or, preferably, in a different context, at a university or in some other way yet to be devised.

Apart from documentation and librarianship, it would be a good thing for future librarians to learn how to advise a craftsman or an industrialist and how to inform him otherwise than by presenting him with exceedingly long and irksome bibliographies. Some of those who will be responsible for national libraries or national documentation centres should learn how to do this. It is still more important for those who are to be in charge of scientific documentation centres, which are constantly dealing with questions of agriculture, industrialization and handicrafts. Even at public library level, the documentalist should think in terms of development, advancement and vocational training as much as in terms of general literature—indeed, more so.

That is not something that can be learnt in schools, especially as many schools do not deal with this aspect of the librarian's calling. In training the first students, arrangements should be made for them to take practical courses in small industrial or agricultural companies which have proved their worth in such matters and can therefore be regarded as centres of development, and also in technical centres or co-operative institutions whose function is to provide information for small- and medium-sized industries in sectors concerned with productivity. In some countries, a sort of course in the art of informing people properly should be introduced, in which students would learn, in addition to modern information techniques, how to find and use, as rapidly as possible, the scientific, technical and commercial information needed by newly established firms.

However, organizing courses will not of itself make people choose this work for their career. Young people should see documentation and librarianship as an honourable profession, like that of teachers, engineers or jurists. Accordingly a multi-level documentalists' code should be prepared and put forward as a model. This is particularly important at the higher level, where requirements are the hardest to meet, for we wish to recruit specialists above the level of the normal technologist or graduate, and at the moment their career prospects are worse than in the case of their colleagues who embark on their working lives without the post-graduate training we have in mind. If care is not taken, the librarians of tomorrow may therefore be technologists, graduates or jurists whom nobody else wants. They will have little impact, and will hardly be recognizable as the nuclei of development referred to in Chapter 1. This will slow down the progress of entire nations.

3   Methodology of study
of the existing infrastructure

3.1   Requirements of users

When examining the question (in section 1.3) of how information and reading could become a powerful factor in development, we were implicitly considering the needs of various categories of users—both expressed (and existing) needs and latent needs which must be discerned, aroused and, as it were, stimulated. In this chapter, therefore, we shall only try to determine how the needs and reactions of the different categories of users may be foreseen in order to analyse them and see what consequences they should have for planning. We shall give special attention to the time factor and to the detection of precursory signs of either an imminent increase in demand or the possibility of making the information network play a greater part in the development process.

Let us first recall the main categories of users:

1. Children (primary and secondary levels).
2. Illiterates.
3. The artificial 'technical-reader' category, in which we include all those who can read and have not yet reached the level of higher studies or assumed the responsibilities corresponding to that level. They often make up the bulk of the population, and their very numbers mean that they have a variety of needs according to their subject of study. The aim for them is threefold: (a) culture and leisure pursuits; (b) vocational training; (c) general lifelong training and retraining.

    They are traditionally divided (though this distinction is tending to become an artificial one) into: people working on the

land; workmen and craftsmen, including drawing-office staff; office technicians (accountants, secretaries, civil servants, tradespeople, artists, etc.).
4. Medium-level and higher managerial staff (engineers, senior civil servants, teachers, works managers, etc.).
5. Retired people.
6. Students.
7. Research workers.

The needs of the users in groups 1, 2, 6 and 7 are the easiest to deal with, and we shall therefore take them first.

3.1.1   FORECASTING CHILDREN'S REQUIREMENTS

In all countries there are now fairly reliable population statistics so that the number of children almost from the time of birth is known. They do not really use school libraries before the age of 8 to 10, so there is ample time to provide for future needs. Moreover, present needs are well known in theory, but they are not always expressed as clearly as is desirable. Children who read apart from their school work are a minority, and secondary school pupils who engage in documentary research are still the exception. It is true that there is a certain degree of correlation between the reading rate and the general level of development, but it is not significant enough for us to be able to see what the situation will be in the next ten years. A change in this attitude depends far more on what schools are like in ten years' time than on general developments in society. Schools, however, are undergoing a transformation as a result of the advent of audio-visual instruction, and the reading matter offered children is changing—comic strips are increasingly popular. These illustrated magazines used to be mere slapstick, but nowadays their artistic and literary quality is such that they really are educational tools, and give an introduction to scientific and technical subjects, while remaining moderately priced. It is probably going a little too far to say that the school library of tomorrow will be only a library of comic strips and a video collection, but wherever this system is applied it will most probably meet with success and may encourage more traditional reading.

Faced with the need to work out a forward-looking programme, planners will therefore have first to ponder the role of illustrated magazines and video cassettes in school libraries. In rich countries these are already distributed commercially, and this will increasingly be the case, the role of the school library being confined to providing more serious reading matter that would not sell profitably. In poor countries, on the other hand, apart from a privileged few, children will scarcely read anything else than what the library has to offer. Since success is guaranteed, if not today at least in a few years, one must work out how many children are intended to be given this reading-matter, and consider, taking a reasonable rate of loss or theft into account, what one may expect the maximum turnover rate to be. In the case of illustrated magazines, this rate is much higher than for ordinary books, since one number can be read in a few days. A rate of at least two readers a week can accordingly be planned for.

As to audio-visual facilities, a reasonable basis to start with might be one session a week for each class. If the classes are some distance apart, transport will of course have to be provided. If each session lasts about three hours, two to three sessions a day can be planned for, depending on local arrangements. This means that the library could provide facilities for between twelve and eighteen sessions a week, each being attended by four school classes. This makes between fifty and seventy-five classes served, or 1,000 to 2,000 children. Reckoning that children in these age-groups account for 10 per cent of the total population, if we take an average country of 20 million inhabitants, 2 million children will be concerned, that is, some 600 audio-visual centres of this type must be planned for.

At the secondary-school age, teaching methods requiring the children to do personal documentary research are making rapid strides in all countries. They do it to prepare for talks that they are to give in class, or for projects or individual or team work for which it is essential to seek out information oneself. We have not estimated this requirement exactly, but it can be put at roughly five books per pupil if a wide variety of subjects is to be offered. For a class of forty pupils this makes 200 titles, and for a secondary school of ten classes 2,000 titles, to which must be added facilities for exchange with the libraries of neighbouring secondary schools. As a minimum, therefore, we can make do with a much lower rate of two books per pupil, and in this case the annual renewal rate will be fairly rapid (on the assumption that a book will not stand up to more than four or five years' use). The figure of five books per pupil would therefore apply to very isolated secondary schools with only a few classes.

Children can of course use public libraries as adults do as well as using school libraries. The advantage of school libraries is that children can borrow books from them without difficulty, while most public libraries will only lend books to children as an exception. In order to assess the needs of schoolchildren we must therefore add:

An expressed demand for general reading-matter in the developed countries of about two books per pupil, which is not expected to increase.

A latent demand for illustrated magazines of one subscription per ten pupils, plus two books per pupil (most of these books incidentally have yet to be written, for good books for children which are instructive, entertaining and artistic are far too few in number and are not suitable for all civilizations).

A latent demand for one audio-visual session a week which will encourage children to read.

A latent demand for two to five books a pupil, in secondary-school classes only, for the preparation of talks, group work and personal studies.

These needs, of course, have to be assessed in the light of local circumstances, namely:

General school attendance rate (school libraries obviously presuppose the existence of schools, and if resources are too scant it is sometimes better to establish one or two more schools rather than libraries).

Nature and outlook of schools (the above-mentioned latent needs are only conceivable where education has advanced somewhat since the beginning of the century).

General level of wealth. Illustrated magazines, for instance, are the most useful in poor countries, and the same applies to audio-visual sessions, particularly in rural areas. In towns, children will increasingly tend to spend their free time elsewhere, and get a general education in other ways (through associations, family life, etc.), rather than through the influence of the school.

3.1.2   FORECASTING LITERACY NEEDS

Literacy needs are directly linked to school attendance, since illiterates are people who could not go to school at the proper time. In sections 1.3.2 and 2.2.4 we have considered how literacy centres might be run. We started on the basis of expressed needs, that is, of the likely attendance of literacy centres by the illiterate section of the population, assuming that such centres exist and that illiterates are suitably encouraged to take advantage of them. We were unable to put this attendance rate above 10 to 15 per cent, but latent needs are certainly at least six times greater. However, with the available resources it will be very difficult to meet all the needs expressed, for one of the main causes of illiteracy is extreme poverty, and it is hard to see how the most destitute regions could miraculously produce the considerable resources needed to educate a very large pro-portion of their population who have had no teaching at all. Moreover, once this effort had been made the countries would find themselves, a generation later, with educational resources that are unused because they are too highly specialized, which were intended to meet a vast but nonetheless temporary need.

While recognizing its inadequacy, it must therefore be concluded that the maximum effort it seems possible to make for literacy work is in accordance with the figures given above, that is: one literacy centre for 5,000 illiterates.

As already stated, this rate corresponds to two sessions a day for the library and to 1.4 sessions a week for the users. In countries with a high proportion of illiterates the rate of using the library can probably be increased to four sessions a day, which would mean one centre for every 10,000 illiterates, who would of course need an adequate supply of the necessary audio-visual material and books.

3.1.3   FORECASTING THE NEEDS OF STUDENTS
         AND RESEARCH WORKERS

The needs of students and research workers have been the subject of more studies than the needs of other categories, and they are therefore among those of which we know most. There are standards which we have discussed in sections 2.2.2 and 2.2.3 concerning the number of books to be provided in university libraries and in docu-mentation centres open to research workers. Services such as this—which can be expressed in terms of the number of books and journals provided—are still all that is generally available for higher education and research. The impression nevertheless remains that, especially in the case of research workers, these services do not meet

their need for information. The selective circulation of bibliographies for special fields of study is a step in the right direction.
Users will perforce make the best of things for a time, but the
situation is undoubtedly changing, and it is difficult today to know
what it will be possible to offer them at an acceptable cost, or how
much more they will be prepared to pay to obtain services more in
keeping with their needs, which are as yet ill-expressed. The level of
wealth of universities and research centres is a relevant factor here;
it is sometimes more convenient to entrust an assistant or a student
with a piece of documentary research, which will be conducted by
makeshift means, rather than to pay the price asked by a centre
which is fully equipped to do the work by the most up-to-date
methods. The time spent by the assistant or student scarcely counts,
for the work is an essential part of his training. A different attitude
would be adopted if the number of research projects increased and
the ratio of students or inexperienced workers to qualified research
workers diminished. This will be the case when university enrolments are more or less stabilized.

The above remarks do not, of course, hold good for industrial
laboratories, where the time spent by research assistants has to be
paid for in full. Nevertheless there will always be a certain need for
rudimentary documentation, just as widespread use of the motor car
does not do away with walking or bicycling. There is still a considerable element of the unexpected in research, and even in the laboratories of large business concerns geared to profitability research
assistants will never be more than partly industrialized.

To ascertain needs we shall first of all take the present number of
students and teachers and the number of research workers in the
public and private sectors.

The former are known and statistics are available for them, for
since students all have matriculation files they can easily be counted.
What is more difficult is looking ahead, especially when it comes
to forecasting numbers in the main fields of study. The holdings of
libraries, if not their infrastructure, are very closely related to the
courses that will be chosen in higher education. In some countries
it used to be possible to go by the number of teachers at a given time,
on the assumption that you did not become a teacher overnight and
that the content of education accordingly had a high degree of
continuity. The present situation is quite different. When a sector
moves into the limelight or when pressing needs arise, which are

related to the country's development (discovery of oil, advent of nuclear power, pollution problems, etc.), it becomes urgent to train specialists accordingly. With international exchanges and the development of newly acquired skills, it will very soon be possible to institute new courses of instruction and laboratories, while others will perhaps be obliged to mark time or even to switch to fresh activities.

Sustained work on forecasting and a great deal of vigilance are therefore essential, in all countries. Fortunately, such changes are heralded by various signs which should always be heeded.

Detailed figures are available for research workers in the OECD countries. Their number will increase slightly in the next few years, but not at a rate very much in excess of the increase in the gross national product, that is, between 5 and 10 per cent a year depending on the present state of research in the various nations.

Similar figures are available for the Eastern European countries, which give a good idea of requirements. The case of the Third World is more complex, as the total number of research workers is not definitely known. Which university teachers do a substantial amount of research? How fast will the teams working with them expand? Should provision be made for research personnel at present working abroad to return to their own country? Generally speaking, there are few industrial laboratories, but their numbers may increase rapidly. When will this occur? And in which sectors?

For want of anything more satisfactory, we propose the following method. In the Western European countries there is one research worker for every 1,000 inhabitants. It may be assumed that this proportion will probably be attained in the Third World after a generation, that is, in about 1993. This assumption, which can of course be disputed, is based on the observation that it takes one generation (twenty years) to produce new mental and social reflexes and subsequently to build up new creative potential. This means, more or less, that the generation now reaching adulthood has assimilated and become aware of science and technology in their present state. It will be for the following generation (that of the children now being born) to make discoveries and add their own contribution towards the progress of knowledge in the world.

If this assumption is accepted, the question remaining is how 1973 and 1993 are to be linked up. Neither an exponential curve nor a straight line seems suitable, for the former gives too rapid a growth in the last years and the latter assumes that the number of research workers will increase in the near future much faster than it does today. The truth therefore lies between the two and is conditional upon the present number of research workers, if indeed this can be assessed. Failing any other evaluation, we can take the number of university teachers of scientific and technical subjects and apply a coefficient to it of between 1.2 and 3, according to the state of private and public research outside the university. We suggest the following equation:

$$X(t) = X_0 + nt + X(t_1) \times (1 + s)^{(t-t_1)} \qquad (1)$$

where:

$X(t)$ is the number of research workers per million inhabitants after a number of years equal to t. This will therefore give us $X(20) = 1,000$;

X_0 the number of research workers per million inhabitants estimated as stated above;

t the number of years that have elapsed since 1973;

n the coefficient proportional to the number of science and technology students per 1,000 inhabitants. Let us suppose that this number is equal to 1 and, for the sake of simplicity, that X_0 is very small. Pure linear growth would correspond to a value of n calculated as follows: $X(20) = 1,000 = n \times 20$; therefore $n = 50$, which means that one student in twenty will become a research worker. This rate is too high and in any case well above that of the developed countries, but a rate of one-quarter or one-third of that is perfectly conceivable in countries seeking to build up a scientific potential. In this example $n = 15$ could be chosen, which means that linear growth would make up about one-third (15 instead of 50) in the assessment of the research potential for 1993;

t_1 is the number of years after which growth would veer from linear to exponential;

$X(t_1)$ is the value of X after t_1 years as from 1973;

s is the growth rate to be assigned to the exponential part of the formula. Let us come back to our example and take $t_1 = 8$, which would bring us up to 1981. This will give us:

$$X(8) = 15 \times 8 = 120$$

and also:

$$X(8) \times (1 + s)^{12} = 1,000 - (15 \times 20) = 700$$

or:

$$(1 + s)^{12} = \frac{700}{120} = 5.8.$$

It follows that $s = 16$ per cent a year.

This growth rate is probably somewhat too high to sustain for twelve years, but it should be remembered that the United States and, later, Europe have known periods of increase in the number of research workers of 10 to 15 per cent a year for some ten years running. In the preceding example we can see that the country in question would probably not attain the objective (although it seems modest enough) of having in 1993 a research worker potential per million inhabitants equal to that of Europe in 1973. Furthermore, we have assumed that the population is constant, which it certainly is not. Therefore to obtain the real rate of increase the population growth rate would have to be added. Information services should keep up with and even if possible anticipate the growth of research.

Similar assumptions can be made in estimating the number of students, except that in some countries the linear term can be disregarded and the exponential curve alone used, and saturation point will often be reached more quickly—within ten to fifteen years in some of the countries and later (twenty years at the most) in the others. Once this period is over, a different formula will have to be adopted which will be applicable to much slower growth.

To come back to research workers, it should be noted that the idea of research and innovation is distinct from that of higher education and that a good many scientific discoveries and still more technical innovations were made outside the universities. This category of research workers still exists today at all levels in the social scale. The most useful inventions can be made by persons with a minimum of knowledge, and creative minds (there are few enough, it is true) thirst for information. Consequently, even in countries where there are not yet any formally qualified research workers, it is highly desirable that technical documentation centres should be capable of giving innovators information. Failing any other estimates, it would appear reasonable to assume that the ratio of practical research workers is at least one per 10,000 inhabitants, that is, one-tenth of the number of research workers found in the industrial countries. This figure seems to us to be a minimum.

3.1.4 REQUIREMENTS OF MEDIUM-LEVEL AND SENIOR 'PRACTICAL' STAFF

In the developed countries, needs here are essentially matched by available funds, which largely keep the book trade going. Three objectives are apparent: (a) general culture; (b) professional activity; (c) lifelong training.

General cultural needs are known and suitably catered for. The present situation is none the less changing, not because people in this sector of the population are reading more, but because their numbers are growing in proportion to the community at large and tertiary activities are being developed. A reason sometimes suggested is increased leisure, but we do not think that actual free time has much to do with the growth of this social category. Even if managerial staff have shorter working hours, their free time is taken up by activities more or less closely connected with their work (associations of all kinds) or by lifelong training or retraining. Many of them spend more time on their work than they are obliged to.

Members of this group amount to only 10–15 per cent of the working population, or 3–4 per cent of the total population, but they purchase 20–30 per cent of the books sold and account for between 30 and 40 per cent of the book-trade turnover (if we include their wives, who are still often classified as 'not gainfully employed'). In so far as this group exists in the developing countries, its members will largely use the public libraries, provided the facilities provided are given adequate publicity and that the conditions for using them are good (ease of access, facilities for borrowing by post, availability of books within a reasonable time, etc.).

Any increase in the size of this group is closely related to the present number of students. For example, the United States has 2.7 students per 100 inhabitants, and the average duration of studies is seven years and of working life thirty-five years. Therefore under normal conditions the proportion of qualified medium-level and senior personnel is 22.7 per cent $\times$ 35/7 = 13.5 per cent, from which we must subtract a certain amount of wastage (married women, failure in examinations, faulty guidance, unemployment, etc.) and to which we must add all such personnel who have not had a higher education. In a country where students represent 0.1 per cent of the population, as in the case mentioned above, we obtain a crude proportion of only 0.5 per cent of senior qualified personnel, a figure that needs to be increased considerably more than for the United States to obtain the true proportion. We can nevertheless see that it will be a long time before it exceeds 1 or 2 per cent and that consequently the book trade will not have the same outlets as in Europe or America.

The second requirement of such personnel is that arising from their work. As a matter of fact, this requirement is fairly close to that of research workers, though less frequent and less specific. It is not customary to count doctors, lawyers or—for the most part—technologists when taking stock of research workers, but everyone knows that in any profession there is a greater or lesser degree of creativity. In industry the transition from research engineer to works manager is imperceptible. Even the latter will always be seeking to improve his production lines, to rationalize operations, to reduce errors and faults, to improve quality, and so on. The documentation he tends to be offered is perhaps not the most useful to him, but there can be no denying that a potential need exists here which probably differs from that of research workers, but which information networks should endeavour to meet. This means not only using better documentary methods but also supplying more— or better—information.

The practical man has less patience than the research worker to go into a question thoroughly. For him time is an essential factor, as he is generally overburdened with a variety of tasks. Consequently he wants to receive the information he needs direct, rather than documents he must analyse, compare and discuss without being sure of finding what he is looking for. This compilation work should be done elsewhere, by competent specialists who must take great care not to distort the content of the information gathered. In large business concerns and government departments, the people in key positions have specialists on hand to do this work and provide them with the information they need in order to take decisions.

Elsewhere, increasing recourse is had to firms of consultants, which seem likely to develop considerably in the future. But, on the one hand, these firms will need the best and most easily usable sources of information and, on the other, many people in positions of responsibiliby will want to be able to obtain information themselves, provided they can do so in suitable conditions—conveniently, quickly and confidently. They will thus turn to new forms of information such as data banks, information-analysis centres and technical centres.

Then there is the need for lifelong training, which is distinct both from general education and from professional documentation. Lifelong training has a medium- or long-term professional objective apart from the actual requirements of one's present work. People need to prepare for economic and social changes, for possible changes in their jobs and for all that new technologies bring with them, as much as for abnormally rapid developments in their own field of work. We have just said that strictly professional documentation is related to that required by research workers. In much the same sort of way, information relevant to lifelong training is not unlike what students need. It includes books, surveys and even audio-visual sessions at which, for instance, an employer can learn about computers, a mining engineer can study the chemistry of coal derivatives and by-products or petrochemistry, and a chemist can assess the importance of exceptional markets for certain plastics.

Actually, there is a difference between the books research workers need and books for university students, because at the age of 30 or 40 people do not think in the same way as when they were 20. They are able to observe relationships and draw on past experience as a student cannot. On the other hand, they will feel ill at ease when documents go too deep into abstract theories. It is true that in medicine certain professional journals such as the *Revue du praticien* or *Concours médical* are widely read both by practitioners and by students. On the whole, the requirements fall within the same range, though they are not identical.

The very idea of lifelong training is in itself new, though many qualified staff have always made an effort to improve their standard of knowledge apart from their jobs. The demand for information used therefore to be somewhat small. Surveys were prepared by governmental bodies or business concerns to keep 'non-specialists' (employers or politicians) informed as to the over-all economic situation and trends in it. Only recently has it been thought desirable to extend the benefit of this to all medium-level and senior personnel. There is therefore a demand for new works in this domain.

To sum up, we have made the following four points:

The number of medium-level and senior qualified personnel can be predicted from the present situation and the present number of students (in law, science and technology) by means of simple extrapolation formulae.

This social category is proportionally that which is the most assidu-ous in keeping up its general culture. It has a considerable impact on the book trade in the developed countries. In the developing countries it would be most desirable for public libraries to be able, at least for a certain time (say five or ten years), to fulfil the same role, special arrangements being made, which may be on a paying basis where appropriate. This is not likely to compete with the book trade. On the contrary, the aim is to form reading habits, and these will subsequently be catered for by the bookshops when this becomes economically practicable.

There is a considerable need for professional technical documen-tation, which meets and extends the demands of research workers.

The advent of lifelong training creates a new problem of the utmost importance, which library structures could easily solve, but for the time being there are not enough suitable books. The problem of finding people to write books of this kind might be partly solved by calling on retired specialists.

3.1.5   REQUIREMENTS OF RETIRED PEOPLE

Our intention was to deal with this section very briefly, since the requirements of retired people are not basically different from those they previously had during their working lives. They could therefore be classified according to their past, though with a marked bias towards general culture and leisure activities. This group of people, however, whose numbers are growing in proportion to the total population and whose health is improving, is playing an increasing role in economic life apart from that of mere consumers. In countries with liberal economies, they own a considerable part of the national wealth. They often hold elective posts (as senators, provincial coun-cillors, aldermen, etc.). Although they have ample recourse to competent advice, their own influence in the business world is far from negligible. It is therefore most desirable that an appropriate information network should keep them informed on: (a) legal, fiscal, banking and similar questions affecting the management of personal and real estate; (b) the trends of scientific progress, so as to make them aware of the general development of technology and of society, and to show them how this affects their own affairs and the decisions they still very often have to take.

The documentation required here comes very close to the needs of lifelong training, and presentation and clarity are all important. The most suitable dissemination channels are certain categories of businessmen (such as notaries, tax consultants and bankers), the medical profession (doctors or nurses with whom one discusses other things than aches and pains) and, above all, associations or clubs of former colleagues (old pupils or alumni, former members of a profession, chamber of landlords, churches, golf and bridge clubs, etc.).

Those of them who help prepare surveys or who continue teaching or personal economic activities will of course use all the services of the information networks, but their relatively small numbers will not markedly affect the infrastructure to be established.

3.1.6   REQUIREMENTS OF AGRICULTURAL,
         ADMINISTRATIVE
         AND COMMERCIAL TECHNICIANS

We realize how artificial it is to lump together occupations that are so dissimilar in their economic functions. To say that their attitudes to reading and documentation are the same would also be wide of the mark. The people we are thinking of are in fact those sometimes referred to as 'the man in the street', who account for most of the population (80 per cent of the working population),[1] barely half of the number of books read each year, a still more modest proportion of the consumption of scientific and technical information (at present a single-figure percentage), and an increasing proportion of 'popular' works.

One of the objectives of progress is that the whole of this section of the community should have full access to culture and knowledge, even if for practical reasons responsibilities must for the time being

---

1. In the developed countries. Virtually the entire literate working population of the poor countries comes within this category, but this unfortunately represents only a somewhat small proportion of the human potential of these nations.

remain concentrated in the hands of relatively few persons. Further-more, this part of the working world is the most vulnerable to economic uncertainty and change (agricultural problems, exhaus-tion of natural resources, sudden technological changes, etc.). It is therefore most desirable that people in this group be given the opportunity to diversify their skills.

Potential requirements are accordingly very great, though present demand is low. In all countries the standard of knowledge and of culture of these 'workers' is an all-important factor in the ease with which they cope with the varied problems of a changing society. Universal basic education and lifelong training are no doubt expens-ive items, but their cost is less than that of a high unemployment rate and chronic inability to adapt to the requirements of progress.

We have drawn a distinction between the notions of culture and leisure, vocational training and lifelong training. But as we have already noted, this distinction, which is valid in Europe, loses much of its meaning elsewhere. Even the reading of a newspaper or of a novel, which in Europe is chiefly a form of relaxation for brain workers, is a means of broadened intellectual attainment for this part of the community. The working world offers few opportunities for self-expression in writing and, above all, few opportunities for reading anything but the routine material produced by certain occupational categories (accounts, work preparation, etc.). Practice in oral expression and the maintenance of proficiency in comprehen-sion and self-expression have to come out of spare time. Failing such maintenance, it is difficult to get promotion at work, since the higher you go the more capable you have to be of communicating. A change of job, when it is necessary, always involves human contact, which is easier for those with a good general education. Similarly, if retraining proves necessary the transmission of new techniques or vocational training always involves using printed material. There are any number of examples—for instance, the awkwardness some-times noticed in country people coming to the city, which is simply the awkwardness of anyone who moves to a place where habits of expression and communication are different from those he is used to. There is a direct connexion between the general educational level and the capacity for resettling. This level is acquired or main-tained principally through reading and, where possible, writing.

What should people read? What they want in their spare time is something interesting and exciting, something in which the reader recognizes more or less a part of himself or the opposite of himself. For a technician who is really interested in his work, anything concerning it and presented in a comprehensible manner is fascinating.

Of course there are many degrading jobs (on factory production lines). It must be said, on the other hand, that jobs (and those in the production line in particular) are up-graded according to the standard of the people it is possible to take on. It is easier to up-grade jobs than to train people for more complex tasks if their initial standard is too low. Even in this case the worker is bound to be interested in his job, in his future and in how he could advance, go on to other work, and so forth.

Contrary to common belief, the technician will readily read or listen to anything concerning his job, even if he curses the time he spends on it. What he requires is not technical documents or surveys but material that is adapted to his needs. Various kinds of 'popular' journals, reviews and books (some of a higher standard than others) have been brought out, as a stepping-stone to a more advanced culture. These types of literature, which already date back several years (indeed several decades), are undoubtedly successful (though much yet remains to be done). The comic strip was invented to induce children to read. Job-oriented literature must be found that is both entertaining and instructive, making the reader want to know more—books that speak of the land to the countryman, of machinery to the worker, of trade circuits to the tradesman, and so on.

As in the case of children, audio-visual methods can play a decisive part.

The mode of dissemination of this information has a political importance which should not be overlooked, because it gives, at least for a time, considerable power to those in charge of it. It can be effected through the public information network of the countries concerned, through firms or landowners, or through trade-union organizations. There can be no question of charging for it at cost price; at the very most, a small token payment may be made.

Furthermore, this group of users provides many future employers. The heads of small- and medium-sized industrial firms are mostly 'workers in their Sunday best', farmers who have grown wealthy or tradesmen and craftsmen who have made their way. Their work and their social advancement will be much facilitated if they have information in keeping with their needs. The information they need will probably not be entirely like that which is useful to their more static colleagues; it will be closer, though with some slight differences, to the documentation required by technologists. They will benefit from information which has already been selected and analysed, but which must be in certain respects, if not in the forefront of scientific discovery, at least well to the fore in the techniques applicable in practice to their kind of work.

Whatever the channel of dissemination and whatever the subject matter, books and other printed material, audio-visual tapes and so on, will always be kept in a library. Alongside university libraries, we shall see the development of documentation centres for the requirements of lifelong training, and they must therefore be planned for as part of the scientific, technical and cultural information networks. The librarian of tomorrow will be not only a depositary but a promoter and an adviser capable of sifting and selecting information in accordance with the varied needs of those who turn to him. One of his most important duties will be to give information and advice and, in certain cases, explanations. His social position will be increasingly reminiscent of that of the village school-teacher in the days when reading and writing were first taught in Europe.

3.2 Services

To meet the very varied needs mentioned above—needs which every government is able at least to assess reasonably accurately, though it may not have an exact knowledge of them—several types of service have come into being, some organized by the public authorities and others by private enterprise, which has long since established what may be called an economic sector (books, periodicals, booksellers, publishers) and, more recently, firms of consultants, information firms, patent offices, technical centres, economic study groups and a variety of associations. These bodies, of course, have other functions besides providing information, but in all of them documentation and information are major items.

On the initiative of the OECD, a very careful survey of the

resources allocated to research and development was made some ten years ago. The question of using similar methods to take stock of the resources available to each country for scientific and technical information has been raised. The funds allocated to libraries and documentation centres and to independent patent services can readily be discovered. But this represents only a fairly small part of all the resources we wish to survey, for many libraries are simply part of a larger complex and they do not usually have separate accounts. Exactly the same difficulties had been encountered when investigating the resources allocated to research (in industrial concerns, for example). By means of a survey system which, it is true, took several years to institute, statistics were eventually obtained. So consideration could reasonably be given to extending the method to the documentation sector.

Such ideas have not so far been taken up, however, for the separation of the expenditure of the bodies responsible for gathering, processing and disseminating data from the time spent by users completing this work was an artificial one. Theoretically, the more you spend on providing high-quality information services, the less time the users should waste. In practice one cannot be absolutely certain of this, for, as stated in the previous section, requirements are by no means fully met, so that improvements in information networks may encourage the user to seek more and better information and, paradoxically, to spend more time in the process.

It is of course not possible to estimate the losses sustained through lack of information (except in a few isolated and striking cases, which are consequently not very significant), and it is equally impossible to work out the proportion of time spent by engineers, research workers and technicians seeking information. In very many cases it is quite pointless to try to ascertain how much of this time is devoted to their general education and how much to their actual work.

Failing a general method of assessing existing services, it is possible to conduct surveys on roughly the same lines as the questionnaires used in estimating resources used for research. The results produce estimates that are admittedly incomplete, but they could be added to. Reference has been made above to a single-figure percentage of resources allocated to research and development. To be a little more precise, let us say between 5 and 10 per cent, according to the field of study. This, however, applies to nations which carry out a great deal of research work. In Canada, a new country which, in tapping its immense natural wealth, draws on methods and technologies originating elsewhere, expenditure on information is proportionally much greater, being comparable to expenditure on research and development.

This example should hold good not only for most other new countries with extensive territories but also for many developing countries whose scientific and technical potential, while not yet capable of major breakthroughs, is able to develop national resources.

Annexed hereto is a specimen questionnaire (Appendix 2) which might be considered for adaptation to each particular case. However, if a similar method could be found which was applicable to all nations an interesting comparison of the figures so obtained could be made.

The various services are theoretically classified as follows: libraries (public, school and university); documentation centres; data banks; information analysis centres; patent rights institutes and patent offices.

This classification, however, is too sketchy and not as full as it should be, so that a developing country establishing a network based solely on the assessment of libraries and documentation centres in a nation taken as a model would achieve nothing like the results expected. For the role played by the private and semi-public sector and by a variety of associations in the dissemination of culture and documentation has a marked effect in the liberal nations, and it is important to note that information services are seldom distinct from other activities. To the summary classification above the information activities of the following bodies must therefore be added:

Publishing houses. That is, if it is possible to distinguish between: expenditure and manpower assigned to the production of books (not to be taken into account here); and expenditure on seeking authors and subsequent storing and distribution (which, on the other hand, are to be taken into account).

It would be advisable to divide up the latter expenditure according to objectives: current affairs (not to be taken into account); general education; scientific and technical material (books and reviews). These figures need not be very accurate, but they are an almost indispensable guide in assessing a nation's effort to obtain culture and knowledge.

Industrial firms. All business concerns have documentation services and libraries; sometimes they employ only half a secretary, but they assume considerable proportions nowadays in large firms. Subscriptions to reviews or book purchases by the various members of the staff are not included, but only orders and subscriptions in the name of the library or libraries.

It is very desirable to have a separate estimate of resources devoted to patent servicing (approximate manpower and expenditure, excluding legal and patent registration costs).

Non-profit-making associations and organizations. Prominent among such associations are learned societies and technical institutions (the best known of which as far as information goes is the American Chemical Society, which produces *Chemical abstracts*, and in the United Kingdom the Institution of Electrical Engineers, which produces *INSPEC*).

Other non-profit-making associations or organizations are principally engaged in research, teaching or advisory activities, but devote a very considerable part of their resources to technical documentation (the associations concerned in France are the professional technical centres, and in the Federal Republic of Germany certain foundations, etc.).

Lastly, in the cultural sphere we find reading circles, sometimes trade unions or even unions of workers or office staff, and so on.

It is generally fairly easy for these organizations to see what proportion of their expenditure and manpower goes on information and documentation.

Management and consulting firms and research departments. Nowadays these firms possess highly developed information tools, usually associated with computers, which many of them own or use on a part-time basis. The data banks which best serve economic development are gradually compiled in these firms and research departments, as well as in large companies and technical centres.

If a complete survey is not feasible, an initial assessment of the situation may be attempted by means of the following method:

The sums spent on libraries are generally easy to estimate, as are those spent on patents and patent rights.

If research bodies exist, it can be assumed that they spend between 2 and 5 per cent of their resources on providing their research workers with information, the lower figure being applicable to fundamental research workers.

In the case of applied technical research conducted on a public, private or co-operative basis, it can be assumed that 5–10 per cent of resources go to information and documentation.

Failing more precise information, it may be said that the proportion of 5 per cent is applicable to major research departments and consulting firms (those with more than about twenty technicians). Small firms may for our purposes be disregarded, unless information is one of their main activities.

As to associations which do not carry out research, the simplest thing is to disregard them unless they show a special interest in the subject.

When studying existing services, special attention should be given to their geographical distribution. It is sometimes the case that capital cities with major universities are fairly well equipped as regards information at all levels, while less-privileged areas lack information facilities, with the result that specialists in these areas feel uncomfortably isolated, and decide to move to an already overcrowded capital.

Not only should a fair balance be struck between services offered in the capital and those existing in the provinces, but the latter should be systematically favoured. Hence the advantage of knowing exactly how activities are distributed between them.

Another important point is the content of book stocks and the sectors covered by the material. In section 2.5 we considered the problem of priority sectors. This seems to us to be an all-important one, because when resources are scarce it is essential to favour in the first place what is the most useful to the country's development. In the above assessment, approximate as it may be, the fields covered by existing services are therefore of considerable interest. If surveys are carried out, the questionnaire prepared will of course include an indication of the approximate distribution, without going into undue detail. If no more than general estimates are attempted, it is possible, from the main activity of the bodies in question, to gain an idea of the subjects on which they supply information.

In addition to the resources brought to bear, an appraisal should be made of the quality of the services actually rendered to the users. Also added as appendixes, as an example, are two questionnaires, one concerning the activity of documentation centres (Appendix 3) and the other on bibliographical publications (Appendix 4). This does not mean that a survey should systematically be carried out, but the questionnaires specify the main points on which it is highly desirable to have information prior to planning. In the case of libraries it is necessary to know not only the attendance rate and the number of loans but also the kind of books or the kind of documents most in demand. The sort of relationship that exists between librarian and user must also be known, as well as what audio-visual facilities are provided, and so forth. For documentation centres the number of subscribers to the bibliographical services and their distribution is of course a basic item, but in addition the replies to questions and the nature of the questions asked are at least as necessary if one wishes to form an idea of the possibility of making these services or new services play a part in the economy.

3·3   Organizations

Appraisal of an existing situation always involves a study of the underlying organization. For a documentation and library network it is no doubt preferable to speak of several organizations, since the network is more or less closely linked to a great many other national activities, public and private, so that in practice several organizational patterns meet in it and are superimposed, creating functional relations which coexist with hierarchical relations. Various ministries are involved, either directly or as the authorities for this or that branch of the economy. Those particularly concerned are the following departments or agencies:

Authority for public libraries: cultural affairs; education; development and natural resources; lifelong training.

Authority for school libraries: education.

Authority for university libraries and for documentation centres: education; technical education; scientific research; industrial development; agriculture; trade; communications, posts, transport, public works; mining and natural resources; environment; defence.

Authority for the publishing trade: cultural affairs; education; trade and industry.

Authority for firms providing services and firms of consultants: industrial development; agriculture; finance; environment; planning.

The OECD had drawn up an organizational plan for all its member countries, showing the principal scientific information services. It was found that in all those countries such services were distributed throughout the various ramifications of the administrative structure, although the largest bodies were attached to the prime minister's office and the departments of education and defence.

It is useful to see what exists, but it is not one of the essentials to smooth operation. Every ministry wishes to have at its disposal one or more documentation centres, capable of informing it and of providing the personnel and bodies under it with the best possible information. Conversely, every library or documentation centre has a duty to maintain the closest possible contact with those whom it is meant to serve. Whether or not there is any hierarchical link, these documentation centres therefore will naturally find themselves close to their main users.

On the other hand, there will be a more or less close link among all these libraries and all these bodies, so that they can communicate satisfactorily and operate as a network. In section 2.6 it has been recommended that, particularly in young nations enjoying freedom of choice, this link should be as close as possible—it should even be hierarchical in nature. In studying an existing situation, it is more valuable to know the main features of this relationship than to be able to say that a particular service is attached to such and such a department. In particular, it is most important to know how co-ordination and co-operation of the various services are organized: Are common working methods used?

Are there common classification schemes or vocabularies? Or how are the linguistic tools used in the different bodies related?

Is there a policy on the choice of materials used or recommended? How is the switch from one system to another effected?

What computers are used? Who takes decisions on the matter? How are the programmes used related to one another? How can they be interconnected?

Has there been any statement of the various aspects of the services to be provided as a matter of priority for the different categories of users (for example the 'man in the street' referred to in section 3.1 above)?

Have the various operations been compared so as to reveal the most effective courses of action (supplies, sources, organization of services)?

Is there any publicity policy? Or any policy of information on the art of obtaining information?

What is the role of national bodies (national library and national documentation centre) in relation to that of the various other bodies or services?

From the answers to these various questions, as much as from organizational charts, it will be possible to deduce how the network functions at present.

3.4   International links and co-operation

The international links in an information network may be a matter of the documents themselves, bibliographies, or direct services to users. Let us take each of these points in turn.

3.4.1   INTERNATIONAL LINKS IN THE MATTER OF DOCUMENTS

Foremost among documents are books. Buying books is no problem in developed countries where the press is entirely free. Publishers regularly supply catalogues to libraries and to all bodies considered potential buyers. The information given about the books is generally sufficient for a choice to be made.

Buying books in the Third World countries is quite another matter. Books must be transported over long distances, sometimes with hazards in both directions, and publishers are reluctant to give notice of their publications to a great many small centres throughout the world which will place only small orders.

Agreements must therefore be made with large publishers or large booksellers taking a special interest in a particular part of Africa or Asia. They select for it lists of books which they know will be suitable, and so maintain a regular flow of business. Like any contract, this system involves greater or lesser constraints, both for the publishers and contracting libraries and for the purchasing bodies. On the other hand, all parties benefit from the regular service so provided. Furthermore, the same body is obliged to have several regular suppliers according to the origin of the books.

It is not desirable to proclaim to all and sundry the content or even the existence of each of these special contracts, but it is most advisable that the governmental authorities should be properly informed of them, for advantage can be taken of pooling arrangements, and in some cases it may be possible to work out a national-based common policy, obtain lower prices and faster deliveries, strengthen certain trends in purchases in co-operation with local bookshops, and so forth.

Besides bulk buying there are individual purchases. For instance, a user asks for a rare book, having obtained the reference elsewhere. If the book is on sale in bookshops, it can readily be obtained by including it in bulk contracts, though supplying it is nearly always a trouble to the bookseller who agrees to obtain it. When, on the other hand, the work is not sold by bookshops but merely brought out by certain specialized organizations, agreements concluded once and for all between bodies of a certain size are infinitely preferable to individual orders, which are quite likely to go astray.

So we come to exchange agreements, which are developing steadily for all categories of documents among the principal libraries of the world. The word 'exchange' is used because accounts are settled only at the end of the year, by balancing the services rendered by each party. If it is thought desirable to simplify accounting, payment can also be made in vouchers. These are bought at the beginning of the year and entitle the holder to specific services. Any surplus is reimbursed.

What holds good for book purchases and exchanges also applies to subscriptions to periodicals. Either the documents themselves or microreproductions are exchanged; the latter, being less bulky, travel faster from one part of the world to another.

Similar agreements are made for unpublished documents collected in several countries by specialized agencies which maintain excellent relations amongst themselves. For countries not (or not yet) possessing such agencies, the correspondent may be a national documentation centre or a national library. Translations—published in some cases and not in others—are generally the subject of separate exchange agreements, for in some large countries they are administered by other bodies than the foregoing.

Several small countries may join together to organize joint purchase centres and to conclude joint exchange agreements—an aspect of regional organization recommended in section 2.6. This involves concluding two agreements in succession, the first regionally based among participating countries and the second between the regional centre and the foreign agencies, but this additional regional step saves time and money.

3.4.2   INTERNATIONAL LINKS
         IN THE MATTER OF CATALOGUING
         AND BIBLIOGRAPHIES

3.4.2.1   *Agreement concerning cataloguing rules*

Most libraries now tend to comply with international recommendations concerning cataloguing procedure. These rules, however, may be interpreted or applied in various ways. We may accordingly find: (a) regional agreements concerning the interpretation, application or simplification of the international rules; (b) on a world scale, similar agreements concerning a particular category of documents. These may be concluded by a far greater number of bodies (as in the case of translations, neutron data, etc.).

3.4.2.2   *Universal bibliographical control*

Going a stage further in this direction, the International Federation of Library Associations (IFLA) and Unesco have both recommended a system of Universal Bibliographical Control (UBC).[1] The aim of this system is to provide information on everything published throughtout the world. In order to achieve this, the relevant bibliographical data must be collected in a short enough time and in a form sufficiently precise and complete to enable all users in every country to make good use of it.

Several countries already publish national bibliographies; this

1. F. G. Kaltwasser, 'Universal bibliographical control', *Unesco bulletin for libraries*, vol. XXV, no. 5, September-October 1971, p. 252–9.

therefore provides a very good starting-point for international bibliographical control—but two conditions must be fulfilled: first, a format must be adopted which will allow these national bibliographical data to be incorporated into a world system; second, such bibliographies must be brought into general use in this common format in all countries which do not yet have them.

The operations to be carried out were summed up by Herman Liebaers in his opening speech to the IFLA, of which we quote the following extract:[1]

At the national level the operation of the system demands first the existence of the necessary means to capture, to seize, each new publication on publication (for example, by legal deposit, or similar governmental regulations, by voluntary deposit, etc.), and thereafter the existence of the necessary means to establish the bibliographic record; in effect, the existence of a national bibliographic agency with the following functions:
To establish the authoritative bibliographic record for each new publication in the country.
To produce those records in a national bibliography which appears regularly.
To produce and distribute those records in a standard physical form (as cards, machine-readable tapes, or acceptable alternatives).
To receive and distribute within its own country, similar records produced by other national bibliographic agencies.
As circumstances permit, to create a retrospective national bibliography.
At the international level, the integration of national bibliographic agencies to form the total system depends upon the universal recognition and acceptance of the two following conditions: that each national bibliographic agency is the organization responsible for establishing the authoritative bibliographic record of the publications of its own country, and that international standards are applied in the contents of the record (elements to be included in the description, the order of those elements, the means of distinguishing those elements and their functions) and the physical form (the standardization of catalogue cards, of machine-readable records or of acceptable alternatives).

With this end in view, a very precise standardization of cataloguing rules is currently being devised, thanks to the co-operation of the major libraries (United States Library of Congress, National Lending Library (United Kingdom), Bibliothèque Nationale (France), the German libraries supported by the Deutsche Forschungsgemeinschaft, etc.). With the common format thus established, it is henceforth possible to draw up co-ordinated national

1. H. Liebaers, International Federation of Library Associations, President's opening speech at Grenoble on 27 August 1973 (54/F/PLE/O).

bibliographies using rules of standardized bibliographical description, and, in each country, to computerize the cataloguing elements of every book and magazine published. In order to facilitate this task and perfect the identification system, it may be convenient to give each work a reference number—International Standard Book Number (ISBN). Any computer will thus be able to verify, very economically, whether a particular work is to be found in a given stock or not, or, alternatively, supply a list of works common to two stocks or, again, a list of standard works missing from a given stock.

Of course, there are still problems to be solved. The first is that of different editions of the same book, to which it is logical to allot different identification numbers (ISBN), since they are in fact different, although their content is the same. It is foreseeable, however, that for a number of users the edition will be of little importance provided that they can get at the text they require. So it then becomes necessary to look under other headings in the bibliographical description in order to find out whether a given text is in stock in one form or another, unless, of course, all the different numbers which the various editions may bear are known beforehand.

Theoretically, Universal Bibliographical Control could work on an entirely manual basis, but the work involved would be heavy and above all a great many problems would be encountered in making use of the corresponding results in libraries. Computerization, to be sure, raises other problems, but the processing power which computer science brings to the tasks of sorting, comparison, combination, updating, dissemination of listings, etc., justifies the effort required to feed the information into a computer.

The system certainly cannot be universal until all countries take a share in it, i.e. until they have the necessary computers which they may own either individually or collectively. This is therefore a gradual and long-term process, which is beginning now through co-operation between national bibliographies and between the main world libraries, and which will spread further through the establishment of regional cataloguing centres (in Europe, North America, etc.) as well as national centres.

Another reason why this system will take shape very gradually is that it can begin only with recent publications, and that libraries will therefore have to inventory their old stock, going further back in time as the means at their disposal allow.

For periodicals, the ISBN is replaced by the International

Standard Serial Number (ISSN). The system is both simpler, because the number of titles is much smaller, and more complex, because a periodical is a continuous collection with a history which cannot be disregarded (changes of title, subdivisions, regroupings, etc.). It also has characteristics proper to its style of publication (periodicity, supplements, if any volume number, etc.). Furthermore, documentalists frequently copy out information on periodicals again and again. In order to simplify this task, over and above the ISSN, standard title abbreviations are used. Bearing in mind the linguistic aspects of this operation, there is an understanding that each country will supply a list, not of abbreviations of its titles, but of standard abbreviations of each of the words which go to make up these titles (such as: journal, *revue*, *rivista*, bulletin, *boletino*, etc.).

The network which is at present being set up has a co-ordinating unit for books at world level, and it also has regional centres; it should be supplemented in all countries by national centres, which may be, quite simply, one of the departments of the country's main library or main documentation centre.

3.4.2.3   *Agreement concerning union catalogues and exchanges by computer*

All the agreements mentioned so far have almost always been concluded between individual bodies without any government intervention. As soon as catalogues of books or documents are computerized and become common property, the bodies concerned must necessarily co-operate more closely and be willing to sacrifice their autonomy to a certain extent. Some of them are in a position to negotiate such agreements at their own level; others prefer them to be set out in a more official instrument, which may even be an intergovernmental agreement. If it be a matter of relations between neighbouring countries or countries with common interests, exchanges of computerized catalogues will form only part of a wider agreement.

3.4.2.4   *Subscriptions to computerized bibliographical services*

Several bodies produce magnetic tapes of computerized documentation, to which it is possible to take out a subscription. However, subscribing to such a service is not like subscribing to a magazine since, apart from the higher cost, the use of such tapes is necessarily subject to detailed formalities.

In some sections, the publisher of such tapes expects the subscriber, in return, to participate in supplying his system with documents. So this involves not only the documentation centre which receives the tapes, but often several other organizations (publishers, indexers, etc.) which are requested to participate by observing rules laid down by the producer of the magnetic tapes.

3.4.2.5 *Agreements for international sharing of documentary tasks*

The only system so far operating in this way is concerned with nuclear energy, and is the subject of an intergovernmental agreement within the framework of the International Atomic Energy Agency (IAEA), to which all countries are free to subscribe.

3.4.2.6 *Agreements for regional task-sharing*

We considered this type of co-operation in section 2.6. Let us observe merely that an intergovernmental agreement is not indispensable, but that it is perfectly possible for several centres to sign such agreements if they belong to nations which are on good terms in other respects.

There are even mixed arrangements, in which some participants are governments, while others are libraries or documentation centres; furthermore, it is possible to introduce international organizations as other parties to the agreement.

3.4.2.7 *Agreements for the distribution of services*

Certain centres from different countries may decide to pool their resources with a view to implementing a policy of distributing their services in their own countries or even beyond their frontiers.

Taken all in all, the agreements made in these various ways form a rather complicated mesh, and it is wise to check from time to time that it does not contain any internal contradictions. What is more, no development programme can avoid taking this into account. As a rule, all these agreements are signed for a limited period, but, unless there is a strong reason for doing so there is reluctance to terminate those which are still in force.

3.5   Manpower

Knowledge of the manpower at work in a documentary network is necessary in order to take stock of its efficiency, in the light of the kind and quantity of the services provided, but it is probably still more useful prior to the launching of training programmes.

From the calculations or estimations mentioned in section 3.2, above, one may deduce (with a greater or lesser degree of accuracy) the figures representing the number of persons employed in information work, by classifying them, first by grade, and then by the kind of services which they help to provide (in particular, distinctions must be drawn between employees of publishing houses, librarians, documentalists, patent specialists, data bank engineers, etc.). Manpower 'ratios' will be established for each production unit.

Different types of units may include the following:

Unit for a literacy centre catering for 5,000 illiterates.

Unit for a public library catering for 10,000 inhabitants.

Unit for a school library catering for 2,000 pupils.

Extra unit for an audio-visual installation holding three to four sessions per day.

Unit for a university library catering for 1,000 students.

Documentary unit for 100 research workers.

Unit for dissemination of knowledge and advice for 20,000 inhabitants in an agricultural setting.

The same in an urban setting.

Data banks of 10 million alphanumeric characters.

Reprography centre supplying 200 reprinted articles per day (i.e. approximately 2,500 to 3,000 pages per day).

Documentary abstracting and indexing centre cataloguing and registering 10,000 documents per annum.

Naturally, in the case of major libraries and centres, their production and the services they provide will be broad enough to include several of the elementary units outlined above. Owing to rationalization of work, the staff employed in them will be proportionately far fewer than in separate units.

This will not be altogether adequate, since it is worth while to have at least a rough idea of the status and career corresponding to these posts (remuneration, which is difficult to ascertain, does not always give a clear indication of an individual situation, as its value is only relative).

Let us recall the main categories of personnel: photocopiers and micro-copiers; stock attendants; sub-librarians; librarians; cataloguers and proof-readers; engineers, graduates or doctors specializing in documentation; specialists in information science; computer scientists in the field of documentation; specialized translators.

Documentation centres and libraries also employ other categories of specialized staff, but these differ scarcely at all from the same specialists working in other sectors (accountants, mechanics and fitters, punched-card operators, computer operators, typists, offset operators, administrators, etc.). All these must, of course, be taken into consideration when weighing up the resources which information centres have at their disposal, but they should not be included in plans for taking on future trainee staff.

3.6   Equipment

The kinds of equipment to be found in an information network fall approximately into two groups: (a) items of equipment which form part of the nation's general infrastructure, whose great importance we have sought to emphasize in section 1.2; (b) equipment belonging specifically to the network and which, if it is not used entirely for information, is at least worth acquiring for this purpose.

3.6.1   GENERAL INFRASTRUCTURE NECESSARY FOR THE NETWORK

3.6.1.1   *Postal service and telecommunications*

First and foremost there is the postal and telecommunications infrastructure. Without a postal and telecommunications service, information work becomes absolutely impossible. If the postal service is slow, and especially if it is somewhat unreliable, the network's organization should be much more decentralized (see section 2.6) than when the mail is swift and sure. It is therefore indispensable to take account of the quality of this service, noting average delays between one point and another and the percentage of mail which arrives either very late or not at all.

It is true that the shortcomings of the postal service may be offset in part by a good telecommunications network, provided that its prices are reasonable. Telecommunications are obviously essential for the use of data banks at a distance, and for automatic registration of books and periodicals in libraries which do not possess computers of their own. For selective dissemination of information, on the other hand, it is less expensive to rely on the post, and this is still more true of sending out information, exchanging documents and dispatching bibliographical bulletins. Nevertheless, one must always bear in mind the need to reach a compromise between cost and speed.

3.6.1.2   *Printing*

Printing does not have a direct part to play in the information network. Theoretically, one could have everything printed abroad. But it is better to avoid this solution, and in any case one must be acquainted with existing printing equipment, the current workload, and exactly what such equipment is like (are traditional casting machines used, and, if so, of which type? Or is there any photo-composition apparatus, and if so, how powerful?).

Besides the main equipment, and without necessarily going into details, it is advisable to know whether auxiliary equipment (type-setting keyboards, machines for collating and binding, etc., and, possibly, specialized computers) is in plentiful supply or, on the contrary, only just adequate or even inadequate in view of the production potential of the main equipment.

3.6.1.3   *Computer network*

To an even greater extent than printing machinery, computers are generally put to quite other uses than library and documentation work, but virtually every documentary modernization programme includes a plan to bring a computer into use. Such a programme depends on what is currently available, as there is a big difference between filling in the slack periods of overplentiful equipment and being obliged to make an additional investment. It also depends on the type of computer which one is in a position to use, for it is fairly difficult, and results in loss of performance, to transfer a programme from one computer to another of a different model. Hence the importance of knowing what types of equipment can be used in practice.

It is necessary to go further, since, as everyone knows, a computer has a short life; when organizations change their computers, they do not always stick to the same make, usually for sound reasons, and the change is planned beforehand. So one has to know not only the present state of the computer population but also, so to speak, its future state. In other words, contact with the departments responsible for planning in computer science should make it possible to assess this situation which, although still in the future, is already a present-day factor in analysis of an information network.

Besides the computers themselves, and linking up with the telecommunications network, it is highly desirable to know the situation of the terminals—their numbers, their cost price, what hypotheses may be put forward concerning their development, etc. There will certainly be a great difference in the presentation of information according to whether there is a terminal in every research department and every agricultural co-operative (for non-documentary uses) or whether, on the contrary, the use of terminals remains confined for years at a stretch to a few private subscribers with heavy outputs (insurance companies and banks).

3.6.1.4 *Reprography infrastructure*

Two types of appliance are gaining ground with remarkable speed—photocopiers and microfilm readers. The existence of the former is making it possible to cut down on equipment in the central document reproduction departments; the extension of the latter is leading to plans for rapid development in microdocumentation. Here, therefore, it is useful to have a general idea not only of the present situation (without going into too many details), but also of the speed with which each of these two phenomena is likely to develop. It is not a matter of making complete inventories of equipment of this kind, but of carrying out a few surveys into the way organizations equip themselves and of being alert to certain indicators, such as, for example, the number of reproductions ordered by a particular group of users and the variations in this number over a period of time.

Another important point is the state of the photographic industry (or craft). How many well-equipped photographers and film makers are there? Are they working to full capacity or not?

3.6.1.5   *Audio-visual infrastructure*

This is undoubtedly one of the best-known factors at national level as far as the number of television sets is concerned but are there other audio-visual appliances, such as minicassette players, or items of equipment producing audio-visual presentations? If they do exist, they are certainly to be found in the possession of educational authorities, but they may also be found in other public or private sectors with which exchanges are possible.

At least as important as the existence of the equipment itself is the population's degree of receptivity to such processes.

3.6.1.6   *Booksellers' networks and book clubs*

This is an interesting factor, as booksellers may be relied on to publicize certain works and, furthermore, they are active in book distribution, and it is unnecessary to do twice over something which already forms part of the services provided by this network.

3.6.2   EQUIPMENT USED STRICTLY FOR LIBRARIES AND DOCUMENTATION

3.6.2.1   *Premises and storage facilities*

Until recent times, buildings alone constituted the main equipment of libraries; space was needed to accommodate readers and to arrange books. Knowledge and culture were preserved within stone walls. It was the user who went to consult them. Nowadays, the effects of progress in microdocumentation and communications facilities are such that there is a growing tendency to bring literature to the customer; in order to give effect to such a policy, there will be a need, not so much for huge buildings capable of stocking thousands of works and accommodating hundreds of people, as for small-scale bases, judiciously placed at strategic points of the economy, and well distributed throughout the territory. Premises may be rented or borrowed as appropriate for temporary or part-time operations. For this venture, storage premises will nevertheless be needed, to be used as archives, but these need not occupy costly sites in the capital cities.

In any case, it is easy, within a documentary network, to make a list of buildings with their potentialities for accommodation and for enlargement where necessary, and their storage capacity (shelving, microfiche libraries, conveyer belts, etc.). For stack rooms above a certain size, transport of documents is now becoming systematically automated, especially in areas where labour is expensive.

3.6.2.2   *Service points and bookmobiles*

Theoretically, the desks mentioned above, which are there to facilitate relations with various categories of users, should be listed together with the buildings. We think, however, that they warrant special consideration, as they represent a larger investment than their value as premises in the narrow sense. There may even be no premises at all, if the library is an outpost in the bush or a travelling library of the bookmobile kind. However, groups of users have been led to acquire a set of habits and expectations, so that these 'service stations'—for this is what they are, either fixed or mobile, but always lightweight—must be considered as an essential part of the network's equipment.

3.6.2.3   *Audio-visual material*

In studying an existing infrastructure, one is likely to come across only a little material of this kind; it is useful to be familiar with its chief characteristics and to know whether only 'receivers' are involved or whether equipment also exists for active photographic work and audio-visual presentations. For audio-visual sessions, the synchronized combination of several systems (projection and mini-cassettes in particular) is worth noting.

3.6.2.4   *Reprography apparatus*

The exact number of photocopiers is not of vital importance; it is simply better to have a general idea of production capacity at the main points of the information network. By contrast, the number of microfilm and microfiche cameras is a significant factor, and so is the number of automatic developers (for microfilms and microfiches) and of duplicators (diazotypes, Kalvar, or equivalent processes).

Of course, large-scale production appliances of the Copyflo type are of central importance in any study of an existing network, as are printing possibilities (plates and offset runs or their equivalents) when they are used mainly by bodies which form part of the network (including printing and binding apparatus). Knowledge about microcopy readers held in documentation centres is of less interest than data on those held by users. Reader-reproducers should be counted, especially if they have a large output or if they are combined with systems of automatic retrieval, of a type such as 'Image system', Synelec, Filmorex or Miracode.

3.6.2.5 *Computers, terminals*
and automatic composition equipment

Some documentation centres have computers of their own, while others share the machines with other centres, usually on a shift basis. A few possess terminals—a simple terminal with a typewriter, a visual-display terminal or a minicomputer with buffer memory, sometimes fitted with a disc or a tape-reader. These terminals may also be used to full capacity or else shared, for example, with the research centre or with the administrative authorities of the university.

Nowadays, one finds combinations of equipment, consisting of a computer built into or connected to documentation apparatus. The following, for instance, have been put on the market with great success:

Photocomposers, or machines for print composition directly controlled by computer (or by magnetic tape). Their rate of production ranges from a few tens of thousands of signs per hour to several millions.

Microphotocomposers, working on the same principle as the former but supplying microfilms or microcards which may also be enlarged for publication purposes. These machines make it possible not only to reproduce the most unusual characters, but also, thanks to the computer with which they are combined, to reproduce diagrams, drawings, chemical formulae, etc.

Apparatus for microfiche or microfilm retrieval, differing only slightly from those mentioned in the preceding paragraph, but which offer a variety of extra possibilities if connected to a computer.

3.7 Supplies and methods

With supplies and working methods, we come to the question of running costs. As in the case of staff, it is advisable to refer to ratios by service unit, such as those outlined in section 3.5. We shall not dwell on the nature of these supplies (paper, typewriters, card indexes, cards for card indexes, punched cards, special paper for reprography, microfilms of various widths (35 mm and 105 mm for microfiches) offset plates, photographic solutions, dusters, ink, shelving, cupboards, filing cabinets, desks, chairs, screens, mini-cassettes, electricity, heating, rubbish disposal, etc.).

A major factor is, of course, the acquisition of books, periodicals and documents which should normally account for at least three-quarters of the running costs in respect of materials of a library which is only a reference library.

When full-scale reprography services are provided, it is usual to exact payment for these in order that they may offset the extra expenses incurred and pay the salaries of the staff employed on these tasks. In theory, by requesting participation in expenses in this way, it should even be possible to pay off investments in reproduction equipment and part of the cost of building construction. It is questionable whether it is right or wrong to include here a part of the purchase price of the document reproduced. We believe that it is right if only in order to avoid competition with the direct sale of documents by those who produce them. Working methods follow naturally from the equipment which exists. Where documentation is concerned, however, it is advisable to know how documentary processing is carried out, and to find out whether there are thesauri, official glossaries, classification systems or other linguistic tools. Similarly, the organization, registration upon receipt, orders, and the arrangement of books in libraries are worth specifying.

Of even greater interest is the way in which these services are made available to users. How are the users received, and how is advertising carried out? What methods are employed to set up dialogues? to find out whether satisfaction is being given? to assess the marked and hidden needs. In a word, how is the marketing of information managed?

3.8 Financial resources

There are three possible sources of funds for documentation centres or libraries, irrespective of whether they have public or private status. They are:

Subventions from public authorities. If these are State bodies, all expenses must be taken into account (materials, staff, running, including the amortization of premises and equipment).

Payment for services rendered (if public bodies are involved this income may not be received by the body concerned. In this case, it is clearly necessary to adjust the amount of the subventions by deducting this income).

Subscriptions, this holds good for all documentation centres or libraries which have associative or co-operative status. Some of these may be attached to a technical centre having such status, and whose funds are provided by the subscriptions of their members. In this case, the technical centre's subvention to its library should be placed in this category.

These subscriptions are sometimes a means of making a global payment for services rendered which one does not wish to set out in detail. This is the case of associations, learned societies, technical centres or schools which draw their financial resources from the contributions of a profession's industries.

In the most highly developed Western European countries, the turnover of the book industry is in the region of 0.2–0.5 per cent of the gross national product (GNP). In France, the breakdown of the above figure, in 1970, was as follows (with the percentage of number of copies on parentheses):[1]

School textbooks, 15 per cent (19 per cent); science and technology, 11 (5); humanities and law, 8 (7); encyclopaedias,

1. M. Troubnikoff, 'Les données numériques', *Le livre français, hier, aujourd'hui, demain*, Paris, Imprimerie Nationale, 1972.

dictionaries and geographical maps, 17 (3); books for young people, 8 (13); general literature and miscellaneous, 35 (52, of which detective novels, 4 per cent, paperbacks, 16; others, 32); the arts, 6 (1).

France exports approximately 17 per cent of the books it produces, and imports an equivalent quantity.

Outlay on documentation and libraries, which is difficult to assess precisely, may be set very approximately at a little more than 0.1 per cent of the GNP, i.e. $3 to $4 per head.[1] A very high proportion of this expenditure comes from public subventions, since all library services are free of charge, and charges for bibliographical services are lower than their cost prices. Only the following are paid for by users at rates corresponding closely to the real costs: reprography services (not in every case); services in connexion with patents; specialized services (bibliographies compiled on request, translations, advice, etc.).

The implicit guiding principle behind the development of these structures is that of popular culture free of charge. At the outset, basic services were made freely available to all, but these did not perhaps afford the convenience needed by users who were pressed for time. Hence, fee-paying services were introduced, geared to the spending power of those who requested them and to the importance which they attached to the additional facilities desired, namely:

Purchasing books in order to keep them at home for an indefinite length of time instead of reading them at the library or borrowing them.

Possessing photocopies instead of coming to consult the original documents.

Having specialized bibliographies at one's disposal instead of plunging into laborious research on one's own.

Having precise and reliable information at one's disposal, in preference to documents which must be read and analysed.

Having access to data banks which provide the necessary guarantees of reliability, speed and accuracy.

It is, of course, possible to call these principles in question, either by planning to make all services fee-paying or, on the contrary,

---

1. A rough estimate based on the libraries' budget, and, for documentation, on the extrapolated results of an already outdated survey (1966).

by raising the level of the basic free-of-charge minimum or, again, by establishing a graded price list according to the degree of 'convenience' required.

3.9 General qualitative and quantitative evaluation of the existing infrastructure in view of the needs to be met

Having examined first the needs, and then the existing services and the means at their disposal for carrying out their tasks, the next step is to make a comparative study by taking, for example, the various types of need, one by one, and the ways in which the existing infrastructure is able to cater for them.

The first task is to make a list of needs which appear to be satisfactorily met.

The second is to find out whether, if certain services were adapted or converted, the latter could be organized to meet a number of unsatisfied needs which are the most pressing and have the closest links with the methods and techniques familiar to the existing staff.

Lastly, the question will arise of gaps and of plans for filling them. Their relative urgency must be discussed, bearing in mind the factors of choice to which we referred briefly in section 2, and in accordance with the unsatisfied needs which stand out as being the most essential to the development of the country. If resources are limited, an attempt may be made to set up a programme for a period of time, paying less attention to a time schedule and rather more to the emergence of certain data which will have a decisive influence on the establishment of the network, such as: school attendance rate; literacy; number of students; coming of age of certain classes of the population; rural and urban development; possibility of releasing extra funds; transformation of the communications network; computer equipment; international agreements, etc.

4   A few examples of the types of need to be met

Without going into detail at this stage, we shall try to give a brief account of the lines on which we think a documentation and libraries network ought to develop as a cultural tool and as a means of promoting economic activities and industrialization. The growth of the network should keep pace with economic and cultural growth, but it is also linked with new possibilities in technology which enable it to play a more important and more active part in the process of growth than it did in the past. We shall take a few examples of different patterns of growth according to the size of the country and its stage of development. In order to illustrate the various kinds of set-up, it may be helpful to refer to the three model statutes contemplated for the U.S.S.R., even if no other country in the world requires such a comprehensive system. The network in the U.S.S.R. is of course headed by a very impressive multidisciplinary documentation centre and a big national library. The following kinds of institute are contemplated as well:

First, a sectoral institute serving the whole of the U.S.S.R. and the various users, but in one specific field, such as metallurgy.

Second, an institute serving a specific locality; it meets all types of need in all sectors but only in Leningrad, for example.

Third, a documentation centre serving an enterprise or organization (on an 'interlocality' and intersectoral basis if necessary) but only meeting the needs of the body to which it belongs.[1]

1. 'Model statutes for information services in the U.S.S.R.', *Unesco bulletin for libraries*, vol. XXV, no. 2, March-April 1971, p. 94–101.

4.1   A medium-sized developed country

This category is typified by the European countries (whether Eastern or Western) most of which are bound by the past so that their freedom of choice is limited and they can only proceed very gradually to reorientate the structure of their information system. The existing situation generally displays the features shown below.

4.1.1   EXISTING SITUATION

4.1.1.1   *Libraries*

One big library or several big libraries holding thousands of books and periodicals, a large proportion of which are very seldom consulted.

A copyright deposit system which ensures that the big libraries hold at least one copy of everything printed in the country.

A very dense network of university libraries, which, however, are not very adequately equipped. (These libraries have had difficulty in keeping up with the very rapid growth of the universities, with the result that their collections are sometimes poor.)

A dense and very effective network of public libraries, used quite intensively in some countries, but much less in others.

In the schools, libraries in nearly all classes, the lending of books being organized by the class teacher or one of the subject teachers.

Stocks of compulsory textbooks, some of which are provided free of charge.

4.1.1.2   *Book trade*

The existence of an active if not flourishing book trade, widely dispensing culture to an increasingly large proportion of the population. However, it still fails to reach between 20 and 40 per cent of the population, depending on the country. This situation is rapidly changing because the 15 per cent of the population regarded as 'avid readers' are to be found chiefly among the young.

The price of books on special branches of science and technology deters many readers. On the other hand, in general literature the price has ceased to be a critical factor (except in a few cases) since the advent of pocket-books. In Eastern Europe even scientific books are very inexpensive.

4.1.1.3 *Documentation services*

The existence of a big documentation centre or several such centres (generally situated in the capital or in a large city).

The existence of specialized documentation centres likewise situated in the larger towns (except in France, where practically all documentation services are concentrated in Paris).

The existence of a central patents service.

Many documentation centres in large industrial firms in the West, which also possess data banks either individually or collectively.

In the West, a network of firms of consultants is beginning to play an important part in the transfer of technical information.

4.1.1.4 *Techniques and methods*

Photocopying is in common use.

Microcopying is employed for some archives work, but has not yet become popular with users.

Inexpensive processes for the duplication and printing of small numbers of copies have made their appearance.

Phototypesetting is in its infancy.

Computers are gradually being introduced into documentation work and into libraries. Their advantages are now appreciated by most services.

Information analysis centres are already functioning (almost without realizing that they are functioning as such).

Audio-visual techniques have only just begun to get a footing (being promoted mainly by young executives).

4.1.1.5 *Organization*

Public authorities are gradually becoming information-minded.

Some efforts at harmonization are beginning to be made by the various bodies concerned.

There is a trend towards some degree of centralization or co-ordination of systems which were originally very heterogeneous.

Studies on planning have been put in hand.

Attempts are being made to interest industry in information services.

4.1.1.6 *International relations*

Co-operation has begun at regional level, and although it is still a small-scale effort it has raised great hopes.

Books, periodicals and microfilms are exchanged between libraries all over the world.

Magnetic tapes of automated documentary material from the United States are being used.

International bodies are actively participating (OECD, International Federation for Documentation (FID), Unesco with its UNISIST programme, International Organization for Standardization (ISO)).

4.1.1.7 *Staff and training*

The employment opportunities open to documentalists and librarians vary from country to country. The situation is not really alarming anywhere. In the countries where it is least satisfactory women are recruited rather than men.

Training courses in librarianship are available (they are being modernized in certain countries).

Many courses are available for library assistants and documentalists (the students sometimes have difficulty in finding employment).

Some advanced post-graduate courses are available (probably still too few).

4.1.2   DESIRABLE LINES OF DEVELOPMENT

The following lines of development are based partly on the recommendations made by OECD and Unesco within the framework of the UNISIST programme, and partly on what is planned or under way in some countries. All the suggestions are of course still subjects of controversy.

4.1.2.1   *Libraries*

4.1.2.1.1   *General extension of union catalogues,*
use of internationally compatible formats,
computerization

This task demands considerable means. If it is not to be too costly, librarians must change their habitual methods of work at all levels (accessioning, ordering of books, loans, etc.). Only integrated mechanized processing enables libraries to take full advantage of a computer without engaging additional staff. Every effort must be made to avoid 'repunching' data already recorded in another form on manual selection index cards. In practice, this reconversion entails acquiring a computer terminal and completely retraining the staff. With this reservation, even small libraries can be modernized without entailing heavy expenditure apart from the investment represented by the cost of setting up the new system.

In point of fact, union catalogues are strictly essential mainly for scientific and technical works and periodicals and for unpublished documents of the same nature. When it comes to literary works, some are so widespread that it can be assumed that all libraries have them and that exchanges are infrequently concerned with them (this applies in particular to classical literature of the sixteenth, seventeenth, eighteenth and nineteenth centuries and contemporary works which have become famous).

Other works are insignificant, in abundant supply and almost interchangeable, so that they can be catalogued by author and the exact titles need not be listed (this applies to detective stories, for example).

Others again are solely of interest to research workers and are only requested by a very few specialists. Systematic cataloguing of these works is very laborious and they may perhaps be consulted only once (early printed books and old manuscripts, rare works, etc.). However, specialists in historical bibliography will find in the course of their research that it is useful to catalogue such works on the computer, so the system must be able to take care of them.

Similarly, as the modernization of libraries progresses, it will become easier to enter new works straight into the automated union catalogue than to continue at the same time to catalogue certain categories of work by hand.

4.1.2.1.2 *Development of book-lending services*
There is a very great need for loans of scientific and technical books. Some countries have worked miracles here. Others have made slower progress. Loans of such books should be available on a paying basis to a large and varied readership. They can be made from any library, especially if there are union catalogues, but experience has shown in the United Kingdom that a central lending service is a very good system, not to say the best, for ensuring the requisite speed and safety. It should be noted that a central lending service presupposes the existence of an efficient postal service.

4.1.2.1.3 *Local library facilities and services*
Reading is now a widespread activity, at least among the young, where general cultural interests are concerned, but people are not yet accustomed to seeking information for the purposes of technical training or lifelong education programmes, nor in connexion with their work.

Here libraries have an important part to play in liaison with bodies dealing with technical training. The services involved (loans, advice, etc.) might be made available on a paying basis.

4.1.2.1.4 *Improvement of holdings*
University libraries are often handicapped by financial difficulties when they wish to build up and modernize their holdings. This reduces their efficiency and at the same time proves harmful to the book trade, which counts them among its good customers (in science and technology, for example). Local libraries have not yet all joined the general movement towards the promotion of scientific and technical culture; nor have school libraries.

4.1.2.2 *Documentation*

4.1.2.2.1 *Organization of the documentation network*
It is mainly the network for circulating particulars of documents which is being reorganized in all countries. There are a great many documentation centres, but since they had difficulty in communicating with one another so long as they were working with manual selection card indexes, they constitute very dispersed networks.

A general extension of the application of the standards should lead to a more rational distribution of tasks. We do not dare to speak of centralization so as not to lose touch with the users, who remain very attached to the individual services they have created to meet their immediate needs.

4.1.2.2.2 *Automation*
Computerization of all catalogues, bibliographical bulletins and other card indexes is imperative. As with the union catalogues of the libraries, it demands a far-reaching change in methods, particularly in cataloguing standards, and also an effort in regard to languages suitable for indexing.

4.1.2.2.3 *Linguistic problems*
There are two aspects to these problems. First, the positively torrential progress of science and technology makes any attempt at classification inadequate. Keywords have to be used to describe the content of documents. These keywords, which can easily be processed by computer, have to be organized among themselves by various types of semiological links which must be known to the computer, just as people using these words have these links more or less consciously in mind. This organization of vocabularies, which leads to the creation of graded but flexible tools known as thesauri, is absolutely essential whatever the method used for feeding the particulars of documents to the computer.[1]

Second, several of the nations concerned speak different languages, produce literature in their respective languages and are generally anxious that the science and technology which they use should be accessible in those languages as far as possible. If people in their country could not think and talk about technology except in a foreign language, the national language would rapidly give way to the language of technology. The latter (which is used at work) is in fact gaining ground as the main vehicle of culture, because it is essential to improve one's knowledge of the language of science and technology by reading novels, short stories and newspapers if one wants to get anywhere in today's society.

On the other hand, whatever the merits of the national pro-

---

1. There are two methods. The first consists in indexing each document at the outset by associating with it keywords or descriptors selected from the theasurus. The second is to use words taken from the natural language of the authors when feeding the computer. In this case the need to resort to the thesaurus is felt when queries have to be answered by the system.

duction, science is international and therefore expressed in all languages, or at least in the principal vehicular languages. Accordingly, it is not enough to compile vocabularies and thesauri in order to process document references on the computer in one preferred language; it is essential to go much further. In the first place, instead of being content to build up national thesauri, it is necessary to co-operate with other countries in producing multilingual thesauri.

In the second place, as it is impossible to translate all documents, it would be worth while to select those to be translated in full, those to be condensed in digest-type periodicals, those of which only a good informative summary will be given, and those which will only be mentioned and indexed until such time as a closer examination is called for by interested users.

4.1.2.2.4 *Provincial network*
In nearly all countries the documentation network is too centralized. Provincial towns feel very isolated and this is all the more true of rural communities. The feeling of isolation is stronger, of course, in some countries than in others. It is at its most acute in France. In most countries an effort is being made, with varying degrees of success, to develop documentation centres based on libraries or local institutes.

4.1.2.2.5 *Analysis centres and their promotion*
As we saw in section 3.1, above, the documentation requirements of a good many potential users cannot be met by bibliographies, but by their subject-matter, in other words, by the actual information. Starting with the various facilities already in existence, documentation services in the countries under review can be expected to make a considerable effort to extract the principal data from documents and present them in an attractive form to potential industrial and rural users who are greatly in need of them. An effort is likewise being made to establish constructive contacts between these potential users and the existing network of libraries and documentation centres. According to the country, potential users are being approached through visiting speakers, technical associations, learned societies, technical centres or various agencies and, in some cases, through credit establishments.

Much of this work has to be done in the provinces where it is even more necessary than in the capitals or the large cities. One of the numerous tasks would be to introduce individual or group projects involving documentary research into general secondary education. School libraries would be used for this purpose after appropriate scientific or technical documents had been added to their collections. Later on, terminals would be installed in secondary schools in order to give pupils practice in consulting stocks of documentation or data banks.

4.1.2.2.6 *International co-operation*

In section 2.6 we dwelt on regional co-operation with neighbouring countries. We think that there is much to be gained by task sharing at this level. We are therefore bound to witness a rapid development of the schemes introduced quite recently. The countries concerned will of course participate widely in world information systems and exchanges with countries in the Third World will be one of their aims.

4.1.2.2.7 *Data base, data bank, distribution centres*

Networks of interconnected computers are beginning to appear. One of the uses of these networks, which often have great capabilities, is to transfer data and bibliographies. The term 'data bank', as we have seen, denotes a fund of specific information which produces a direct answer in figures, or the equivalent, when a question is put to the system. A data base, on the other hand, is a fund of references which makes it possible to obtain such information after going through another procedure. Thus, a documentation network supplying bibliographies constitutes a data base (at present, it must even be described as the principal form in which this idea has materialized, inventories being the other form). The base could be piloted by a centre for the dissemination of knowledge in liaison with a regional network. This pilot centre would collect the data introduced into the network by the various centres existing in the country and would add magnetically recorded contributions from foreign systems.

4.1.2.2.8 *Training and status of specialists*

In the countries under review, there is a trend in favour of changing the training courses for high-level specialists to keep abreast of the evolution of methods and technology. Fairly intensive retraining will probably be necessary in view of the number of librarians and documentalists at present employed. As regards status, documentalists are unlikely to organize themselves formally into a separate profession; they seem to aim instead at a qualification (information science specialists) which would be additional to such other degrees as they may hold.

4.2   A small developed country

All the foregoing applies on the whole to the small countries, with a few reservations which are set forth below.

4.2.1   EXISTING SITUATION

The libraries and documentation network is much more closely organized than in the larger countries. There is usually a multi-purpose body (the national library, for instance) which plays a preponderant role. Some centres existing in small countries have, however, won an international reputation in certain specific fields (for example agriculture and medicine).

4.2.1.1   *International relations*

Relations with foreign countries are particularly close. Sometimes there are relations of a preferential character, joint research projects or even common services having been organized in some cases.

4.2.1.2   *The book trade*

The book trade necessarily assumes a very international character since the market is not large enough in the country itself. Some categories of literature are always imported, but it is possible, on the other hand, that in other branches local publishing houses have come to the fore on the world market. Several of the big international publishers are established in small countries.

4.2.2   LINES OF DEVELOPMENT

4.2.2.1   *Organization*

In so far as organization is concerned, the problems are often much easier to solve than in larger countries for there have been fewer independent or isolated efforts, everything having been done with a view to national and nearly always international co-operation.

4.2.2.2   *External relations*

Connexions with international networks are the rule. Co-operation at regional level is often given top priority. The only difficulty does not arise from the internal situation but from such agreements as may have been concluded with foreign systems incompatible with each other and with the standards which the regional or international network is absolutely obliged to take into account.

4.2.2.3   *Provincial network*

Paradoxically, it is fairly easy to serve the provinces, for in such countries there is often a rather more federalist structure than in larger countries and poles of attraction for development efforts exist outside the capital, which have assumed responsibilities with regard to information work.

4.2.2.4   *Analysis centres and data bases*
             Training of specialists

As a rule all these new problems arise in the same way as in medium-sized countries, but the action which could be taken in those countries at the strictly national level can only be taken in small countries in close co-operation with their neighbours. There are forms of investment in intellectual and material equipment (training schools, data-processing programmes, computer networks, linguistic tools) which are not a paying proposition except in a larger community.

4.3 A large developing country

4.3.1 EXISTING SITUATION

4.3.1.1 *Organization and 'political' structure*

Most large developing countries have a federal political structure, so that combined efforts are made at the level of the central authorities and by local governments. This has the great advantage of making it possible to share the work on all projects which are only justifiable for a very extensive information network (and in particular to launch studies on advanced techniques such as the use of audio-visual equipment). At the same time, maximum use can be made of the available means for the dissemination of culture and information at the local level.

4.3.1.2 *Relations between libraries and documentation services*

Libraries in several of the developing countries are among the oldest in the world and have rich collections of early works. Examples of such libraries are found in Asian, Latin American and Arab countries. The copyright-deposit system is very widespread, so that the national libraries hold a very large part of the national literature in their archives. At the same time, documentation centres have grown up alongside research centres or have been set up at the suggestion of national science and technology advisory boards for the purpose of operating an information service for research workers. As a result, separate national science libraries have come into being and in several countries there are two organizations, one of which is still carrying out its original mission of an essentially cultural nature, while the other seeks to meet as far as possible the needs of technologists and research workers. This situation exists in developed countries too, but since the means available are much more considerable, the separation (which can be expected to become less marked as time goes on) is far less critical.

4.3.1.3 *Literacy training*

In many cases, the illiteracy rate is still high. In view of the size of the populations of large developing countries, this means that there is such a great number of illiterates that it warrants the development of perfected tools for literacy training. The production of such books and material would be an economic proposition since millions of copies or units would be required and consequently the unit cost of each item could be kept very low. For this there is an historic precedent: in the U.S.S.R. in the 1920s several million copies of only a few dozen books of general cultural interest were distributed.

4.3.1.4 *Industrialization*

One of the interesting features of large developing countries as compared with other developing countries is the existence of already powerful industries in several sectors of the economy. These industries, of course, employ only a minority of the population, the majority remaining agricultural, but they constitute a sufficiently large group of potential users of the documentation network to justify an investment of capital for the purpose of meeting their needs alone.

4.3.1.5 *Libraries*

There are still very few school libraries. They have to compete for priority with the needs for school buildings, teachers, textbooks and educational supplies, which are very difficult to meet. It is also rare to find a children's section in a public library.

The position seems rather better with regard to public libraries, although its needs are very far from being met and there are still not nearly enough libraries. Furthermore, their status, which varies from country to country and even within the same country, is not yet clearly recognized.

As a rule, university libraries were organized on rational lines at the outset when the universities were set up. They are now faced with three main problem areas:

The increasing number of students, which leads to a critical shortage of copies of available books.

The expansion and diversification of knowledge, already referred to in section 2.1.2, which makes it impossible to purchase all the works required.

The difficulty of recruiting qualified staff.

4.3.1.6   *Audio-visual media*

The effectiveness of audio-visual media is universally recognized in developing countries, whereas it is still a matter of controversy in highly developed countries. When adequate means can be devoted to this method of disseminating culture and knowledge it spreads very quickly. Several public libraries have acquired audio-visual equipment and they find that its use is increasing at about the same rate as the reading of books.

4.3.1.7   *The book trade*

The book trade is progressing slowly because there is a shortage of printing plant. There is also a lack of locally produced good-quality paper, so that it is all too often necessary to import supplies at additional cost. Furthermore, there is no certainty that any given work will attract enough readers, in the absence of some planning or some authoritative recommendation to the effect that this or that book should be used in preference to others.

4.3.1.8   *Documentation*

Documentation networks are organized on the basis of industrial technical sectors and on the basis of university libraries. This has led to the appearance of specialized networks (each serving a particular branch) to meet the needs of certain users. At the same time, however, some governments have realized the tremendous amount of duplication which would result from the dispersal of efforts, and have set up national documentation centres. At least one of these governments is studying an integrated information system for science and technology.

4.3.1.9   *Documentation techniques*

The ratio between the reprographic devices used for documentation work and those used for the other library activities is almost the same as in the more developed countries. On the other hand, the new techniques in microphotography and especially in printing have not yet been introduced on a significant scale. Computers are relatively numerous, but are only just coming into use in librarianship and documentation.

4.3.2   LINES OF DEVELOPMENT

4.3.2.1   *Organization*

As stressed by all the experts, to set up a centralized organization headed by a national agency wielding authority is clearly one of the essential aims. This is possible because of the still relatively modest scope of the various bodies which have sprung up when circumstances permitted. Such an organization has become indispensable owing to the paucity of the resources available—human, financial and material.[1]

It is even regarded as highly desirable by some experts that the same agency should be in charge of both the libraries and the documentation network, for there is no essential difference between the needs of university libraries, which aim to train future research workers and engineers, and the needs of documentation centres, whose purpose is to help practising research workers and engineers. Nor is there any fundamental difference between libraries for the general public and school libraries, and a part of their holdings ought to be the same as those of the libraries of technical education establishments and those of documentation centres designed to serve workers practising the corresponding trades.

4.3.2.2   *The planning of accessions and union catalogues*

As we have seen, exchanges play a vital role in documentation networks, but if exchanges are to be easy the holdings of other libraries or other centres must be known, either exactly (and this brings us to the need for union catalogues) or approximately (the approximate scope and content of holdings being transcribed by hand or printed for exchange purposes).

---

1. See in particular P. H. Sewell, *The planning of library and documentation services*, Paris, Unesco, June 1969, 87 p. (IIEP/S 20/1); *Final report of the Meeting of Experts on the National Planning of Library Services in Asia (Colombo, 11–19 December 1967)*, Paris, Unesco, June 1968, 30 p. (Doc. COM/CS/190/6); *Main working document of the Expert Meeting on National Planning of Library Services in Asia (Colombo, 11–19 December 1967)*, Paris, Unesco, November 1967, 90 p. (Doc. COM/CS/190/3); P. Lazar, *India: a national information system for science and technology*, Paris, Unesco, March–April 1972 (Doc. 2717/RMO/RD/DBA).

At all events, accessions as a whole have to be planned (in broad outline for current books and periodicals, in detail for rare and expensive works) at the level of the national agency (national library, documentation centre, or co-ordinating authority).

4.3.2.3   *Development of national production*

Large countries can produce books, periodicals and audio-visual materials by technical processes which are not beyond their means. A great effort must therefore be made in this direction and it will of course be accompanied by concomitant creative work consisting in the production of written or audio-visual material much better suited to local needs than the textbooks imported from abroad.

4.3.2.4   *Connexion with economic planning*

The means available for the documentation network are likely to remain inadequate for some time to come. Some machinery for determining priorities must therefore be established to ensure that the latter are consistent with the priorities fixed for education and social development.

4.3.2.5   *Abstracting, indexing, translating*

If there is a national documentation centre and if the size of the country permits, specialists in the main branches of science and technology can be brought together at the centre to perform the following tasks: to prepare abstracts of the nationally produced literature with a view to making it known at home and abroad; to help national users to extract the maximum information from certain works selected from the foreign literature to meet the most current or most urgent needs.

With this end in view, the scope of one of the tasks already being performed in certain countries by the national centre's abstracting and indexing service would be extended and the existing facilities would be strengthened (in those large countries where there is no national documentation centre, the required facilities would be created).

Translation work would likewise be intensified in countries where it is already going on and a start would be made in the others. In this connexion, international co-operation between nations belonging to the same linguistic group might be very rewarding, for documents would then be translated only once.

4.3.2.6 *Automation, research*

At the level of a national documentation centre, a research unit fully justifies its existence. Its main tasks would be: to study the automation problems of the libraries and documentation network including union catalogues; the drafting of national cataloguing rules in accordance with the internationally agreed system; any transliteration questions that may arise; the fixing and checking of vocabulary to bring it into line with the thesauri compiled at international level; and practical procedures for computerized information processing, as well as to study the adaptation of the potential output of computers to actual needs.

4.3.2.7 *International co-operation*

International co-operation is less vital for large developing countries than it is for small countries because the number of users is always large enough to justify the outlay on an organization supplied with extensive planning, research and training facilities and on equipment which soon pays for itself. So it is chiefly for the collection of information material that it is necessary to use the world network. Three kinds of exchanges are therefore developing:

Those made between libraries on a reciprocal basis for the purpose of obtaining rare documents on subjects which are not regularly handled by the national services.

Those made with documentation centres in the same linguistic area (co-ordination of translations, exchanges of compendiums, exchanges of document references with abstracts and indexing material, co-operation with regard to vocabularies and thesauri).

Those made between members of world-wide networks (participation in UNISIST and more specialized world networks).

4.3.2.8 *Training and status of librarians and documentalists*

In respect of training, the needs are the same as in the more developed countries. The number of existing schools and institutes varies widely from country to country. Practically nil in some countries, it can be regarded as fairly satisfactory in others. There is a shortage of specialists nearly everywhere. However, it must be remembered that a documentation network has to be built up almost from scratch so that far more people will have to be recruited during the first few years than it will be necessary to train later when the organization has been run in. Accordingly, those responsible for initial planning must beware of being too ambitious, for there is a risk of setting up a training system which, in a few years' time, might be turning out too many graduates for the openings available.

Training programmes should take into account the considerations set out in section 2.7, above, and in particular the following points:

A distinction should be drawn between specialized technical functions (those of cataloguers, reprographers, stack-attendants, sublibrarians) for which it is not necessary to have followed a course of scientific training, and fields of high-level specialization in which training in documentation and librarianship is additional to university level scientific studies.

In training at both levels, but more particularly the latter, the bias should be towards modern methods (use of reprography and microphotography, audio-visual techniques and, above all, use of computers, etc.).

At both levels, but more especially at the higher, stress should be laid on the part libraries can play in stimulating and advising readers and serving as a nucleus of development of crafts, agriculture, cottage industries, public health and even rural organization and home economies. Without going so far as to train 'hostesses for cultural, economic and social development', librarians ought to make their contribution to such development in so far as the dissemination of books and documentation permits.

4.4 A medium-sized developing country

Much of what was said in the previous section applies here too, of course, so we shall dwell only on the differences.

4.4.1   EXISTING SITUATION

4.4.1.1   *Organization*

Since the political structure, with certain exceptions, is fairly centralized, most of the efforts have so far been made in the capital, where the principal university is located. In many cases, adequate solutions have not yet been found to the problem of providing documentation and library facilities at local level and establishing units in outlying areas.

4.4.1.2   *Libraries*

Some of the libraries are very old, while others have been recently created. Most of them have so far existed only in skeletal form (they do not always have a copyright deposit system) so there is great freedom to choose the most rational form of organization. Hence a tendency to prefer an integrated organization comprising both documentation services and libraries and using very modern methods from the outset—in so far, of course, as the necessary means can be made available.

4.4.1.3   *Literacy training*

Literacy training is not always very advanced either, but in this field the country is not large enough on its own to warrant the development of the necessary modern materials. It is essential to join forces with other countries with the same needs, or else to adopt some of the books or audio-visual materials used by the largest countries.

4.4.1.4   *Industrialization*

Industry is usually weak and what little industrial plant there is has been concentrated, in many cases, on a few dominant activities. Undoubtedly, these activities have a special claim to the services of the documentation network. The information sectors to be given planning priority should accordingly be selected on the basis of a study of the country's potential resources and of all its latent needs.

4.4.1.5   *State of documentation techniques*

The new documentation techniques have made their appearance in those countries only very recently. The book trade is still rudimentary in most of the countries in this category. On the other hand, there are printing presses for newspapers.

4.4.1.6   *International co-operation*

Although it is realized that international co-operation is a very real need, the effort in this direction has not yet been fully effective. Some countries have obtained assistance from international organizations (Food and Agriculture Organization (FAO), International Labour Organisation (ILO), Unesco, etc.), but this assistance has necessarily been devoted to some specific goal, sometimes involving several nations, but not forming a part of a comprehensive programme. The same applies to exchanges at the regional level.

4.4.2   DESIRABLE LINES OF DEVELOPMENT

4.4.2.1   *Organization*

The national agency already recommended for the large countries is even more essential here. It should perform the function both of a national library and of a national documentation centre. This body, which should receive a copy of everything printed in the country under the copyright-deposit system, would also be organized to receive as many foreign books and periodicals as possible, excepting those already held by other libraries in the country. It would serve at the same time as the co-ordinating body for the whole network of libraries and documentation centres. It would represent this network at international level and act on its behalf. It would also work out the methods and standards to be used at national level.

4.4.2.2   *Union catalogue*

The union catalogue will be easier to keep up to date than in the largest countries, since fewer bodies are involved and their collections are smaller. On the other hand, it is of vital importance to compare the union catalogue with similar catalogues in neighbouring countries and this will be one of the main tasks of the national library, together with the planning of accessions.

4.4.2.3 *Development of national production*

The development of national printing presses is particularly urgent here because little has been done in this direction. Not only must countries have this medium of communication but they must also be able to produce by their own means some of their textbooks and general educational works. Needless to say, it will not be possible to go as far as the largest countries; the market is limited and becomes even smaller at each successive level of education and specialization. The national library and the education ministry could enter into task-sharing agreements with their counterparts in neighbouring countries to produce the necessary textbooks and audio-visual materials.

4.4.2.4 *International co-operation*

Regional co-operation should be one of the bases of the national information policy in science and technology. This is even more important for the countries under review than for the more developed ones. No documentation system can survive today unless it serves the needs of a sufficiently large population. If we had to give some idea of the size, we would say 100 million inhabitants, although we are aware that this is a very relative and debatable figure. In any event, it would have to be modified in the case of the library network, for each library could of course function independently. Limitations will soon be reached with regard both to technological progress and to the size of collections of documents. All the points made in section 2.6.3 apply here in most of the fields considered (cataloguing of books, information retrieval, working methods and standards, training). It is true that the setting up of data banks mentioned in section 2.6.3.3 will not be placed high on the list of priorities until such time as industrialization has reached a certain stage, except for data concerning natural resources. These, on the contrary, are particularly valuable and it would be advisable to keep them and make use of them in conjunction with the Unesco-sponsored work being done in this branch (an international data bank for the natural environment).

Sharing tasks with other countries also implies signing special agreements. Although it may take time to reach agreements covering a whole region, it is quite feasible to conclude bilateral agreements to which other countries would subsequently accede, or which might be revised later if the basis of co-operation was extended to a multinational group.

4.4.2.5   *Local documentation centres and libraries*

Outside the capital and one or two other large cities, there is a growing need for local centres which would work in liaison with such libraries as may exist (school libraries, public libraries, technical libraries), in order to guide and advise them, submit proposals for the creation of new services to the competent authorities, and provide them with the means of making themselves known to the public. Furthermore, these centres would keep in contact with all the dynamic elements in the local economic life, encouraging their efforts, supplying them with information and at the same time drawing them into a web of technical and cultural relationships capable of promoting nuclei of development.

This would mean fulfilling the functions of what is known in Europe as a documentation centre (or sometimes a 'specialized documentation centre') and in the OECD as an 'information-analysis centre'. For the sake of simplification, we shall adopt the former term, while fully aware that it covers both of these ideas and also includes a third function, which is to guide libraries so that they can become centres for the dissemination of knowledge and culture.

4.5   A small developing country

It must be said at the outset that it is not easy to give a very precise definition of what we mean by a small country in this context, for many developing countries with small populations have large territories and potential wealth which put them in the preceding category. Here we have in mind, *inter alia*, a few States (very dissimilar in other respects), whose small size is a dominant feature, such as some of the islands in the Pacific or in the Indian Ocean, the States bordering on the Himalayas, the emirates on the Persian Gulf, certain countries in Central or South America or certain African States. There are many others in different parts of the world. Almost all of them have the political advantage either of being the neighbour of a powerful nation or of being situated in the same geographical area as other nations with a similar system (in the Persian Gulf, Central America, Oceania). None of them has the means nor the need to equip itself with a network of libraries. As mentioned earlier in section 2.6.1, there will be a single body performing all the principal functions. In particular, it will co-ordinate the work of the various public and school libraries, as also that of university libraries and specialized centres when several exist. In most of these countries the economy is geared to one main activity (mining, oil-production, agriculture, fishing) on to which a cluster of subsidiary activities has been grafted (mechanical engineering, repairing of equipment, generation of electricity, operation of hydrological services, rural and urban development, tourism, etc.). It is self-evident that this economic pattern will be borne in mind when collections of books and documents are being built up.

Clearly, international co-operation assumes great importance here, either because there are close links with institutions in other countries (for example, through the 'twinning' of universities) or because a group of documentation services grows up around a national library which is more dynamic than the others and comes to the fore at regional level. In the first case, there will be an especially intensive flow of exchanges with the institutions to which these in the type of country under consideration are linked.

In the second case, there will develop a sort of federation or club headed by the library chosen as the pilot institution. The procedures employed for sharing out tasks and for agreeing on accessions, the selection of equipment, standards, union catalogues, staff training and exchanges of all kinds will be rather more unwieldy than in a highly developed nation, since they will be based entirely on voluntary co-operation and the sources of finance will be found through a different channel than that of the federating body. In some regions, however, there is evidence of a marked trend towards the adoption of this solution, for its effectiveness is coming to be more and more widely recognized.

5 Ways of meeting needs and planning

5.1 Summary review of objectives and their integration into general planning projects

As we have already said, documentation services and libraries contribute to national development; they are a factor in the promotion and support of economic activities and the exploitation of natural resources. Their objectives are therefore parallel to the general planning objectives, as is shown in Table 4.

If the objectives of the documentation network are to be effectively attained those in charge of each of the general planning projects will have to participate in the management of the services listed above. It will be incumbent on them, just as much as on the librarians, to provide guidance for accessioning programmes and indications as to the way in which they wish the services to operate for their purposes.

While maintaining the indispensable hierarchy of authority within an organization such as seems to be advisable in the light of the foregoing considerations, it will be necessary to give these users a priority right to express their views.

The problem of resources will inevitably arise. If the objectives set out above are closely co-ordinated with the general planning objectives, it is reasonable to suppose that the resources which it should be possible to devote to them will bear some relation to the amounts spent in attaining the general objectives. The proportion which can be allotted to information work will vary according to

TABLE 4

General objective and planning	Objective of the documentation network
Literacy	Literacy centres using modern techniques of the audio-visual type
Primary and secondary education	School libraries, audio-visual centres for children
Higher education	University libraries
Technical training	Documentation centres, public libraries
General and vocational lifelong education	Public libraries, centres for dissemination of knowledge
Research, innovation development of crafts agriculture and cottage industries	Documentation centres, centres for dissemination of knowledge, university libraries
National technical development programmes (dams, roads, buildings, forests, etc.)	National library, national documentation centre, documentation centres
Culture	Public libraries

the kind of economic, educational and cultural agents to be aided by the documentation network. Let us attempt to make an assessment.

First, let us consider public expenditure. We know that it represents a proportion of the gross national product (GNP) which varies according to the degree of development. The proportion may range from 20 to 40 per cent in the most highly developed countries, and will necessarily drop to a much lower figure in the poor countries, whose resources are too meagre to enable them to be drawn upon to any significant degree in order to finance a collective infrastructure effort. For priority programmes, contributions in kind (hours of work) have sometimes been obtained and have given good results. In the case under review, it must be admitted that such contributions are sure to be very limited.

Education, which is one of the community's first tasks, absorbs as much as 20–30 per cent of budgetary resources. In principle, documentation services and libraries are an integral part of education and should systematically receive at least 3–5 per cent of the resources allocated to the latter.

In Sri Lanka, for example, it is forecast that by 1978 the funds devoted to libraries will have reached only 0.84 per cent of educational expenditure; we shall round this figure up to 1 per cent.[1] But in some Central American States, this rate seems already to have reached 1.5 per cent in 1972.[2]

Furthermore, the general development programmes for town planning, infrastructure and the harnessing of natural resources, which form another of the priority chapters of the budget, might consider devoting up to 1 per cent of their resources to the dissemination of up-to-date technical information, not only in order to meet immediate needs, but also in preparation for the future (needs in the fields of technical training, lifelong education, aid to innovation projects, etc.).

Recapitulating the various objectives listed above, we can now draw up the following assumptions (Table 5) regarding resources,

TABLE 5

General objectives	Percentage of the GNP allocated to general objectives		Percentage of the GNP allocated to documentation objectives			R
	Maxi-mum	Mini-mum	Maxi-mum	Mini-mum	Aver-age	
Education	8[1]	3[1]	0.48	0.03	0.25	1–6
Research. Innovation	3	0.5	0.30	0.02	0.15	5–10
Investments directly productive	15	5	0.03	0.01	0.02	0.2
Investments indirectly productive (roads, dams, forests, etc.)[2]	4	1	0.04	0.01	0.02	1
Defence	7	1	0.02	—	0.01	0–0.2
Culture	0.5	0.1	0.1	0.01	0.05	10–20
	37.5	10.6	0.97	0.08	0.50	0.50

1. This percentage is reached only in the cases of Canada, Sweden and the U.S.S.R. In the other developed countries, it is closer to 5 or 6, but to this figure must usually be added private contributions or expenditures on technical training or lifelong education. In the developing countries it varies between 1.5 and 5 per cent. After, *Unesco statistical yearbook, 1970*, p. 465–95, Paris, Unesco, 1971, 786 p.
2. Excluding education and housing.

1. C. V. Penna, *The planning of library and documentation services*, 2nd ed., p. 72, Paris, Unesco, 1970, 158 p.
2. Ibid., p. 32.

letting R stand for the percentage of expenditure on general objectives which ought to be used for documentation services.

If we compare the results of Table 5 with the means at present allocated to libraries and documentation services, we see that these means are generally much smaller. For example, the figures collected in Colombo for Sri Lanka[1] show that in 1967 libraries accounted for only 0.46 per cent of educational expenditure; this figure was not expected to rise to 0.72 per cent until 1973, and to 0.84 per cent until 1978; we see therefore that it is lower than the 1 per cent which we consider in Table 5 to be the minimum. Yet Sri Lanka is a fairly advanced country in this field, since it already had 150 public libraries in 1968. This shows that the full scope of the problem has not been appreciated in itself; nor has sufficient attention been given, perhaps, to the 'profitability' aspect, which should never be lost sight of. In the same country, the funds granted for education amount to approximately 5 per cent of the GNP—in other words, the need for an effort in this sector has been properly understood.

5.2 Assessment of needs in comparison with existing services. Guidelines and tentative planning

The examples of Ecuador, India, the Ivory Coast, Senegal, Sri Lanka, Uganda, and many other countries, show that an effort has been made almost everywhere; but this should be compared with the conclusions which might be drawn from the needs assessed in section 3.1. Adopting the usual calculation methods of financial experts, we have arrived in section 5.1, above, at an idea of the funds which there might be hope of raising for libraries and documentation services according to the general picture which emerges of the importance of this sector as compared with others.

1. *Meeting of Experts on the National Planning of Library Services in Asia, Colombo. Final report*, op. cit.

5.2.1   ATTEMPT AT AN ASSESSMENT
          BASED ON A HYPOTHETICAL EXAMPLE

We shall take a hypothetical example (a country of 20 million inhabitants with a *per capita* GNP of $400) and we shall see that the minimum needs are much higher, if reference is made to the usual standards.

In fact, these needs are still not completely covered even in some comparatively wealthy countries (such as France), but even when they are halved we shall see, that they can only be met by the poor countries at the cost of a great effort which, for many reasons (resources and available staff), must be sustained for many years to come.

The following figures should, of course, be adjusted to take account of the wage level in the country concerned by applying a formula which we shall give, and also according to the density of the population. We assume that out sample nation occupies a territory of 500,000 km² so that d represents 40 inhabitants per km². If the density is different, the figures might be altered as follows: density less than 15, suggested multiplier 1.4–1.5;[1] 15–30, 1.2; 30–50, 1; 50–100, 0.8; more than 100, 0.7.

We shall work from an ideal model which we shall then attempt to adjust to take account of such means as may be found to be available by discussing possible priorities.

Let us consider our example: a country developing at an average rate with a population of 20 million inhabitants and a mean *per capita* GNP of $400. Let us suppose in the population 25 per cent are illiterate (i.e. 5 million); 10 per cent are children of primary-school age (i.e. 2 million); 5 per cent are children of secondary-school age (i.e. 1 million); 0.1 per cent are students (i.e. 20,000); and 0.01 per cent are research workers or equivalent (i.e. 2,000).

Although this last figure may appear high, since there may not be many research centres as yet, we believe that it is too low if we include all those inhabitants who have inventive minds, are able to read and are trying to collect the documentation they need.

---

1. If some countries consist of two zones, one densely populated and the other almost empty, each zone should obviously be considered separately.

If we recapitulate the needs, we arrive at the following figures:

One literacy centre for every 5,000 illiterates, i.e. in this example, 1,000 literacy centres.

One children's audio-visual centre for every 2,000–3,000 pupils, i.e. 600 audio-visual centres.

One school library for every 1,000 pupils, i.e. 3,000 libraries.

One public library, or, better still, one centre for dissemination of knowledge for every 10,000 inhabitants, i.e. 2,000 such centres.

One university library unit for every 1,000 students, i.e. twenty units, which may be grouped together, since there will probably be four or five universities with 4,000 to 5,000 students each.

One documentation and information analysis centre for every 100 research workers, i.e. twenty centres. Each of these centres would also direct and co-ordinate the activities of several centres for the dissemination of knowledge.

To these should be added the central bodies and the co-ordinating bodies which we mentioned above. We shall assume that these are a high-level science information council and a national library which also serves as the national documentation centre and as the general loan and reprography agency for any material not readily available in the country.

We shall now proceed to examine the order of magnitude of the cost of setting up these various services:

5.2.1.1   *Literacy (for one centre)*

Premises: 200 places (allowing 0.5 m² per place), i.e. 100 m² at $150 per m², hence $150 \times 100 = \$15,000$.

Investments in equipment: $10,000 for projectors, television unit, readers, etc.

Books: initial outlay, $5,000 then $1,000 per annum.

Films, magnetic tapes and running expenses: initial outlay, $10,000 then $2,000 per annum.

Maintenance of equipment: $500 per annum.

Staff: three persons, one at $3,000 and two at $1,500, i.e. $6,000 per annum.

Total (investments):
$$\$15,000 + \$10,000 + \$5,000 + \$10,000 = \$40,000;$$
(operation):
$$\$1,000 + \$2,000 + \$500 + \$6,000 = \$9,500 \text{ per annum.}$$

5.2.1.2   *Children's audio-visual centre (for one centre)*

The figures and expenses may be taken to be the same as for a literacy centre, except that the allowance must be made for a little more audio-visual material and no books.

5.2.1.3   *School libraries*

Premises. We have two figures which coincide. (a) The report on the planning of library services in Asia gives $25 per pupil;[1] (b) the report on the planning of library services in Africa[2] suggests that we take 5 per cent (in terms of expense) of the 3.5 m² allotted to each pupil for education, i.e. 0.17 m² per pupil.
   Taking the price per m² to be $150, we find: 0.17 × 150 = $26 per pupil,[3] i.e. for 1,000 pupils, $26,000.

Books. Five books at $1 per pupil, i.e. for 1,000 pupils, $5,000. The report on the planning of library services in Asia gives $8, but this includes audio-visual equipment. The above-mentioned figure of $5 is already higher than the current figure. We can therefore accept it as a first estimate. We should add approximately $1,000 for microfiches and viewing apparatus.

Shelving and equipment. The price of these items is usually taken to be one-quarter of the price of books in the case of university and specialized libraries, and one-third in the case of public libraries. The inclusion of modern equipment of the audio-visual type or microfiches, with which children should become familiar, would make it necessary to increase this proportion. As our figure of $5 per pupil is lower than the figure recommended, we shall take the cost of the initial equipment to be two-fifths of this figure, i.e. 1,000 × 2/5 = $2,000 for 1,000 pupils.

Operation, binding and renewal. Although the figures given amount to $5 per pupil per annum, which would result in $5,000, we

1. *Meeting of Experts on the National Planning of Library Services in Asia. Main working document*, op. cit.
2. *Meeting of Experts on the National Planning of Documentation and Library Services in Africa*, Paris, Unesco.
3. Penna, op. cit., p. 68.

believe that it is possible to keep a library running properly without spending more than 30 per cent of the initial outlay, which we have estimated at $6,000 + $2,000 = $8,000. In round figures, we woudl therefore have operating costs amounting to $2,500 per annum for 1,000 pupils.

Staff. Theoretically, planning provides one librarian for every 1,000 pupils, but this would result in an expenditure amounting to approximately $3,000 per annum. In France and in many other countries, school libraries are run by class teachers or subject teachers. In Latin America, it has been suggested that they might be paid a special allowance in addition to their normal salary. We think that this is the best solution, since the three persons appointed on a full-time basis to the audio-visual centre should also find it possible to run a service for rotating supplies to neighbouring school libraries. Therefore we need only make provision for allowances to be paid to teacher/librarians equivalent to one-sixth of the staff item per library, i.e. $500 per annum.

We see, then, that the heaviest expenditure is uncurred for premises, which should clearly be built at the same time as the school premises. The equipping of school libraries (nearly 3,000) and literacy centres (600 to 1,000) may, in view of their numbers, raise a problem in regard to imports of books, and hence, in some cases, a foreign-currency problem. It should be remembered that books for school libraries are of the kind which can easily be produced on local printing presses (because large quantities are required, the titles are foreseeable in advance, etc.). At the rate of one book per child for 3 million pupils, the quantity to be produced comes to 3 million books, comprising only a few hundred titles. In the case of those which are most in demand, print runs of up to 50,000 copies are justified for one country alone. In the case of those which are less widely used (being suitable at secondary level), equally large print runs may easily be attained by joining forces with other nations to form a more extensive cultural unit.

To sum up, we arrive at the following totals for 1,000 pupils: investments, $26,000 + $8,000 = $34,000; operation, $3,000 per annum.

5.2.1.4 Centres for dissemination of knowledge and culture (one for every 10,000 inhabitants)

Although their aims are not the traditional ones of public libraries, a substantial proportion of the figures applying to the latter can be taken to be relevant to these centres as well.

Investments. We refer to the figure of $120,000, which is broken down as follows: buildings, $55,000 (300 to 400 m²); books, $40,000 (two books at $2 per inhabitant); equipment, $25,000 (including $10,000 worth of audio-visual materials). It is nevertheless possible to make some savings on buildings, owing to the difference in aims.

Operation. $22,000 per annum, broken down as follows: books, $10,000; audio-visual materials, $2,000; equipment, $3,000; staff, $7,000 (four persons, i.e. one at $3,000, two at $1,500 and one at $1,000).

5.2.1.5 University libraries (one for every 1,000 students)

Investments. $725,000, broken down as follows: buildings, 0.25 m² per student, i.e. 250 m² and 1 m² for every 100 books, i.e. 500 m²; totalling 750 m² at $150 per m², i.e. $112,500, rounded down to $100,000; books, fifty books per student at $8, or twenty books or their equivalent in periodicals at $20, i.e. for 1,000 students, $400,000; audio-visual materials, $100,000; shelving and equipment, $125,000.

Operation. The reports allow for $170,000 (United States' standards) in Asia and $125,000 in Africa. In the present case we suggest $100,000 per year, broken down as follows: books and audio-visual tapes, $50,000; equipment, $20,000; librarians, $30,000 (ten persons, i.e. two at $5,000, four at $3,000, four at $1,500, giving a total expenditure of $28,000, rounded up to $30,000).

5.2.1.6 Documentation and information analysis centres

Investments. $250,000, broken down as follows: buildings, $30,000; books and periodicals, $150,000 (100 volumes at $15 per research worker); audio-visual materials, $20,000; furniture and equipment, $50,000 (including reprographic equipment).

Operation. $75,000 per annum, broken down as follows: subscriptions to periodicals and additional accessions, $20,000; audio-visual materials, $5,000; furniture and equipment, $5,000; staff (ten persons, i.e. five at $6,000 each and five at $3,000 each), $45,000.

The figures given above are higher than the usual estimates, as it is essential to renew the tools of the services in order to keep abreast of current developments. It may be necessary to undertake translations. Above all, the promotion work demands great drive, skill and enthusiasm. This accounts for the large expenditure on staff, since the personnel, although not necessarily of outstanding scientific calibre, must be highly qualified and very active in the work which they are called upon to do.

5.2.2   NATIONAL LIBRARY
         AND CO-ORDINATING BODY

The only detailed study we possess in this field concerns Ecuador,[1] a country with 6 million inhabitants. We cannot take it entirely for granted that for this body the costs are all in proportion to the size of the country. The study on Ecuador provides us nevertheless with an excellent working basis. We shall use a variable factor in the region of 2 when dealing with equipment or structures which are little affected by the number of users. On the other hand, the usual coefficient of 3 should be used for staff and operating expenses. Lastly, some items seem to us to have been greatly underestimated, namely, acquisition of books and building up of the initial stock, as well as the procurement of modern equipment. These national libraries must benefit without delay from the new techniques which are currently applicable. We can thus draw up the figures as shown in Table 6.

1. 'Meeting of Experts on the National Planning of Library Services in Latin America, Quito, 7–14 February 1966. Report', *Unesco bulletin for libraries*, vol. XX, no. 6, November–December 1966, p. 278–95.

TABLE 6

	Figures for 6 million inhabitants	Suggested coefficient	Figures to be considered for 20 million inhabitants
Investment ($ thousands)			
Premises	1,000	2.25	2,250[1]
Initial stock	120	5	600
Equipment	70	4.3	300
Computer	—	No provision	1,000
TOTAL	1,190		4,150
Operation ($ per annum)			
Increase of stock	20,000	5	100,000
Staff	63,000	5[2]	315,000[2]
	50 posts	3	150 posts
Day-to-day running expenses	10,000	3	30,000
Audio-visual materials and peripheral computer equipment	No provision	—	50,000
TOTAL	93,000		495,000
Management and co-ordination advisory service	37,000	2[2]	75,000[2]
	14 posts	1.4	20 posts

1. 15,000 m² at $150.
2. In the imaginary country which we have taken as our example, salaries are significantly higher than in Ecuador.

The 150 posts for library staff would be broken down as follows: two directors, $10,000; five engineers, $6,000; four computer experts, $5,000; twenty specialists, $3,000; twenty-seven librarians, $2,200; forty-six sub-librarians, $1,650; forty-six reprographers and stack attendants, $1,050.

If we compare these figures with those noted for the national library of Sri Lanka, for which we have an estimated over-all operating budget of 400,000 rupees (for 1978), i.e. $68,000[1] for 12 million inhabitants, we see that our estimate of $480,000 is

1. In calculating the rupee as $0.17.

approximately 1.4 times higher, having regard to the difference in rates of pay (salaries are probably three times higher in a country with a *per capita* GNP of $400 than in a country where it is only in the region of $100) and the difference between the population: $68,000 × 3 × 20/12 = $340,000 instead of $480,000. This gap is largely accounted for by the computer and the modern equipment ($50,000 per annum) and those items which we had considered to be underestimated for Ecuador.

Construction costs will rise or fall, of course, with the wages level of each country, and so will staffing costs. In order to allow for this in accordance with the different degrees of wealth, we propose to adopt coefficients calculated as follows:

The figures above are assumed to correspond to a *per capita* GNP of $400. If the GNP is different, the adjustment factor would be the result of a formula such as: $K = a + bP/P_0$, where P_0 stands for the *per capita* GNP of the hypothetical reference nation; P stands for the *per capita* GNP of the country under consideration; a stands for a fixed quantity taking into account the factors which are unaffected by the mean national wealth figure, and b stands for a coefficient of proportionality equal to $(1—a)$.

The value of coefficients a and b depends on the item considered: For building, we would have:

$a = 0.6$ and $b = 0.4$;

for books, materials and equipment, $a = 1$, $b = 0$;

for staff, $a = 0.4$, and $b = 0.6$.

The reason for the existence of the fixed quantity a in staffing costs lies in the fact that the salary range is generally much wider in the poorer countries, owing to the relative scarcity of specialists.

5.2.3   RESULTS

The example described in section 5.2.1 results in Tables 7–10.

TABLE 7. Public libraries[1]

Country	Number of volumes (stock)	Registered readers as percentage of the population served		Number of readers which a library can serve
		Adults	Young people	
Australia	2	30	45	3,000[2]
Belgium	3–4	20	40	3,200
Czechoslovakia	3			
Denmark	2	—	—	2,000
France	1.5	5	32	8,000
Federal Republic of Germany	2	15		
Hungary	2–3	20–25		
New Zealand	—	40		2,000
Norway	1.5–2	—	—	
Poland	1–2	30–40		
South Africa	1–3			2,500
Sweden	2–3			
United Kingdom	1.5			2,500
United States	2–4	15		2,000 to 2,500

1. Norms generally accepted by the various countries. Floor area per thousand readers served: 40–60 m² for a population of 10,000–20,000 inhabitants served (excluding lecture halls).
2. One for over 10,000 inhabitants, 30 per cent of whom are registered readers.
Source: F. N. Withers, *Standards for library service* (rev. ed.), Paris, Unesco, July 1971. (COM/WS/151.)

TABLE 8. School and university libraries

School libraries	University libraries (developed countries)
Floor area: 3.5 m² per pupil for teaching, to which 5 per cent should be added for the library.	Floor area: 3 m² per reader present, i.e. 0.3 m² per student.
Number of books: 5 (Denmark) to 15 (Canada) books per pupil.	Stackroom area: 12.5 volumes per metre on shelves accessible to readers; 40 volumes per m² in the stackroom (German Democratic Republic).
Expenditure: (United States) 6 per cent of the cost of teaching, i.e., for example, $41 per child per annum.	Number of books: 70,000 volumes to 1,000 students (some older universities have much larger collections); 4,000 periodicals for 10,000 students.
Staff: one librarian to 500 children.	Staff: for 1,000 students, approximately 5 persons including 1 to 2 librarians.
	Expenditure: approximately 5 per cent of the university budget.

Source: Withers, op. cit.

TABLE 9. Cost of setting up a library network in a country of 20 million inhabitants (in thousands of dollars)

Services	Number of units	Investments								Total	
		Buildings		Books and periodicals		Audio-visual		Equipment			
		Unit cost	Total cost	Unit cost	Total cost	Unit cost	Total cost	Unit cost	Total cost	Unit cost	General total
Literacy centres (for 5,000 illiterates)	1,000	15	15,000	5	5,000	10	10,000	10	10,000	40	40,000
Audio-visual centres (for 3,000 children)	600	15	9,000		—	10	6,000	10	6,000	35	21,000
Centres for dissemination of knowledge (10,000 inhabitants)	1,500	55	9,000	40	6,000	10	15,000	15	20,000	120	175,000
School libraries (1,000 pupils)	3,000	26	78,000	5	15,000	1	3,000	2	6,000	34	102,000
University libraries (1,000 students)	20	100	2,000	400	8,000	100	2,000	125	2,500	725	14,500
Documentation centres (100 research workers)	20	30	600	150	3,000	20	400	50	1,000	250	5,000
National centre[1]	1	2,250	2,250	600	600	100	100	1,200	1,200	4,150	4,150
TOTAL			186,850		91,600		36,500		46,700		361,650

1. Co-ordination of the network: on the premises and with the materials of the national centre.

Table 10. Cost of operating a library network in a country of 20 million inhabitants (in thousands of dollars)

Services	Number of units	Books and periodicals		Audio-visual		Material maintenance		Staff — Number of persons		Staff — Costs		Total	
		Per unit	Total	Per unit	Total	Per unit	Total	Per unit	Total	Per unit	Total	Per unit	General total
Literacy centres (for 5,000 illiterates)	1,000	1	1,000	2	2,000	0.5	500	3	3,000	6	6,000	9.5	9,500
Audio-visual centres (for 3,000 children)	600	—	0	2.5	1,500	0.5	300	3	1,800	6	3,600	9	5,400
Centres for dissemination of knowledge (for 10,000 inhabitants)	1,500	10	15,000	2	3,000	3	4,500	4	6,000	7	10,500	22	33,000
School libraries (1,000 pupils)	3,000	1.5	4,500	0.5	1,500	0.5	1,500	0.15	—	0.5	1,500	3	9,000
University libraries (for 1,000 students)	20	40	800	10	200	20	400	10	200	30	600	100	2,000
Documentation centres (for 100 research workers)	20	20	400	5	100	5	100	10	200	45	900	75	1,500
National centre	1	100	100	50	50	30	30	150	150	315	315	495	495
Co-ordination	1	—	—	—	—	—	—	30	30	30	75	75	75
Total			21,800		8,350		7,330		11,380		23,490		60,970

5.2.4   COMPARISON BETWEEN NEEDS
         AND POSSIBLE RESOURCES

We shall now look at the figures shown in the Tables 9 and 10 set
out above, relating them to the *per capita* GNP, which we have
taken to be $400.

TABLE 11

Services	Investments			Operation and staff				
	Total	Per inhabitant ($)	Percentage of GNP	Staff	Operation	Total	Per inhabitant ($)	Percentage of GNP
Literacy	40,000	2	0.5	6,000	3,500	9,500	0.48	0.12
Audio-visual (children)	21,000	1.05	0.25	3,600	1,800	5,400	0.27	0.07
School libraries	102,000	5.1	1.25	1,500	7,500	9,000	0.45	0.1
Centres for dissemination of knowledge	175,000	8.75	2.1	10,500	22,500	33,000	1.65	0.4
University libraries	14,500	0.72	0.2	600	1,400	2,000	0.1	0.03
Documentation centres	5,000	0.25	0.05	900	600	1,500	0.07	0.02
National centre	4,150	0.21	0.05	315	180	495	0.03	0.01
Co-ordination	0	0	0	75	—	75	—	—
TOTAL	361,650	18.08	4.5	23,490	37,480	60,970	3.05	0.75

It will be recalled that in developed countries the funds allocated to education represent approximately 5 or 6 per cent, or
more, of the GNP; in the poorer countries, the proportion cannot
always be so high. If we consider that it is possible to earmark
for libraries a maximum of 10 per cent of all educational funds,
we see that we are likely to have at our disposal a maximum of:
$400 × 0.05 × 0.10 = $2 per inhabitant; i.e. $40 million for our
entire sample country instead of the $60 million needed for normal
operation.

First, the figures of $18.08 for investments and $3.05 for *per
capita* operational expenses seem less ambitious if compared with
other common day-to-day expenditure of a much less useful nature.
For $18 spread out over five years would come to $4 per annum,
added to the $3 operational expenses; this represents an outlay of
only $7 per inhabitant in order to organize an efficient library and

documentation network. It is far from being out of the question.

Second, the sum of $40 million, which represents only one-quarter of what would be necessary, stands no chance of being attained in a country such as the one we have been considering. The objective sought is, for the time being, out of reach, since this inaccessible sum does not even cover operational expenses.

An information campaign must be launched with a view to securing at least the $2 *per capita* for the poorest countries (whose GNP is in the region of $100 to $200 *per capita* instead of $400), and the slightly wealthier countries (*per capita* between $200 and $500) must be urged to make a greater effort.

In order to be realistic, we shall study the choices to be made if the imaginary country we have taken as an example had the following amounts available:

Hypothesis 1: $4 *per capita*, i.e. $80 million per annum.
Hypothesis 2: $2 *per capita*, i.e. $40 million per annum.
Hypothesis 3: 0.35 per cent of the GNP, i.e. $1.40 *per capita*, i.e. $28 million per annum becoming available by degrees.

In the case of hypothesis 1, 1 per cent of the GNP would be earmarked for libraries and documentation; in that of hypothesis 2, only 0.5 per cent; and in that of hypothesis 3, 0.35 per cent.

5.2.4.1   *Hypothesis 1*

We have $4 *per capita*. Clearly, operational expenses of $3 would be too heavy, as there would be only $1 per annum left for the investments needed to set up the network. It would not be reasonable to reduce expenditure on university libraries or on documentation centres. Similarly, the national centre represents only a small outlay compared with the whole, and it is absolutely indispensable. We may therefore attempt to make a saving on centres for dissemination of knowledge, literacy centres and, finally, school libraries.

Children's audio-visual centres, it seems to us, have a very important part to play in familiarizing young people with up-to-the-minute methods of communication, and we believe that they should all be maintained for as long as possible in their present form. If a suitable balance is to be struck, as much, on average, should be allotted to investments as to operational costs, i.e. $2 *per capita* to each; in other words, one must either save on operational costs or cancel one-third of the programme (see Table 12).

TABLE 12[1]

Services	Investments			Operation and staff			
	Initial budget	Reduction	Final budget	Initial budget	Reduction	Final budget	Rate of reduction (%)
Literacy							
1,000 centres	2	1	—	0.48	0.23	—	48
500 centres	—	—	1	—	—	0.25	—
School libraries							
3,000 libraries	5.1	1.7	—	0.45	0.15	—	33
2,000 libraries	—	—	3.4	—	—	0.30	—
Centres for dissemination of knowledge							
1,500 centres	8.75	3.3	—	1.65	0.62	—	38
900 centres	—	—	5.45	—	—	1.03	—
Other services	2.23	0	2.23	0.47	0	0.47	0
TOTAL	18.08	6	12.08	3.05	1	2.05	33

1. Figures are in dollars *per capita* except column 'Rate of reduction' which is a percentage.

This plan is not, of course, as full as the basic theoretical plan, but it may be anticipated that the network will be fully established within five years, in fairly favourable circumstances, especially if part of it has already been set up. Allowance should be made for the venture to gather momentum in the second half of the decade. This programme can in fact be applied to nations which are already highly developed and enjoy a large portion of these services. In this case, the figures should be transposed, using the formulae given in section 5.2.2, as the *per capita* GNP will be, for example, $1,500.

The literacy centres, on the other hand, must be eliminated. Building costs will be:

$$P = P_0 \left(0.6 + 0.4\,\frac{1,500}{400}\right) = 2.1\,P_0. \qquad (2)$$

Salaries will be:

$$S = S_0 \left(0.4 + 0.6\,\frac{1,500}{400}\right) = 2.55\,P_0. \qquad (3)$$

It will be observed that, in Table 9, buildings represent very nearly 50 per cent of the investments, i.e. in our final investment budget, approximately $6 *per capita* (12.08 × 0.5). This figure will become: $6 × 2.1 = $12.60 *per capita*, to which should be added $6.08 *per capita*, i.e. $18.68 *per capita* (instead of $12.08) from which should be deducted approximately $1.50, the sum which was set aside for literacy work. The *per capita* investment would therefore be $17.

Similarly, as regards operational expenses, Table 10 shows that salaries represent a proportion of 23,490/60,970 = 38.5 per cent of the total operational expenses, i.e. in our final *per capita* budget: $2.05 × 38.5/100 = $0.79 which should be multiplied by 2.55, i.e. $0.79 × 2.55 = $2.01, which should be added to $2.05—0.79 = $1.26, i.e. $1.26 + 2.01 = $3.27 from which must be deducted approximately $0.38, the sum which was intended for literacy work. We are therefore left with $3.27—0.38 ≈ $2.90 *per capita*.

Evidently, these expenses are still very heavy, but fortunately in these countries all that needs to be done is to complete a network, a large part of which exists already. There is therefore very little proportionately to be invested.

5.2.4.2   *Hypothesis 2*

The reduction to be made to the original plan is more drastic than in hypothesis 1, since this time it is necessary to save at least $1.50 of the final operational expenses; this cuts the programme by a half. At the same time, this half-programme should be spread over approximately ten years. This is a long time, and it is preferable to divide it into two phases, i.e. an initial five-year programme which would represent only one-third of the present programme, and a further programme which would be revised in the light of developments in techniques, achievements and the results obtained.

If we still maintain the documentation centres, the university libraries and the national centre intact, we shall be obliged to reduce expenditure on all the other items—chiefly the centres for dissemination of knowledge and the literacy centres.

Actually, even if this programme is reduced to one-third, it still entails employing a great many people: 11,380/3 ≈ 4,000 employees.

In France, by way of comparison, the budget for public libraries alone is in the neighbourhood of $55 million ($25 million in running expenses and $30 million in salaries), i.e. approximately $1 per inhabitant. There are 6,500 employees. We arrive at the following programme, still in dollars *per capita* (Table 13).

TABLE 13[1]

Services	Investments			Operation and staff			
	Initial budget	Reduction	Final budget	Initial budget	Reduction	Final budget	Rate of reduction (%)
Literacy							
1,000 centres	2	1.6	—	0.48	0.38	—	80
200 centres	—	—	0.4	—	—	0.10	—
Audio-visual centres							
600 centres	1.05	0.47	—	0.27	0.12	—	45
330 centres	—	—	0.58	—	—	0.15	—
School libraries							
3,000 libraries	5.1	3.4	—	0.45	0.30	—	66
1,000 libraries	—	—	1.7	—	—	0.15	—
Centres for dissemination of knowledge							
1,500 centres	8.75	—	—	1.65	1.05	—	65
650 centres	—	5.53	3.22	—	—	0.60	—
Other services	1.18	—	1.18	0.20	—	0.20	—
TOTAL	18.08	11	7.08	3.05	1.85	1.20	60

1. Figures are in dollars *per capita* except column 'Rate of reduction' which is a percentage.

We shall see that this programme cannot possibly be carried into effect, even in ten years, unless a large number of the services advocated exist already (such as university libraries, for example). A deduction will be made for these, and hence, if the same sum is available, it will be possible to implement the programme more rapidly. In the same way, if external assistance is provided to launch the programme, it could cover the cost of part of the investments planned for the first year.

5.2.4.3   *Hypothesis 3. System of grading*

In many countries, university libraries are the most advanced. Priority should therefore be given to documentation centres (which would be given a technical bias) and to the national centre. Let us take a closer look at this hypothesis and attempt to see exactly how the funds provided for equipment and operational costs will be spent, as we have indicated them year by year above. Existing services no longer have to be financed, but operational expenses should be included in the budgets which we have shown. Let us suppose that there are five university library units, instead of the twenty which we have allowed here; the most urgent task, of course, will be to set up a national centre, or to bring the latter up to the required standard if it has been established previously, and above all to set up centres for documentation and information analysis.

In order of priority, the amounts received in the first year should be allotted as follows:

1. National centre (first phase $\frac{1}{4}$), $1,000,000.
2. Documentation centres (6), $1,500,000.
3. University libraries (additions), $3,000,000.
4. Centres for dissemination of knowledge, with a technical bias (25), $3,000,000.

Total phase one investments, $8,500,000.

Staff needed for this first phase are as follows:

National centre ($\frac{1}{4}$), 40; documentation centres (6), 60; university libraries (additions), 20; public libraries, 100; giving a total of 220 persons.

For the most part, these staff are not yet available. Training takes approximately one to two years for the lower grades, and more or less the same amount of time for specialists, assuming that graduates and technologists are available who have already had the necessary basic training. Allowance must also be made for at least two years' preparation before spending large sums, in order to make plans, choose the best sites, study the best lists of works to be ordered, examine the most suitable materials and work out, in the light of all this information, plans for the architecture of the whole, etc.

It can be seen that one of the bottlenecks will be that of training properly qualified staff. It will be fairly easy to train subordinate staff (stack attendants, reprographers and assistant librarians). It will be much more difficult to train documentalist staff (information scientists). But the most critical part will be to ensure that technical documentation centres are sufficiently polyvalent to be in fact focal points of creative thinking and innovation.

The second phase would include:
5. Children's audio-visual centres (60), $2,100,000.
6. Literacy centres (20), $800,000.
7. School libraries (100), $3,400,000.
Total phase two investments, $6,300,000.

Number of persons employed are as follows: 60 audio-visual centres: $60 \times 3 = 180$; 20 literacy centres: $20 \times 3 = 60$, i.e. 240 persons.

A third phase might be planned to include:
8. Documentation centres (10), $2,500,000.
9. National centre ($\frac{1}{4}$) $1,000,000.
10. Public libraries (50), $6,000,000.
11. Audio-visual centres (60), $2,100,000.
12. Literacy centres (20), $800,000.
13. School libraries (100), $3,400,000.
Total phase three investments, $15,800,000.

The grand total of investments will therefore be: $8,500,000 + $6,300,000 + $15,800,000 = $30,600,000.

It is still lower than that forecast for the first year of the theoretical model.

The extra staff needed will amount to: documentation centres, $10 \times 10 = 100$; national centre, 40; centres for dissemination of knowledge, $50 \times 4 = 200$; audio-visual centres, $60 \times 3 = 180$; literacy centres, $20 \times 3 = 60$; giving a total of 580 persons.

Grand total of persons employed: $220 + 240 + 580 = 1,040$ persons.

Let us assume that two preliminary years of preparation and three years corresponding to the three 'running-in' phases shown above have passed. Only at this point do we embark upon the plan proper. Expenditure for the first two years (preparatory installation expenditure estimated at 5 per cent of the first phase) has been as follows: $30,600,000 \times 5/100 = $1,530,000; being $580,000 for the first year and $950,000 for the second.

These amounts will be spent on the recruitment of management staff, purchase of sites, surveys, and various optional activities. To these items should be added staff training; we shall return to this subject later.

If the first phase of work coincides with one year, this will be the budget for the third year. It represents: $9,500,000/20,000,000 = $0.47 *per capita*, i.e. 0.47/400 = 0.12 per cent of the GNP.

After this has been completed, we shall have to deal with operational expenses. We have established a proportion of the final programme amounting to: $0.47/7, i.e. 6.71 per cent.

We can therefore expect to pay in the following year approximately 4.42 per cent of the total operational costs, i.e. in dollars *per capita*: $1.20 \times 6.71/100$ = $0.08 *per capita* which must be added to investments in the second phase (if the latter takes one year) and to the operational expenses of the five university libraries, i.e. $0.025 *per capita*.

In dollars *per capita*, for this second phase, these investments come to: $6,300,000/20,000,000 = $0.31.

Expenditure in this second year will therefore be: $0.31 + 0.08 + 0.025 \approx$ $0.42 *per capita*, i.e. $0.42/400 \times 100 \approx 0.1$ per cent of the GNP.

This is a little lower than in the first year, and we can take advantage of the fact to forge ahead with a programme of specialist training, since we now have the necessary administrative staff, and since needs will have to be met in the years to come if development is continued in this sector.

All these expenses, as well as those for the third year which we shall calculate in the same way, are much lower than the figure of 0.35 per cent of the GNP which we originally took to be possible. So, clearly, the speed of establishing the network is limited by the need for progressive growth and by the shortage of specialists.

5.3   Machinery for planning and assessment

The foregoing is of course only an example, and doubtless does not apply to any actual case. It is intended merely to demonstrate, in a hypothetical case, the factors which must be taken into account. When planning, it will be as well to optimize not only the financial costs but also the objectives. In our view, this task should be entrusted to those in charge of policy-making in education and development, assisted, where appropriate, by financial experts or technicians. The procedure set out below might perhaps be adopted.

A top-level committee would lay down the general guidelines; it would comprise: one official from the Ministry of Education, one official from the Ministry of Agriculture, one official from the Ministry of Health, and one official from the Ministry of Industry or Commerce.

Even if the ministries are organized in different ways, it will be possible to form a group of individuals closely concerned with the fields for which the four ministries mentioned above are responsible. This committee would be assisted by two specialists in documentary problems and one financial expert, who might, in the early stages, make a very rough estimate of the over-all cost of the programmes which could be undertaken.

The work of this committee would consist in making proposals to the government, based on an analysis of the situation as it is and on a study of needs. When the government has taken its decision, the proposals chosen should be examined and worked out in greater detail, with the help of a commission of specialists, before they are put into operation, so as to determine exactly what needs are to be met, what kind of infrastructure is needed, which sites are to be chosen, what materials are required, how the necessary staff are to be trained, etc. In addition to specialists in documentation or librarianship, this commission would include representatives of those users who are most directly concerned. Even if the latter are not in the majority, their opinions should at least carry considerable weight in discussions.

This commission would continue to operate in order to keep an eye on the building and investments thus planned, and it would also supervise the way in which the services are carried out and would lay down criteria of efficiency. Statistics on the number of books consulted, the number of documents on loan, and the social category of borrowers and users, should be drawn up frequently and kept up to date by the existing or newly created organizations, while these organizations are making their service available.

Further information should be collected with a view to gauging the repercussions of the measures adopted, for example:

Expenditure on documentation derived from funds not supplied by the government.

Progress in regional or local economic development (expressed in terms of turnover, for example).

National or local production of information or documents.

Development or changes in agriculture or certain industries.

Number of patents taken out, etc.

Growth of certain categories of firms or appropriately selected activities.

Activities and trends of labour in the major economic branches.

Most of these statistics concern economic matters, and the needs of the present study alone are not, of course, sufficient justification for drawing them up; but they exist in most countries. In some circumstances it may be advisable to add one or two questions to the surveys or to modify slightly some of the 'indicators' used by statisticians, as has already been done in an attempt to see how research and teaching activities are related to the economy as a whole.

It is particularly desirable that these over-all statistical results should be constantly related to what is being done to develop libraries and documentation; this is essential as a basis for continuous assessment.

The aforesaid group of experts and users' representatives will adjust the programme in the light of this assessment. However, it is not advisable, unless a fresh piece of information of paramount importance comes to light, to alter a programme that is being carried out before it has had time to produce results. Information influences national activities indirectly, just as it does educational activities. Being well informed is not a direct source of wealth, but merely provides ideas as to how to produce fresh riches. One is therefore obliged to wait until a beginning has been made on the execution of some of these ideas before one is in a position to appreciate the advantages of the information network at all levels. For this reason, users are very slow to realize that it is necessary to 'waste time' in acquiring information. Only when they have had one or two practical examples of what is to be gained from having recourse to documentalists will they return in order to consult them have a look at books, place orders for others, ask questions, etc.

The public authorities and planners, for their part, will not observe any remarkable change in users' behaviour for two or three years. On the contrary, after an initial period of enthusiasm, there will be a phase of disillusionment, and in the second or third year the statistics will probably show a decline. Similarly, no significant variation will be noted in the economic and social data for four or five years. Nevertheless, one should persevere and, at the end of the second or third year, attempt to produce a number of specimen cases from which it can be seen whether or not the information supplied by the network is appropriate to the situation of the country.

Invaluable assistance both for this attempted evaluation and for the promotion of the documentation network, could be provided by professional associations: engineering associations, agricultural associations, trade guilds and learned societies. Theoretically, it is better to accept the assistance of associations which have no, or few, material interests to defend, since, in the case of the others, defence of the profession may take precedence over the impartial thinking that documentation planning requires. However, greater drive may be found in certain groups which are engaged, in other ways, in a professional conflict (for example, agricultural workers or certain craftsmen, etc., in some countries). Documentalist associations or technical research associations can, of course, also assist planning by giving their enlightened advice. It should always be borne in mind that service should be the aim of planning and that care should consequently be taken to ensure that the study of needs and of the means to be employed is not carried out solely by librarians.

The part that these associations, and users, can play is particularly valuable when local institutions are set up, such as school libraries, public libraries or, better still, the centres for the dissemination of knowledge referred to above. Such centres should be organized in close liaison with these local associations which ought, where necessary, to be encouraged. The latter should contribute actively, if not to the management, at least to the guidance of the services. They should serve, furthermore, as a forum for an exchange of views with all those to whom information and reading will be of benefit.

Side by side with over-all planning, it is often desirable to provide for the possibility of direct action, in the form either of research designed to test this or that kind of material, or of an occasional pilot project or, again, of steps to secure the co-operation of two or more organizations. A fund for such operations representing some 10 per cent of the amount allocated to general planning is thus particularly useful. The pattern will therefore be as follows:

At the top: interministerial committee or council of ministers. Will meet once a year.

Ministerial subordinate body (could be set up jointly with some other authority): high-level committee of seven or eight members (including three experts). Will meet first to define main objectives, and then again at the time of the budget.

Commission responsible for detailed planning and implementation: group of specialists comprising ministerial representatives, users, information specialists (this commission will provide detailed guidance in regard to international relations). Will meet once or twice a month.

To ensure the functioning of these various bodies, there would be a permanent secretariat or co-ordinating unit, with responsibility for the execution of the committee's decisions. This unit might be either completely independent or incorporated in the national library or national documentation centre, or else in the single body which would, in some countries, assume the two functions.

In certain developed nations, the high-level committee does not exist in its own right as it forms part of other organs responsible for other tasks such as, for example, the planning and co-ordination of scientific and technological research. It is conceivable that, according to the characteristic structures of each nation, this committee will be the same as the body responsible, for example, for the planning of education or of industrial development.

6   Conclusion

6.1   The needs served by information and documentation

Having given some thought to what is beginning to be called 'I & D' (Information and Documentation) by analogy with 'R & D' (Research and Development), one is almost taken aback to see how comparatively meagre the resources allotted to this sector are, considering the vital part that it plays in social development. Up to now, it has been possible to acquire information at little cost in proportion to the amount that has to be expended on the necessities of life. However, as the importance of the so-called 'tertiary' sector has grown in economic activities in relation to the direct exploitation of natural products (primary sector) and resources for processing them (secondary sector), increasing budgetary provision is going to be made for information services and these will become all the more indispensable in that basic needs (food, housing, etc.) will be met more effectively.

At the same time, it has become apparent that I & D is a powerful development factor, on condition, of course, that it be organized and planned towards that end. Even the poorer countries will therefore be compelled to set aside the necessary resources from their already inadequate revenue in order to encourage reading and to spread knowledge.

It is too early to set out objectives as a percentage of the gross national product as was done, a few years ago, in the case of research expenditure (R & D). The financial objective cannot, in any case, have any meaning as such; it is only the content of the corresponding programmes or plans that can be usefully compared with other economic and social development programmes, both in order to appreciate their importance as users of resources and also, and this is all-important, to achieve the homogeneity which is essential. For information and libraries are not self-sufficient activities; they are always concomitants (and sometimes prime movers) of priority economic and social activities (education, agriculture, mining, industry, health, administration, and so on).

However, whatever the sector involved, the methods employed to obtain information are virtually the same, the documents and instruments used are of the same kind, and sometimes even identical to a large extent. And so I & D techniques, while they are distinctive and make up an integral part of the various economic and social sectors that they have to serve, form a whole and constitute a horizontal branch of the economy on the same footing as, for example, computer science (data processing and computation).

6.2   Need for a continuous survey

To follow the progress of this branch (which, if not new, is at least changing very fast), we do not possess, in general, sufficient data to provide a picture of the present situation. That is why a continuous survey should be conducted in all countries, beginning of course with the most developed in which a great many documentary activities are dovetailed and intermeshed in such a way that, more often than not, no clear picture at the national level can be obtained. To secure knowledge of present expenditure, methods, staff and services other than that available to us as colleagues, subsidizers or users seems to us to be of prime importance. Such a survey would not take long to conduct in the poorest countries which still have only a few libraries, but they will probably be extremely glad to have fuller information about structures and costs in the more developed countries.

Proceeding from these starting points and also knowing the present situation and planning forecasts in the main sectors to which I & D can afford assistance, we can highlight a number of objectives which, although set out in still rather general terms, will give us, even now, facts and figures at every point where there are priority needs to be satisfied or provided for in the coming years.

6.3   Resources and personnel

At the same time we shall have, in accordance with what we have tried to achieve, a preliminary idea of the expenditure on information which is likely to be required; but as we have seen, this expenditure is not always the most crucial issue in the developing countries. The need to have really qualified personnel is a more difficult obstacle to overcome, because the training of such staff takes time, and must be very varied.

If priority is assigned to scientific and technological information, as will be the case in many countries, the personnel concerned will have to include a proportion of engineers and scientists who are trained in documentation techniques as well.

If wholly or partly automated information systems eventually prevail, as seems likely, the presence of computer specialists familiar with the problems of libraries and documentation centres will be essential.

For the training of staff, teachers will be needed too, of course. Fortunately teachers can be found in other countries, but techniques and methods have to be adapted to take into account differences in traditions, specific needs and divergencies between levels of development and means actually available, the latter being usually much more limited in poor countries where efficient services must nevertheless be set up.

Planning must therefore provide for an 'arborescent' sequence of logically connected stages, some more easily described in numerical terms than others, which will be rationally timed and co-ordinated as far as possible. While these processes are taking place, it is particularly advisable to pay close attention to change occurring in the planning of the objectives set for 'I & D', since a shifting of emphasis in such fields as education or regionalization, or the fluctuating importance of a priority sector of the economy, has a direct impact on information needs, involving not only the nature of the documentation to be supplied, but also the qualifications required of the staff to be trained, the siting of libraries or documentation centres, etc.

6.4   Looking ahead

An attempt was made in section 5.2 to show by means of figures that it takes time to develop an information network. As we have seen, the minimum period required is from three to five years, including the preliminary discussions. During that period techniques evolve, so that it is worth while to try to visualize what an information network might be like ten or fifteen years hence. People must be trained and equipment planned in the light of the situation as it is expected to exist ten years later, even if estimates are a long way out. This is better than taking the present state of information technology as a basis, for this will be out of date as soon as the equipment and staff foreseen by planners today become operational.

   In this connexion, we have taken some of the findings of a Delphi survey conducted recently in Sweden[1] by the Swedish Agency for Administrative Development, which forecasts a rapid evolution of the working methods of libraries from 1975 on. The causes of this evolution lie, on the one hand, in the scientific breakthrough achieved by information processing and telecommunications, combined with expanding needs and the shortage and increasing cost of manpower, and on the other hand, in the greater affluence of users, who are becoming less hesitant about investing in equipment in order to obtain more useful information or a faster and more convenient service.

   According to this survey, the following situation is likely to prevail in 1977 or 1978.
Public libraries will disseminate information for adult education (including textbooks and audio-visual aids).

---

1. U. Wennerberg, 'Using the Delphi technique for planning the future of libraries', *Unesco bulletin for libraries*, vol. XXVI, no. 5, September-October 1972, p. 242-6.

They will become responsible for disseminating information for university education at undergraduate level.

They will set up joint purchasing services.

All this accords with what was deduced by an ordinary extrapolation process from the existing situation, in sections 2, 3 and 4 of the present study. The year 1978 is still covered by short-term planning; what is more interesting is the situation predicted for the years 1979, 1980 and 1981.

Library purchases will be handled semi-automatically. A computer will provide the staff in charge with purchasing proposals based on frequency of loans, costs and various factors initially fed into the computer, or derived instead from the performance statistics of the network of centres using this method.

On-line data transmission connexions between automated documentation systems and with libraries and firms will have become operational. An information system network with terminals connected to joint computers will begin to operate in Sweden.

The existing organization will change, in that libraries and documentation centres will tend to split up into production and processing units, on the one hand, and service units in direct contact with users, on the other hand. These units may operate at considerable distances from each other. The first-mentioned type may be assigned the function of rationalizing acquisition and processing procedures; while the service units may concentrate on providing individual or specialized services.

Official documents (regulations, information on citizens' rights and duties, etc.) will be stored on microcopies, as also theses, reports and other documents which are not widely circulated.

It is even thought that scientific papers will be presented in a standardized form to enable abstracts of their contents to be stored in data banks. Around 1983, a rapid increase in the use of the videophone for consulting audio-visual documents seems to be anticipated. Thus, by the end of the present decade, media other than books will occupy a prominent place in networks for the dissemination of information. This will not abolish reading, nor books, but it seems essential even now to allow for this rise of other media, represented at present by micro-documents and audio-visual materials, when planning the future and organizing staff training.

6.5 Contributing as a producer to information networks

Whether books, bibliographies or materials other than books are involved, it is highly desirable not to join the world information network merely as a consumer. If it is true that information contributes greatly to development, then the production of at least part of the information supplied should be geared by the internal services to objectives set at the national level. All countries, whatever their level of development, have scientific and cultural contributions to make. It is important that they should make them, on the one hand, in order to become better known and, on the other hand, because the rest of the world needs all contributions, however modest. Going a step further, we can say that such contributions should be made through national channels (or, in the case of very small nations, regional channels), which means that each country owes it to itself to encourage not only reading and the dissemination of knowledge but also the production of information and its publication in printed form or, possibly at a later stage, its communication by other technical media (for example, audio-visual or micro media).

This applies to bibliographies too. While it may be indispensable to subscribe to outside services, it is impossible to over-emphasize the importance of independent activity wherever this is possible and reasonable.

6.6 Acquiring equipment suited to actual needs

Whether a new information network is to be set up or a network of documentation units or libraries is to be modernized, the necessary equipment must be selected in the light of anticipated trends in the techniques available, the needs of users and the working methods of staff. Programming the acquisition of this equipment is beset with special difficulties, for in addition to the three factors already mentioned, it is necessary to consider the socio-economic context, taking into account certain administrative constraints such as those due to the condition of communication facilities including the general telecommunication network, the country's trade balance, its policy, climate, etc. Fortunately, equipment can be supplied without undue delay, usually within a year, so it is possible to adopt a very gradual purchasing policy whereby the decision to procure a given item must not be taken before it has become clear that the optimum conditions for its use will shortly obtain. Computers and data transmission equipment are the most expensive items, but such equipment, with some exceptions, is not intended solely for documentation services. In a sense this is irksome, for it means coming to an agreement with other users in order to justify the purchase of such items, but on the other hand there is less risk of under utilization in the event of unexpected circumstances arising.

In many cases, quite new situations will have to be met and it is difficult to foresee exactly what response there will be to the measures taken on the lines recommended above to promote reading and access to knowledge. For this reason, more stress is laid here than in other fields on the need for 'rolling' plans which can be frequently revised. The total figure for the means required may remain much the same, but the uses to which they are put will have to be adapted to the existing situation almost every year, although each experiment will have to be given enough time (at least three years) to yield useful guidance for decision-makers.

6.7   A sector with a promising future

Whether library and documentation networks are already flourishing (as in Europe or North America), or whether the reading habit has not yet become widespread in all sections of the population in the country concerned, the I & D sector is full of promise and can be expected to expand very significantly in the next few years. Rapid changes are already under way, but it is very hard to know at what rate they will progress in the more developed countries and how the developing countries will organize their services in order to benefit from this evolution. The growing numbers of highly educated members of their population will wish, at all events, to equip themselves with the means of improving their knowledge, disseminating it as widely as possible and communicating the results of their studies in books or through other media. Exchanges of information, books and documents will play an increasingly important part in international relations.

Appendixes

Appendices

Reading and paper consumption

For some countries an attempt has been made to compare various data taken from Unesco statistics[1] with those of the recent survey by the International Federation for Documentation. Once again this is a very rough comparison as the figures given for the various countries do not always mean the same thing.

It appears that the data given for OECD countries regarding population and GNP per inhabitant are more up to date than the others, which affects their homogeneity but does not noticeably alter the disparities—in any case there are far more serious discrepancies in other areas. In fact the only figures which we can compare for all countries are those for paper consumption. (Only a few gave statistics for the number of volumes published.) On the assumption that a book containing 1 million characters weighs on average 330 grammes, we used an admittedly very arbitrary coefficient to estimate the relative amounts of printing paper and print used for books on the one hand and leaflets which are read on the other. This arbitrary coefficient was 0.2 in Western countries where much correspondence is typed and where publicity leaflets actually read represent a very small proportion of the paper consumed. Also the weight of paper used for each page in these countries is greater. A coefficient of 0.5 was adopted for Eastern countries and countries less developed in this respect. Where the number of volumes published was known, this figure was used to establish a comparison, but it is interesting to note that it is always smaller (often a half or a third) than that deduced from the figures for paper consumption.

When calculating how much material is read, newspapers must inevitably be taken into account, but here again very broad approximations were the rule. In the first place we assumed that a newspaper contained 6 million characters to the kilogramme and, in order to take account of publicity, we adopted regression coefficients of 0.2 for North America, 0.5 for Europe and 1 for Eastern countries and developing countries. Should this assumption be correct, it would appear that, for every book, two or three newspapers are read.

The figures given in the following table are based on these estimates. The following is the key to the column headings:

P   population in millions of inhabitants
GNP/h   gross national product in thousands of dollars per inhabitant

1. *Unesco statistical yearbook 1970*, Paris, Unesco, 1971.

pj	annual consumption of newsprint in thousands of metric tonnes
kj	regression coefficient chosen
kpj	the product of the two preceding columns
Tj	corresponding number of printed characters in milliards
Tj/h	number of printed characters per inhabitant in millions
pi	annual consumption of printing paper and print in thousands of metric tonnes
ki	regression coefficient chosen
kpi	the product of the two preceding columns
Ti	number of corresponding printed characters in thousands of milliards per year
Ti/h	number of printed characters per inhabitant in millions (i.e. number of printed books per inhabitant)
Ni	number of copies of books published supplied directly by statistics, where available (in millions of copies)
Ni/h	number of copies of books published per inhabitant (to compare with column Ti/h)
Ti + Tj/h	the sum of columns Ti/h and Tj/h in millions of characters per inhabitant per year, i.e. approximately the number of books (or equivalent in periodicals and newspapers) presumed read per inhabitant. (In fact only large books have a million characters; average-sized books have 200,000 to 400,000 characters in general)
NT	the number of titles published per year, to be compared with the preceding figures
NT/h	number of titles (new or re-prints) published per million inhabitants per year
E%	proportion of students as a percentage of the total population
AL%	proportion of illiterates as a percentage of the total population.

The results of this attempt are rather encouraging, as will be seen. It will be noted that countries such as Switzerland with high book exports have a very high pi + pj per inhabitant.

Country	Order no.	P	GNP/h	pj	kj	kpj	Tj = 6 kpj	Tj/h	pi	ki	kpi	Ti = 3 kpi	Ti/h	Ni	Ni/h	Ti + Tj/h	NT	NT/h	E %	AL %
United States	1	203	4.6	8,911	0.2	1,800	10,000	50	10,000	0.2	2,000	6,000	30	—	—	80	62,083	300	2.7	2
Canada	2	21	3.2	473	0.2	90	540	27	593	0.2	120	360	18	—	—	55	3,659	180	—	3
Federal Republic of Germany	3	61	2.5	1,034	0.5	500	3,000	50	2,000	0.2	400	1,200	20	—	—	70	33,454	550	0.5	0
France	4	50	2.5	572	0.5	300	1,800	36	1,440	0.2	280	840	17	—	—	53	21,958	440	1	3
United Kingdom	5	55	2	1,554	0.3	450	2,700	50	1,339	0.2	270	810	15	—	—	65	32,321	600	0.5	3
Japan	6	102	1.6	1,772	0.3	500	3,000	30	1,500	0.2	300	900	10	—	—	40	31,009	310	1.3	—
Australia	7	12	2.3	419	0.2	80	540	45	210	0.2	42	130	10	—	—	55	3,939	320	0.8	3
Belgium	8	10	2.3	169	0.5	85	510	50	310	0.2	62	186	19	—	—	70	5,089	500	—	0
Switzerland	9	6	3	150	0.5	75	450	70	260	0.2	54	162	27	—	—	97	7,506	1,200	—	0
Portugal	10	9.5	0.6	35	0.5	18	110	11	41	0.5	20	60	6	—	—	25	5,760	600	—	0
Austria	11	7	1.7	95	0.5	47	280	40	113	0.2	23	69	10	—	—	50	5,204	700	—	3
Spain	12	33	0.9	194	0.5	100	600	20	270	0.5	13	40	12	166	5	32	20,031	600	0.7	0
German Dem. Rep.	13	17	1.6	85	1	85	510	30	200	0.5	100	300	18	—	—	48	5,568	320	1.9	3
U.S.S.R.	14	241	1.2	872	1	872	5,200	22	1,000[1]	0.5	500	1,500	7	1,276	5	30	74,611	310	1	3
Czechoslovakia	15	14	1.4	57	1	57	340	24	148	0.5	75	230	16	56	6	40	8,103	550	0.4	3
Hungary	16	10	1.1	39	1	39	234	23	86	0.5	43	129	13	—	—	36	4,831	500	1	—
Argentina	17	24	1.1	210	0.5	105	630	26	110	0.2	22	66	3	—	—	30	4,000	170	—	—
Italy	18	53	1.7	307	0.5	155	930	17	1,024	0.2	205	615	12	93	2	30	8,440	160	—	—
Mexico	19	49	0.5	163	0.3	50	300	5	198	0.2	40	120	3	—	—	8	2,966	150	—	—
Brazil	20	91	0.3	250	0.3	75	450	5	225	0.2	45	150	2	—	—	7	—	70[1]	0.3	34
Cuba	21	8	0.3	26	0.5	13	80	10	25	0.5	12	40	5	26	3	15	995	120	0.4	25
Egypt	22	32	—	24	1	24	140	4	41	0.5	20	60	2	—	—	6	1,695	50	—	—
Ghana	23	9	0.2	6	1	6	36	4	5	0.5	2.5	8	1	6	0.6	5	446	50	0.06	79
Ethiopia	24	2.5	0.1	0.4	1	0.4	2.4	0.1	3[1]	1	3	10	0.5	—	—	1	—	15[1]	0.02	70
Zambia	25	4	0.3	3	1	3	18	4	2	0.5	1	3	1	—	—	5	—	8[1]	0.02	—

1. Estimates.

Order no.	Country	P	GNP/h	pj	kj	kpj	Tj = 6 kpj	Tj/h	pi	ki	kpi	Ti = 3 kpi	Ti/h	Ni	Ni/h	(Ti + Tj)/h	NT	NT/h	E %	AL %
26	Nigeria	64	0.1	5	1	5	30	0.5	12	0.5	6	18	0.3	5	0.1	1	1,099	15	0.01	—
27	Kenya	10	0.1	4	1	4	24	2	7	0.5	4	12	1	—	—	3	193	20	0.02	40
28	Senegal	4	0.2	0.3	1	0.3	2	0.5	2	0.5	1	3	1	—	—	2	38	15[1]	0.1	—
29	Ivory Coast	4	0.3	1	1	1	6	1.5	0.5	0.5	0.3	1	0.3	0.05	0.01	2	—	10	—	—
30	Morocco	15	0.2	3	1	3	18	1	9	0.5	5	15	1	—	—	2	300	60	0.02	—
31	Tunisia	5	0.2	0.6	1	0.6	4	1	3	0.5	1.5	5	1	—	—	3			—	—
32	Iran	28	0.4	14	0.5	7	42	1.5	50[1]	0.5	25	75	1.5	9	3	26	1,341	50	1	—
33	Israel	3	1.6	33	0.3	10	60	20	28	0.2	6	18	6	63	3	29	2,038	700	—	ε
34	Yugoslavia	20	0.6	62	1	62	372	20	117	0.5	60	180	9	5	0.2	12	8,708	450	—	—
35	Republic of Korea	31	0.2	92	0.5	46	276	9	50	0.5	25	75	2.5	8	0.7	7	2,501	75	0.1	25
36	Sri Lanka	12	0.2	23	0.5	11	70	6	10	0.5	5	15	1.2	—	—	4	1,586	130	—	70
37	India	537	0.1	195	1	195	1,200	2.5	377	0.5	200	600	1.2	—	—	2	13,733	25	—	57
38	Indonesia	116	0.1	19	1	19	120	1	50	0.5	25	75	1	—	—	2	2,457	70	—	—
39	Thailand	34	0.2	33	0.5	16	96	3	13	0.5	7	21	1	—	—				—	—
40	Singapore	2	0.8	14	0.3	4	24	12	20	0.2	4	12	6	4	2	18	533	260	0.3	22

1. Estimates.

Alphabetical list

Country		Country	
Argentina	17	Mexico	19
Australia	7	Morocco	30
Austria	11	Nigeria	26
Belgium	8	Portugal	10
Brazil	20	Senegal	28
Canada	2	Singapore	40
Cuba	21	Spain	12
Czechoslovakia	15	Sri Lanka	36
Egypt	22	Switzerland	9
Ethiopia	24	Thailand	39
France	4	Tunisia	31
German Democratic Republic	13	U.S.S.R.	14
Federal Republic of Germany	3	United Kingdom	5
Ghana	23	United States	1
Hungary	16	Yugoslavia	34
India	37	Zambia	25
Indonesia	38		
Iran	32		
Israel	33		
Italy	18		
Ivory Coast	3		
Japan	6		
Kenya	23		
Republic of Korea	16		

2 Preliminary draft questionnaire
on resources devoted
to documentation

1. *General information*

1.1 Name of body or firm
1.2 Full address
1.3 Annual turnover or budget
1.4 Total number of employees
1.5 Total number of technicians[1]
1.6 Number of research workers or research technicians
1.7 Number of teachers

2. *Expenditure on acquisitions*

You purchase books, magazines and other documents. Some of these are stored in the library or at the documentation centre or in a patents section, others are stored elsewhere or destroyed. Could you indicate:
2.1 Total expenditure in 1973 on the acquisition of all these documents
2.2 Total expenditure in 1973 on the acquisition of books and periodicals only
2.3 Total expenditure on the acquisition of books, periodicals and documents to be stored in the library or at the documentation centre
2.4 Total expenditure on the acquisition of documents, books and periodicals to be stored in the patents section

3. *Resources of the library and of the documentation centre*

3.1 Have you at least one library?[2]   yes ☐   no ☐
3.2 If you have more than one, how many?
3.3 Have you at least one documentation centre?[2]   yes ☐   no ☐
3.4 If you have more than one, how many?
3.5 Total number of persons employed in your library (libraries) or in your documentation centre (centres) (full-time equivalents)

1. The total number of technicians may include research technicians or teaching technicians.
2. Tick the appropriate box.

3.6 How many of these persons are:
    3.6.1 Technicians[1]
    3.6.2 Librarians or documentalists[1]
    3.6.3 Other technicians and workmen[1]
    3.6.4 Administrative staff[1] (secretaries, accountants)
3.7 Expenditure on staffing your libraries and documentation centres
3.8 Expenditure on the acquisition of documents (figure already given under 2.3)
3.9 Other expenditure on running your libraries or documentation centres
3.10 General expenditure and amortizations chargeable to your libraries and documentation centres
3.11 Total expenditure on these services in 1973 (total of entries 3.7–3.10)

4. *Resources of the patents section (other than purchases of licensing rights)*

4.1 Have you a patents section?   yes ☐   no ☐
    If yes,
4.2 Number of persons employed in the section (full-time equivalent)
    Of these persons how many are:
    4.2.1 Technicians[1]
    4.2.2 Documentalists or librarians[1]
    4.2.3 Other technicians and workmen[1]
    4.2.4 Administrative staff[1]
4.3 Expenditure on staffing this section
4.4 Expenditure on the acquisition of documents (figure already given under 2.4)
4.5 Other expenditure on running the patents section
4.6 General expenditure and amortizations chargeable to the patents section
4.7 Total expenditure in 1973 (total of entries 4.3–4.6)

5. *Expenditure on documentation outside the library, documentation centre and patents section*

5.1 Could you estimate the number of persons who devote a considerable portion of their time to documentary duties (apart from those employed in the departments dealt with under 3 and 4)? (full-time equivalents)
5.2 Could you estimate the corresponding expenditure on staffing?
5.3 Expenditure on the acquisition of documents (difference between entry 2.1 and the sum of entries 2.3 and 2.4)
5.4 Sum of lines 5.2 and 5.3

6. *Recapitulation*

6.1 Total expenditure on documentation (total of entries 3.11 + 4.7 + 5.4)
6.2 Staffing employed in documentation (total of entries 3.5 + 4.2 + 5.1)

7. *Name of the person who answered the questionnaire*

Address:
Telephone:

1. Full-time equivalents.

3 Survey of scientific and technical documentary services

1. *Identification of documentation centre or service*

1.1 Name
   (initials or abbreviation in common use where appropriate)
1.2 Full address
   Telephone number
   Telegraphic address
   Telex number
1.3 Country
1.4 Name of director
1.5 Name of director of documentation centre
   or of head of documentation service
1.6 Name of establishment to which the centre is attached
1.7 Date of opening of the documentation service
1.8 Staff (approximate total)
1.9 Activities and aims of the documentation centre or service

2. *Subjects covered*

2.1 Terms of the macrothesaurus or headings of a classification system
   The UDC may be used to indicate the various areas of activity. However,
   for specialized centres it would be very helpful to add a description using the
   terms of a macrothesaurus, as this would give immediate access without
   passing through the process of computer selection.

INFORMATION PROCESSING

3. *Sources: number of documents processed per year per category*

Amount per year[1]	From 0 to 10	From 10 to 100	From 100 to 1,000	More than 1,000
3.1 Titles of periodicals	☐	☐	☐	☐
3.2 Books	☐	☐	☐	☐

1. Mark the appropriate box (one only) with a cross.

Amount per year	From 0 to 10	From 10 to 100	From 100 to 1,000	More than 1,000
3.3 Theses	☐	☐	☐	☐
3.4 Reports	☐	☐	☐	☐
3.5 Conference proceedings	☐	☐	☐	☐
3.6 Patents	☐	☐	☐	☐
3.7 Offprints	☐	☐	☐	☐
3.8 Standards	☐	☐	☐	☐
3.9 Other	☐	☐	☐	☐

3.10 Number of current periodical titles

4. *Documents*

4.1 Language of documents

4.1.1 German ☐		4.1.5 Arabic ☐
4.1.2 English ☐		4.1.6 Japanese ☐
4.1.3 Spanish ☐		4.1.7 Russian ☐
4.1.4 French ☐		4.1.8 Chinese ☐
		4.1.9 Other ☐

4.2 Analysis of documents

    4.2.1 Documents received and simply indexed ☐

    4.2.2 All documents received systematically analysed ☐

    4.2.3 Documents analysed on a selective basis ☐

4.3 Co-operation

    4.3.1 Do you exchange primary documents?

    Do you exchange abstracts (per year)?

	Less than 1,000	From 1,000–10,000	More than 10,000
4.3.2 On paper	☐	☐	☐
4.3.3 On tape	☐	☐	☐

    In co-operation with other documentation services or centres:

    4.3.4 Co-operation at the national level ☐

    4.3.5 Co-operation at the regional level ☐

    4.3.6 Co-operation at the international level ☐

    4.3.7 Bodies with which you co-operate:

5. *Methods used*

5.1 Document storing:

    5.1.1 Conventional manual card files ☐

    5.1.2 Edge-notched cards, punched cards ☐

    5.1.3 Microfiches ☐

    5.1.4 Microfilms ☐

    5.1.5 Machine-operated punched cards ☐

    5.1.6 Punched tape ☐

    5.1.7 Magnetic tape ☐

    5.1.8 Magnetic discs ☐

    5.1.9 Mass storage systems ☐

5.2 Number of references stored per year:
    5.2.1 From 0 to 1,000   ☐
    5.2.2 From 1,000 to 10,000   ☐
    5.2.3 From 10,000 to 100,000   ☐
    5.2.4 Over 100,000   ☐
5.3 Automatic documentation:
    5.3.1 Name of the automatic documentation system used:
        Method of use:
    5.3.2 Batch prossessing ☐
    5.3.3 Tele-processing ☐
    5.3.4 Oral   ☐
    5.3.5 Name of the computer programme (or programmes) used:
    5.3.6 Can this programme be acquired? ☐
    5.3.7 Do you use magnetic tape from outside? ☐
    5.3.8 From which bodies are these tapes obtained? (name the five most
        frequently used):
5.4 Thesaurus:
    5.4.1 Do you use documentary lexicon?   ☐
    5.4.2 Do you use one or more printed thesauri? ☐
    5.4.3 Give the name and date of the last edition of this (these) thesaurus(i):

6. *Dissemination of information*

6.1 Bibliographical dissemination (in the form of cards (1), bulletins (2), microfiches (3), magnetic tapes (4))

	(1)	(2)	(3)	(4)
6.1.1 Enumerative or annotated bibliographical bulletins	☐	☐	☐	☐
6.1.2 Primary periodicals containing a bibliographical section	☐	☐	☐	☐
6.1.3 Contents list bulletins	☐	☐	☐	☐
6.1.4 Cumulative indexes	☐	☐	☐	☐
6.1.5 KWIC indexes	☐	☐	☐	☐
6.1.6 KWOC indexes	☐	☐	☐	☐
6.1.7 KWIT indexes	☐	☐	☐	☐
6.1.8 Citation indexes	☐	☐	☐	☐
6.1.9 Cross indexes	☐	☐	☐	☐

6.2 Give the titles of these publications, followed by their frequency of issue
6.3 Indicate the number of references published per year:
    6.3.1 From 0 to 1,000   ☐
    6.3.2 From 1,000 to 10,000   ☐
    6.3.3 From 10,000 to 100,000   ☐
    6.3.4 More than 100,000   ☐
6.4 Other publications of the centre or service:
    6.4.1 Bibliographical monographs   ☐
    6.4.2 Lists of periodicals received   ☐
    6.4.3 Lists of translations   ☐

6.4.4 Printed catalogues showing the centre's collections ☐
6.4.5 Others ☐
6.5 Selective distribution by profile:
    6.5.1 By individual profile ☐
    6.5.2 By group profile ☐

7. *Information retrieval*

Does the centre carry out retrospective retrieval?
7.1 From its own documentary collection ☐
7.2 From a collection obtained from external sources ☐
Is there an 'at-your-service' information desk giving rapid replies?
7.3 On the spot ☐
7.4 By telephone ☐
7.5 In writing ☐
Is there a department which prepares 'state-of-the-art' reports or reviews of progress of various matters?
7.6 Regularly and systematically ☐
7.7 Only on request ☐
7.8 Does the centre possess and information-analysis service?[1] ☐
7.9 Does the centre possess a data bank service? ☐

8. *Access to primary documents*

8.1 Does the centre possess a library? ☐
    8.1.1 Library with automated control ☐
    8.1.2 Library with automated cataloguing ☐
    8.1.3 Library open to the public ☐
    8.1.4 Library open to students and academics only ☐
    8.1.5 Library open to other members of the public with special permission only (teachers, research workers) ☐
8.2 Consultation of documents on the premises:
    8.2.1 By members of the public ☐
    8.2.2 By authorized persons only ☐
8.3 Loan of documents (frequent[2] (1), occasional (2), rare (3))

	(1)	(2)	(3)
8.3.1 Loans to individuals	☐	☐	☐
8.3.2 Loans to students and academics	☐	☐	☐
8.3.3 Loans to members of the public with prior permission	☐	☐	☐
8.3.4 Internal loans only	☐	☐	☐
8.3.5 Inter-library loans	☐	☐	☐
8.3.6 Loans abroad	☐	☐	☐

1. That is, is it in a position to give technical or scientific replies to questions and not merely lists of documents, and does it carry out criticism and make syntheses?
2. That is, in numbers corresponding approximately to the quantities of new documents acquired in the course of a year.

8.4 Scientific and technical translations carried out by the centre
Total number of translations per year:
8.4.1 Less than 100 ☐
8.4.2 From 100 to 1,000 ☐
8.4.3 From 1,000 to 10,000 ☐
8.4.4 More than 10,000 ☐
8.4.5 Are these translations carried out systematically? ☐
8.4.6 Are these translations carried out on request? ☐
8.4.7 Are they written translations? ☐
8.4.8 Are they oral translations? ☐
8.4.9 Are they translations on magnetic tape? ☐
8.5 Reproductions supplied by the centre
Total number of reproductions carried out per year:
8.5.1 Less than 1,000 ☐
8.5.2 From 1,000 to 10,000 ☐
8.5.3 From 10,000 to 100,000 ☐
8.5.4 More than 100,000 ☐
8.5.5 Reproductions supplied in the form of photocopies ☐
8.5.6 Reproductions supplied in the form of microfiches ☐
8.5.7 Reproductions supplied in the form of microfilms ☐
8.5.8 Other media (indicate which):

9. *Give any other important information concerning the documentation centre or service:*

4   Survey of bibliographical periodicals

1. Title of the wholly bibliographical secondary periodical:
   Previously published under the title:
2. Date of establishment:
3. Frequency of publication:[1] weekly □, monthly □, quarterly □, half-yearly □,
   10 times a year □, annual □, irregular □, other (give details):
4. Organization:
   Editorial board and name of chief editor of the periodical:
   Name and address of the body responsible for publication:
   Publisher and publishing address:
5. Description of current bibliography:[1]
   Is it a contents list bulletin? □ An enumerative bulletin? □ An annotated
   bulletin? □ Other type (give details):
   Length of summaries: less than 5 lines □, between 5 and 10 lines □, more than
   10 lines □
   Classification system used for summaries (or references): UDC □, systematic
   internal classification □, alphabetical classification (subject-words) □, other
   classification (give details):
   Order of the references within one category of the classification system used:[1]
   by author □, by title □, by date □, by language □, haphazard □, other:
   For titles in languages other than that of the periodical, what method is used?
   original title followed by translation □, translated title followed by original
   title □, original title only, without translation □, translated title only,
   followed by indication of the language □, modified version of original
   title □, transliteration of original title □, other (give details):
   What rules are observed for the abbreviation of titles of periodicals?
   Are descriptors given with every summary? yes □ no □
   Are they taken from a thesaurus? yes □ no □
   Which thesaurus?
   Are they taken from a documentary lexicon? yes □ no □
   Are they taken from a different source, and, if so, which?

---

1. If possible, enclose with the questionnaire one copy of the periodical, giving details
   of the classification system.
      Mark reply with a cross (×).

Number of references (or summaries) published in each issue:
Number of references (or summaries) published per year:
Is a subject index supplied with every issue of the periodical? yes ☐ no ☐
Is an index of authors supplied with every issue of the periodical? yes ☐ no ☐
Are there cumulative indexes?

	Monthly	Quar-terly	Half-yearly	Annual
By author	☐	☐	☐	☐
By subject: permuted words				
(KWIC type)	☐	☐	☐	☐
Keywords	☐	☐	☐	☐
Subject headings	☐	☐	☐	☐
By country	☐	☐	☐	☐
By language	☐	☐	☐	☐
By source (periodical, body, symposium, laboratory[1])	☐	☐	☐	☐

6. Inventorying and coverage:
   What fields are covered? check the attached list of disciplines
   What percentage of periodicals is fully abstracted?
   Who selects the articles, and by what criteria?
   Is more importance attached to selectivity ☐, or to comprehensiveness ☐
   In the field covered, are the concerns mainly: scientific ☐, technical ☐, or economic ☐
   Number of titles of national periodicals abstracted:[2]
   Number of titles of foreign periodicals abstracted:[2]
   Number of other documents abstracted each year:[2]

	National	Foreign
Books:		
Patents:		
Theses:		
Reports:		
Reports of conferences:		
One entry only for the conference:		
One entry for each paper:		
Offprints:		
Standards:		
Other documents:		

Classification by language of the documents abstracted (expressed as percentages):
French:
English:
German:
Russian:
Other languages:

---

1. Strike out whichever does not apply.
2. If possible include a list of the periodicals abstracted.

7. Preparation of the bibliographical periodical

What indexing language is used for documents? Ordinary language □, subjects or subject headings □, descriptors □, class marks □

By whom are summaries made (state whether full-time or part-time)?

Qualifications of translators/abstractors:

Number of persons employed internally:

externally:

Is there a drafting committee? yes □ no □

Is there any co-operation with other centres or bodies? yes □ no □

With which national bodies?

With which regional bodies?

With which bodies in other countries?

What form does this co-operation take?

Is your periodical published with the help of a computer? yes □ no □

What equipment and procedures are used?

For printing:

For the preparation of indexes:

For the preparation of summaries:

For other purposes:

Is your periodical published: on sheets 75 mm × 125 mm □, A6 (105 mm × 150 mm) □, different format □, on magnetic tape □, on punched cards □, in any other form (microfiche, microfilm, etc.) □, give details:

What is the approximate interval between the publication of an article and the appearance of a notice on it in your secondary periodical?

8. Circulation and financing of the periodical:

Print run:

Circulation by means of subscriptions (express as percentages):

Exchanges:

Gifts:

Other means:

Selling price:

How and by whom is the periodical financed?

Who are the periodical's principal readers?

What are the readers' means of access to original documents? reproduction □, translation □, consultation on the premises □, loans □

Name of person replying to the questionnaire:

Telephone number:

The questionnaire should be returned to: Centre National de la Recherche Scientifique, Centre de Documentation, Service Relations PASCAL, 26 Rue Boyer, 75200 Paris.

Reminder: (a) please enclose with the questionnaire one copy of your periodical together with an outline of the system of classification if the latter does not appear in the periodical; (b) please also attach a list of the French and foreign periodicals of which abstracts are made for publication in the periodical.

5   Disciplines[1]

Biological and medical sciences
Biochemistry
Animal biology
Cellular biology
Plant biology and physiology
Biophysics
Ecology
Genetics
Biomedical engineering and
    medical informatics
Hygiene
Immunology
Pathological medicine
Veterinary medicine
Microbiology
Biological oceanography
    see Earth sciences
Parasitology
Animal physiology
Physiotherapy
Psychology
Agricultural sciences
Pharmacological sciences
Forestry
Technology of agriculture
    and food production
    see Exact and technical sciences
Therapeutics
Toxicology
Virology
Zootechnics

Earth and space sciences
Astronomy and astrophysics
Atmosphere and meteorology
Geochemistry
Geodesy
Geography
General and regional geology
Geophysics
Hydrology and surface-water
    formation
Mineralogy and crystallography
Oceanography
Paleontology
Petrography
Tectonics

Applied mathematics and information
Econometrics and economics
Computer science and automation
Operational research. Management
Information science and linguistics

Exact and technical sciences
Acoustics
Architecture and town planning
Analytical chemistry
General chemistry and physical
    chemistry
Mineral chemistry
Organic chemistry

1. Mark 2 crosses ($\times\times$) for main disciplines and 1 cross ($\times$) for subsidiary disciplines.

Electronics and quantum electronics
Electro-technics
Energy: production and transformation
Atomic engineering
Chemical engineering
Civil engineering, public works, building
Agricultural and food industries
Mechanical engineering industries
Mining and oil industries
Parachemical industries: wood, cellulose, paper colouring, dyes, fats, soaps, perfumes, leathers, polymeric substances (plastics, rubber), coating materials, paint, varnish
Chemical products industries
Building materials, pottery, glass

Mechanics
Metals and metallurgy (casting, smelting, welding)
Meteorology
Optics
Atomic and molecular physics
Nuclear physics and chemistry
Mathematical physics
Physics of plasma
Physics of solids and fluids
Pollution (air, water, soil)
Spectroscopy
Aerospatial techniques
Telecommunications
Textiles
Thermodynamics, heat
Land and sea transport
Others

Bibliography

Ad Hoc Working Group on Information Requirements of Developing Countries in the Framework of the UNISIST Programme. Final report. Paris UNISIST/Unesco, 5 July 1972. 12 p.

ADISESHIAH, M. S. *Let my country awake.* Paris, Unesco, 1970.

ANDERLA, G. Future needs for information specialists—a forecasting study. In: *Information in 1985.* Paris, OECD, 1973. 131 p.

ARUTJUNOV, N. B. The requirements to be met by national scientific and technical information systems. *Unesco bulletin for libraries,* vol. XXVII, no. 5, September-October 1973. p. 246–9.

CAIN, J.; ESCARPIT, R.; MARTIN, H. J. *Le livre français hier, aujourd'hui et demain.* Paris, Imprimerie Nationale, 1972. 406 p.

CASADIO, F. *Journées d'études internationales sur la documentation des Nations unies et autres organisations internationales, Genève, 21–23.8.72.* Geneva, UNITAR.

DUCAS, M. *L'ingénieur et l'information. Congrès National des Ingénieurs Français.* February 1973. 40 p.

Economic and social aspects of educational planning. Paris, Unesco, 1965. 264 p.

Expert Meeting on National Planning of Documentation and Library Services in Africa, Kampala, Uganda. Final report. Paris, Unesco, 17 March 1971. 26 p. (See also *Main working document,* 14 August 1970. 79 p.)

FAURE, Edgar et al. *Learning to be.* Paris, Unesco/Harrap, 1972. 299 p.

GARDNER, F. M. *Public library legislation: a comparative study.* Paris, Unesco, 1971. 285 p.

International standardization of library and documentation techniques. Paris, Unesco, 13 March 1972. 241 p.

KALTWASSER, F. G. Universal bibliographical control (UBC). *Unesco bulletin for libraries,* vol. XXV, no. 5, September-October 1971. p. 252–9.

LAZAR, P. *National information system for science and technology. India.* Paris, Unesco, July 1972. 49 p.

LIGUER-LAUBHOUET, K. L. *Rapport sur la planification et l'organisation des bibliothèques. Conférence de l'Association Internationale des documentalistes et des bibliothécaires africains. (AIDBA) Sept. 1972. Abidjan.* (AIDBA BP 375 Dakar.)

Meeting of Experts on the National Planning of Library Services in Asia, Colombo, Ceylon. Final report. Paris, Unesco, 26 April 1968. 30 p. (See also *Main working document,* 15 November 1973. 90 p.)

Meeting of Experts on the National Planning of Library Services in Latin America: report. *Unesco Bulletin for Libraries*, vol. XX, no. 6, November-December 1966. p. 278–95.

MEYRIAT, J.; BEAUCHET, M. *Guide for the establishment of national social sciences documentation centres in developing countries.* Paris, Unesco, 1969. 72 p.

Model statutes for information services in the U.S.S.R. *Unesco bulletin for libraries*, vol. XXV, no. 2, March-April 1971. p. 94–101.

PENNA, Carlos Victor. *The planning of library and documentation services*, 2nd rev. and enl. by P. H. Sewell and H. Liebaers. Paris, Unesco, 1971. 158 p.

POIGNANT, R. *The relation of educational plans to economic and social planning.* Paris, Unesco: International Institute for Educational Planning, 1967 and 1971. 51 p.

Review of national scientific and technical policy: Canada. Paris, OECD, 1971. 162 p.

The role of science and technology in economic development. Paris, Unesco, 1970. 216 p.

SAMUELSON, K. *Automated international information network.* Stockholm, FID/TM, 1969. 58 p.

——. *Mixed multimedia: development potentials.* Stockholm, FID/TM. 68 p.

SEWELL, P. H. *The planning of library and documentation services.* Paris, Unesco: International Institute for Educational Planning, 17 June 1969. 87 p.

Les statistiques des bibliothèques municipales. *Bulletin des bibliothèques de France*, vol. XVI, no. 6, June 1971. p. 309–50.

Study on national structures for documentation and library services in countries with different levels of development. FID. Committee for Developing Countries. Budapest. Paris, Unesco, 254 p.

Study report on the feasibility of a world science information system (UNISIST). Paris, Unesco, 1971. 158 p.

TARABOÏ, V. *Organisation, fonctionnement et activités des systèmes nationaux d'information documentaire.* Bucharest, 1973. 93 p.

Unesco statistical yearbook 1970. Paris, Unesco, 1971.

WENNERBERG, U. Using the Delphi technique for planning the future of libraries. *Unesco bulletin for libraries*, vol. XXVI, no. 5, September-October 1972. p. 242–6.

WITHERS, F. N. *Standards for library service: an international survey.* Paris, Unesco, 1974. 421 p.

Archives

by B. Delmas

Keeper, French National Archives

Foreword

All planning forms part of a policy. But at the level of the establishment and development of the national archive services, the lead must be taken by governments. Moreover, governments must have a clear idea of what they may gain by an archival policy in terms of administrative efficiency, their own information, their sovereignty and also the enhancement of their national identity. Perhaps Unesco and the International Council on Archives have an historic role to play, for they could foster such an ambition by organizing an International Archives Year. This could have immense repercussions, particularly in the Third World countries, and could ensure the preservation of source material for the national history of each country, which is the common heritage of all mankind.

It will be the aim of archivists to help people become aware of the specific role of archives and, on the basis of a serious and thorough study of the problems raised by this policy, to formulate realistic proposals incorporated in a programme.

In many countries, however, the planning of archives services is a relatively new field which has not yet been systematically studied and which has only very rarely been tackled as such.[1] There are, however, many studies of the usefulness of archives, methods of dealing with documents and the material means of preserving them. These, whether detailed or more general in nature, are of very great value as documentation.

---

1. Unesco, *Consultation on the planning of national archives services, Paris, 4–6 December 1972*. ICA, Direction des Archives de France and Unesco, *Colloque sur la planification des infrastructures d'archives dans les pays en voie de développement, 28–30 May 1973*.

My own experience relates to European countries and to French- and English-speaking countries in West Africa, and I have endeavoured to obtain information as to the situation in the other countries in the world. Being familiar with the extent to which the archival situation varies with each country, but at the same time convinced of the universal character of archival problems, I have sought to deal with the subject in a sufficiently general manner for everyone to be able to find something useful in my remarks. I have gone into details only in cases where basic problems were involved which could be usefully clarified; my fundamental aim was to give the reader a clear picture of the problems to be resolved, the means to be used and the methods to be applied.

In concluding this foreword I should like to express my gratitude to all those who helped and advised me during the writing of this study. In particular, I should like to mention the members of the International Council on Archives, Unesco, together with J. R. Ede, Keeper of the Public Records of the United Kingdom, and his colleagues, Mr Mabbs and Mr Bell, for enabling me to visit the Public Record Office, and Guy Duboscq, Director-General of the Archives of France and his colleagues.

Introduction

Why archives?

Man enters his estate only through self-awareness, through being conscious of what he is and of his evolution. But if he is to be aware of himself and of his past he needs landmarks, he needs documents.

When one looks at it closely, however, everything is a document, that is to say everything testifies: the earth testifies to the history of the universe, man's body testifies to the originality of our species, our chromosomes testify to our heredity. Everything in its degree and in various ways remembers and bears witness to what it has been and to what it is.

What are archives? 'All documents, regardless of their nature, which are automatically and organically collected by any administrative body, any person or corporate entity, by virtue of its (or his) functions or activity.'

Archives are documents bearing on man as a social being; they are the proofs of his continuity and of his adaptation to the deep-seated changes in his living conditions on earth. Thus archives are the foundation of that conscious memory that man has of himself, through history. Whatever adds to the history of mankind enables us to know more about man and understand more of human nature. Such is the basic social role of archives.

Thoughts, desires and actions were first of all expressed in writing on stone, clay and metal and, for about a thousand years, principally on paper. But since the beginning of the twentieth century the hand-written document has ceased to be the pre-eminent form of archives. The development of printing and, later, of the typewriter and of duplicating machines and lastly the invention, some decades ago, of new types of documents—audio-visual documents (films, photographs, sound recordings, magnetic tapes) and mechanically produced documents (punched tapes and cards, documents produced by computers, etc.)—all this has considerably enlarged the concept of archives.

In terms of the definition given above all these documents can be properly called archival documents, even if their preservation calls for new techniques. Thus in the U.S.S.R. the central State archives and the central archives of the republics administer specialized repositories containing cinefilms, photographic holdings and sound recordings.

Moreover, the specific character of archives appears even more clearly if they are compared in terms of their methodology and their purpose with libraries and documentation centres, which, while commonly considered to be closely related to archives, are based on the concepts of selection and collection.

It is the function of libraries to collect and to preserve, so that they can be read, works which are the products of self-sufficient intellectual activity. In performing this task the librarian chooses books to suit the requirements and the taste of his readers.

The main functions of documentation are similar, for they consist essentially in selecting and collecting as much information as possible to meet present or foreseeable requirements. What is important for documentation is the use that will be made of it in a clearly defined area. Its functions, then, are short-term ones and its scope limited.

The function of archives is quite different and has grown steadily throughout the ages. Archives were first of all services attached to the chancellery, and as such they were the guardians of the documents of title and rights of the State. It logically followed that they very soon became the memory of institutions and the guardian of documents important for their history. Today, with the development of the modern world and the proliferation of documents of all kinds, they have a new mission to fulfil. For the greater the number of documents organically produced by an administrative department becomes, the more the proportion of documents without historical significance increases. Not only is this useless body of documents a great burden, but it also, as it were, snows under the documents which are of historical value.

As it is not possible to keep everything, it now becomes necessary to sort out from the great mass of documents those which are of general importance (always a relatively small part of the whole) and those which are useless. A scientific reply must be given to the almost philosophical question, 'What information should we keep and be able to find again concerning ourselves; what will our society have need of tomorrow?' This question obliges archivists to have their gaze turned towards the future, and the task of elimination and weeding out becomes a choice fraught with consequences.

In answering this question, and because documents are mostly unique in nature, archives indeed exercise the right of life and death over information, for what is destroyed will be lost for ever. Thus the modern world entrusts to archives an important part of itself, since society makes its archivists responsible for choosing on its behalf what its memory will be tomorrow.

For lack of the material and human means necessary for the accomplishment of their mission, modern archives, with very rare exceptions, are unable to fulfil their role. A decision of paramount importance remains to be taken at the level of governments: whether to abstain from action and accept the destruction of archives or not. But what head of state, what chief executive can reasonably deprive himself of a tool which is so vital to his economic and social action and to his political goals? How could he run the risk of destroying his country's memory by neglecting its archives, allowing ancient archives to be done away with and threatened more gravely as each day passes, and failing to safeguard for the future evidence of the great changes taking place at the present time? The level of civilization of a society can be judged from the interest that it shows in its past.

It is therefore the duty of governments to set up and to maintain the necessary infrastructures.

Why should archives services be planned?

When one speaks of the modernization and development of national archives services, one has in mind the optimum use of funds, the reduction of wastage of time and money; one is concerned with efficiency, which implies the idea of planning.

Yet, it must be recognized that planning does not mean drawing up a programme for the development of existing structures, but rather establishing an archives system aimed at solving the problems of the future.

It is important that archivists should define their policies for themselves, with their eyes on the future, and that they should know what they want, since policy cannot be divorced from volition, and the deep-seated conviction which is theirs and the rational choice which they make will have to be presented in such a way as to gain the support of others.

First of all, the facts must be ascertained and foreseeable requirements must be considered, so as not to calculate in terms of the present but rather to pave the way for the future. Volition needs this if it is to lead to action, and volition is also needed in drawing up a plan.

Planning means deciding upon certain essential goals and working out what tools, what funds and what work will be needed to attain them. Its value—a value at once material, psychological and social—is that:

Planning makes us consider: (a) Where are the possibilities? (b) Where are the contradictions, and how can they be overcome? (c) What chances have we of succeeding, and on what conditions?

Planning makes us look at habits and routines in a new light. No administration undertakes such a re-evaluation of its own accord, and yet every administration is obliged to do so if it wishes to continue playing its part in a continually changing society and in a constantly evolving State: What are the reasons for my services, and in what ways are they of use? How are public funds being used? How efficient am I?

Planning enables us, through investigation, to define and see clearly the goals of a national archives service: We collect public papers, we weed out those which are devoid of interest, we classify and preserve those which are of permanent value—why, how? We wish to play our part in administrative life by facilitating the control and assisting in the management of the ever-increasing volume of documentation produced in public offices—why, how? We wish to make the documents which have been preserved available to all those who request them, or rather to all those who may be interested by these documents—why, how?

Planning makes us try to see which sectors of activity could be made better or brought up to date. Our task is to preserve the historical heritage of the nation, increase administrative efficiency, extend the quest for information and promote its dissemination.

Planning enables us to modernize archival activities and adapt them to the needs of the modern world. Archives, apart from merely preserving documents, have a part to play in furthering the grand designs of the nation. They must make their specific contribution to the administrative, social and economic, educational and cultural, and even political action of the State.

Planning encourages a forward-looking state of mind. Planning makes it necessary for a national archives system to be worked out, as a coherent and more or less structured whole, which can cope with the problems of the future.

Planning makes it necessary to determine the aims of production and to lay down priorities.

Planning gives the profession goals, which are of prime importance to any profession—and goals worth striving for.

What is meant by planning archives services?

Many countries have had relatively little experience of the planning of archives services, and neither basic concepts nor methods have yet been defined. Two quite different levels of concern are in fact involved in the expression 'the planning of archives services'. They are: (a) the level of structures, the drawing up of development plans for national archival infrastructures in the context of the national development plan; (b) the level of functions, the programming of the activities of the State archives services.

These two aspects of planning cannot very well be dissociated, since the whole point of developing infrastructures, their sole justification, is to enable actions which are useful and beneficial to the nation to be carried out. Consequently, the development plan should be conceived in such a way that all investments become 'productive' within a reasonable period of time.

Where and when to plan

The question may arise as to whether it is advisable to plan the archives services at the present time. Is there a particular point or stage when planning is best done? When should one plan? This is not where the problem lies. It follows from what was said above that one should plan in order to pave the way for the future. One does not pave the way for the future tomorrow, but straightaway. We must remember that, if a library is destroyed, its bookstock may, with patience and money, be built up again. But if archives are destroyed or allowed to be destroyed (too often such destruction still takes place, regrettable as it may be), their loss is irreparable, for they are usually made up of unique documents. This is why any delay in modernizing archives means the disappearance of documents.

Once we become aware of this time factor, we can answer the question of space—in what country should we plan? Once we have a policy—that is to say once we are no longer content with living from day to day, but have decided to assemble the means and acquire the methods of solving the problems of the present, whilst preparing to solve those of the future—irrespective of the country concerned, we will use planning as a tactic and a strategy.

However, the problems met with vary with the economic level of the country. Where the economic level is high, certain more or less complete elements of the system will exist already; at the very least, it will be possible to find a rapid solution to the problem of preserving documents. Archives services already exist in such countries and the sole task of planning is to make good deficiencies and to pave the way for the future.

Nevertheless, in the developed countries, the structure of the public archives system is complex just as their institutions are. With a few exceptions, it is the result of a long administrative and political history (national or federal archives; more or less autonomous ministerial archives; archives of local authorities, dependent or not, etc.). But generally speaking, although they often have no hierarchical links with each other, they form a homogeneous whole, because the persons in positions of responsibility in them have the same training, conform to the same laws and regulations and are confronted by similar problems.

In countries which are relatively underdeveloped and irrespective of the institutional form of these new States, situations which are in fact much the same exist; there is a strong central authority with local powers representing the power of the capital city, having little independent authority and far more closely linked together than in the traditional federal systems. Often the archives services exist only in an embryonic state; they have been too recently set up for it to be otherwise, they have no archival traditions and their infrastructures are rudimentary.

The problems to be solved, then, are those of setting up, organizing and developing national archives services. However, as there are no restrictions imposed by the past, one has more freedom, and one can establish an organization with a new life of its own, rather than a system which retains the same old habits, not to say the same old prejudices. Whilst the problems of these states may be on a smaller scale than those of the more advanced nations, they are more widespread and more general. We think it best to approach the subject bearing this in mind.

When planning an archives service one should first examine the question of its purpose—that is to say, one should clearly define its administrative, economic, social, educational and cultural objectives—then determine its requirements and finally draw up a timetable to meet these requirements. But such planning must be incorporated into the national development plan if it is to benefit from decision-making at the national level and receive external aid—in a word, if it is to have any chance of being implemented.

1 The requirements
of the community
and the necessary means:
rational choices

1.1   Archives: a luxury or a necessity[1]

Considered by many as a relatively inexpensive luxury, but solely
for the use of a small number of scholars, archives are often
deemed to be useless. If, however, one asks who it is that archives
are meant to serve, one has no difficulty in pinpointing the needs
they can meet—those of: private persons and citizens; economic
and social life; the administration, by the reduction of overheads;
the government, as a particularly rich source of information; the
State, as the guardian of the titles of its sovereignty; the nation,
as its memory; the international community, as an inalienable
part of the heritage of mankind.

1.1.1   CATERING FOR THE NEEDS
OF PRIVATE PERSONS AND CITIZENS

In our time the development of our civilization places increasing
importance on archives on account of the increasingly large role
played by the State in all sectors of economic and social life. So
when laws and regulations are to be passed, the administration
finds itself confronted with a growing number of questions to be
answered and files to be dealt with in order to meet citizens' needs.

1. The title of this section is the same as that used for the white paper published by the
Association Professionnelle des Archivistes Français in 1971. Certain passages in this
text are based on Mr Kecskemeti's essay: 'Archives, développement et souveraineté
nationale' (1971).

It happens increasingly that citizens must or can request, for one reason or another, the recognition of their rights, authorization to take certain action, the granting of a loan, State assistance, etc. If these requests are to be granted in accordance with the rules, precautions must be taken which entail observing certain formalities, establishing files and examining their contents.

In our society, which is based on the written word, these files are made up of documents required as proof of citizens' rights or permanent obligations: papers containing evidence of birth, marriage, and death, legal and medical documentation, certificates issued by schools and universities, documents relating to financial, fiscal or professional matters, titles to property, etc.

I.I.2   THE ROLE OF ARCHIVES IN ECONOMIC
         AND SOCIAL LIFE

What has just been said and what is about to be said about the usefulness of archives in the life of citizens, in the conduct of administration and in the service of the community also applies to public corporations and private companies, particularly in view of the growing role played by the State in the economic and social spheres. But to this should be added all the documents produced in the past on these subjects which may help us to solve present-day problems of the same kind.

I.I.3   THE REDUCTION
         OF THE OVERHEAD EXPENSES
         OF GOVERNMENT DEPARTMENTS

Whatever the level of economic development of the country, the contemporary world is characterized by the ever-increasing production of documents and by the considerable enlargement of the tertiary sector (the provision of services). The growth of services involves a parallel growth of government departments. The latter may serve equally to spur on or to curb this expansion depending on whether they are well or badly organized.

These phenomena, marked as they are in the advanced countries, are proportionally even more pronounced in the developing countries, and for this there are two reasons: these countries, which have newly established economic systems, have neither deeply entrenched administrative traditions nor a long established infrastructure; these countries, which are usually newly established States as well, have to set up, in place of the fairly loose colonial administrative infrastructure,[1] a more complete and more closely knit system in order to cope with the problems posed by development.

Consequently, although they have little experience, these countries have to develop their administrative systems rapidly, starting from the slenderest foundations. As a result, administration, that is to say the functioning of public services, tends to absorb an enormous part of the national budget.

On top of this burden on the national economy, which is difficult to reduce, there are also the internal problems arising from rapid growth which the administration has to contend with: the increasing cost of establishing files; a growing lack of control in file management.

The lack of organized archives in offices gives rise to operational dislocation (in the form of administrative delays), loss of time (with a harmful effect on productivity), financial expenditure (office equipment and accommodation used to no purpose), and extra work in searching for or re-establishing files that have been mislaid or lost.

In the field of records management, however, archives have a specific function to fulfil, which should be distinguished from that of 'organization and methods' services. In most countries, 'organization and methods' services study the functioning of the administration in conjunction with the *bureaux d'ordre* or the 'registry services'. They are concerned with the production of files (administrative channels, decisions, printed forms, procedures) and their day-to-day management. Archives should share in this concern with administrative efficiency and, abandoning their present attitude, which is still too passive, they should, in future, in accordance with the situation of each country, assume clearly defined responsibilities in the field of records management, taking over all or part of the role of 'organization and methods' services. This is dealt

1. The head of a province was often the sole representative of the colonial administration for a huge area and a large population.

with below, in the section on 'The setting up of intermediate repositories'.

In the absence of premises set apart for the preservation of documents and fitted out for this purpose, papers are one of the causes of that unproductive expenditure which is associated with the building of offices; more space must continually be provided, in particular so as to be able to accommodate new storage units. The fitting out of a small archives repository would cost the department ten times less.

Thus, for a modest initial outlay, the organization of archives services in offices should make it possible to reduce considerably the cost and inconvenience of badly kept archives. Furthermore, the general level of expenditure incurred in the functioning of government offices is often greatly reduced and, apart from this material gain, greater efficiency results and there is an improvement in the quality of its services.

Archives services are the basic tool which governments have at their disposal to carry out their administrative task.

The role of archives services is not confined to the satisfactory management of the material basis on which information is preserved, for the satisfactory management of information has consequences which, likewise, are not to be discounted.

1.1.4   INFORMING THE GOVERNMENT

Once files have been established, they are of interest to the archives services; however, the usefulness of such files is not always very obvious, especially in countries without firmly established administrative traditions. Nevertheless, often those in positions of responsibility would like to consult again documentation whose existence they are aware of. But sometimes weeks of searching are necessary before one can lay one's hands on a document, if it can be found at all. Would it not be preferable to make an effort to keep to the order (or registry system) which was established when the file was assembled?

Studies which are carried out more than once are another and even more inadmissible aspect of administrative wastage. Often the execution of a project has to be postponed, for instance on account of financial or monetary problems, or because fluctuations in the price of raw materials suddenly deprive a State of resources on which it previously counted. When the situation improves, the project may be taken up again, but by then it is very likely that it cannot be found. There are many instances of studies which have had to be carried out again in this way as many as three or four times.

The waste of time and money is no less serious, for example, when projects of various kinds are concerned (roads and railways especially) which have in the past been prepared in very great numbers, usually by colonial administrations. These studies can and should be used again. And what of the files relating to roads which have in fact been constructed and which, when in need of repairs, require large-scale operations (geological readings, checking the line of the road, structural work, etc.)? Thus even for the purpose of maintenance or development it is necessary, often through lack of records, to go a very long way back over work already done.

Governments in every country have to take decisions whose consequences grow daily more far-reaching because they involve increasingly large sums of money, affect society more and more profoundly and reach out further and further in time and in space (national construction work, development plans, reforms, etc.). It is quite obvious that in these conditions errors of judgement are disastrous and that all the important information must be found if economic and social development is to be satisfactory. Everyone is convinced of the desirability of having as much information as possible. Few people acknowledge, however, that archives, because they constitute the largest bank of political and economic information that is to be found in a country, can provide the wherewithal for making a decision that is realistic because it is based on full information (being grounded on the most exhaustive collection of public papers)—a decision which is at once relevant, because it is the result of selection, and considered, because it looks back at the past. In this way archives may constitute an exceptionally effective tool for government planners and leaders to use in decision-making, for they will thereby have access to the main facts on which their decisions are to be founded.

Because of this, however, archives must be constantly added to so that they are a living memory, and arrangements must be made so that it is increasingly easy for everyone to have access to them and to be able to use them.

It follows that it is profitable to invest in archives. Archives are not in themselves a priority goal or a sectorial goal such as education or housing. Archives are an indispensable tool for improving the economic and administrative management of a State, for they relate at one and the same time to all the sectors of the life of a country and the ways in which they function. Lastly, if records cannot be constantly referred to, there is not, nor can there be, continuity in action, nor can decisions be well-founded or lasting.

1.1.5 THE SOVEREIGNTY OF THE STATE

Archives, being an excellent source of information for the State, by virtue of the increased facilities which they place at its disposal, and a spur to greater productivity on the part of the administration, constitute, as do the other public services, a part of its sovereignty.

Originally, even before being considered as a means of information, archives were established by States in order to preserve the titles on which were founded their rights, their prerogatives and even their claims. It is therefore the duty of every State to collect the documents relating to its sovereignty, internal as well as external—for they are necessary to it—to preserve its constitution and also the deeds and evidences attesting to its dominion, the documents relating to each of its citizens, etc. These documents are the means by which it can preserve its rights to the full. On the other hand, the loss of these documents will always give rise to political difficulties or to endless administrative disputes.

Treaties and international or other conventions, which lay down the exact position of frontiers, define a geographical area, and may acquire considerable economic importance when rich mineral deposits, of oil for instance, are discovered. Here too, if the documents have been mislaid, political difficulties, which may have very grave consequences at the international level, and which are not readily settled, are bound to arise.

1.1.6 ARCHIVES AND THE NATION

Into contemporary nationalism are channelled energies of every kind; it is the over-all expression of political, economic, social and cultural aspirations. For, in the developing countries especially, the movement towards national independence is bound up with the goals of economic and social progress.

In contrast with old countries, where the State is the emanation of a nation formed over the centuries, young countries derive their present existence from a colonial period (it could perhaps be said that every nation arises from a colonial period) which, owing to the increasing pace of history, has bequeathed to them the structure of a State before they have been able to forge a national soul.

Major achievements in economic and social developments and the spread of education and professional training are essential factors in the formation of modern nations, and these factors may be planned and organized. But the evolution of mental attitudes, which results in the formation of a nation, follows its own logic. No doubt the use of the mass media may be of assistance to governments in promoting this evolution.

But States that are searching for their identity may be said to suffer from personality problems, and they will not surmount them until they know themselves better. This is why research of every kind whether carried out by nationals or foreigners, which makes it possible to understand fully the essential nature of a country, should be encouraged (geography, anthropology, ethnology, arts and traditions of the people, etc.) and above all history, which encompasses all the other human sciences. The teaching of history and historical research should be accorded priority attention by every recently established State.

Besides being a focal point for historical research, archives are also amongst the great centres for the dissemination of national historical culture, through their publications and the exhibitions and educational activities which they organize.

I.1.7   ARCHIVES AND INTERNATIONAL LIFE

The contemporary world is characterized by the rapid development of international life greatly stimulated by the spread of the communications media. Continents, regions, populations, civilizations and men, hitherto ignorant of each other, are more and more frequently in contact and are getting to know each other better. Archives are a storehouse from which all research workers may acquire greater familiarity with the history and culture of every people and a better understanding of the unique destiny of each. In this sense, the future of archives concerns mankind.

From whatever point of view one looks at it—at the individual level, at the economic and social levels, at the governmental, national, international or cultural level—the setting up and organization of modern archives services has become a matter of unprecedented necessity.

The problems which arise at the level of the management of public and private papers have become so great that they cannot be indefinitely ignored with impunity.

It is for this reason that the functions of archives must be scientifically re-examined so as to ensure that documents to be preserved are selected with the greatest of care, that administrative files are properly maintained, and that the information which they contain is readily accessible. To the quantitative challenge presented to archives by contemporary information needs, a qualitative response must be found; in the face of these new needs, new means are called for.

1.2   The necessary infrastructures: some standards

If archives are to perform their task in meeting the needs of the community, a number of facilities are called for which are the constituent elements of a modern archives service. The problems of providing these and the proper conception of their role in the economy of archives planning will also be considered.

The first point, and one which should not be overlooked, is that the problem is primarily a problem of dimension: the magnitude of the problem of archives, the ability of the country to meet the financial, material and human requirements of archives. In the face of the need for archives, such is the reality with which we must come to terms.

The second point is the question of men and machines. In the developing countries—that is to say, the countries where professional qualifications are rare but there is a plentiful supply of manpower, where equipment is expensive, deteriorates rapidly and is difficult to keep in good repair, and where, finally, even if there is no shortage of money, it is drained off, as in the more developed countries, by projects which are considered to possess greater prestige—the archives system to be planned must take these factors into account. The type of service to be aimed at is one in which a large staff can be employed (thus helping to solve the employment problem). The staff, which will be more highly qualified in some countries than in others, will usually have to be trained on the spot. Likewise, equipment must be simple and sturdy, and it will therefore be less costly to acquire. If machines are chosen by applying the same criteria, they will be easier to manipulate and keep in good repair. The most up-to-date methods should not be overlooked, but one should always bear in mind the difficulty of obtaining spare parts and other supplies and that of maintenance.

In the more developed countries, on the other hand, machines are often less expensive than men, and there are less problems in keeping them in running order, whilst men are generally qualified, but scarce and expensive. At all events and however far mechanization goes archives services will require more men than machines.

Having noted these points, let us now consider what infrastructures need to be set up.

Legislation and regulations that will assist the efficient functioning of the archives network.

An archives network adapted to the constitutional and administrative structure of the country.

Financial means commensurate with the tasks assigned to the archives services.

Qualified personnel and adequate manpower.

Equipment to meet requirements and new means to cope with new tasks.

I.2.I   LEGISLATION AND REGULATIONS

The archives plan will include a section on legislation to be enacted at such time as is considered appropriate and regulations to be introduced in the course of the implementation of the plan. So new provisions, adapted to a new situation, will considerably augment the new means available to archives services. Incorporating the legislation in the plan in this way will prevent it from remaining a pious hope.

In a new State it will be easier to draw up a satisfactory law relating to archives and to get it passed. This law should be conceived in such a way as to take into account the constitution of the State, the realities of the country's administrative system and its past.

Finally, a clear distinction must be made between the area covered by the legislation, which is very general in nature, and the more practical and more easily amendable area covered by the regulations.

1.2.1.1 *Legislation*

Clearly set forth in a fundamental law, the general principles relating to the structure and the organization of the archives services will not only serve as a frame of reference for it but will also need to be observed by all the other public services. They embrace:

The definition of the concept of archives and of archive groups, comprising documents of all types to which the law applies (including archive groups of government departments and private archives over which certain rights of control may be exercised).

A statement of the major principles relating to archives: the inalienable and imprescriptible character of public papers and the confidentiality attached to them; the public character of public archives and restrictions on access to them designed to protect the interests of the State and third parties (generally for a period of thirty years, which may be reduced or extended in certain cases), and to safeguard the documents; the authenticity of archive documents and possibilities of authentication; the principle of keeping archive groups intact.

A statement of responsibilities with regard to archives: the responsibility of departments with regard to the management of their documents (implies the designation in each department of a person to be responsible for archives); the right of the archives service to examine administrative documents (departmental records) with a view to their being transferred and to supervise all weeding operations; the duty of departments to transfer their papers to the archives service when no longer in use or after an agreed period (normal closure period and variations from it); the drawing up of lists or schedules of papers to be destroyed, by joint agreement of the archives service and the department concerned, and the necessity for authorization from that department of the destruction of all papers less than thirty years old.

The parent authority under which the archives service will be placed. There is no ideal solution, and the country's political situation and traditions will have to be taken into account. Generally speaking, the archives service will have to come under a governmental institution possessing extensive interministerial powers.

The organization of the controlling authorities: a superior archives council appointed to help the parent authority or the archives directorate; an archives directorate responsible for the autonomous management of the service and for legally determining its competence, role and status in the administrative system; an archives inspectorate responsible where the need arises for supervising the operation of dependent repositories, in the case of extensive archives networks, or for co-ordinating archival activities on the national scale.

The organization of the archives network. The law determines the structure of the archives network. It determines the method of operation of the central State archives (the national archives) and of the archives of government departments and responsibility for source materials for the history of the country. It defines the status and the responsibilities of the other archives repositories. Irrespective of the country's constitution, there are signs of a trend, in the new states especially, towards the nationalization of archives repositories.

The situation of non-public archives. This will vary with the degree of autonomy of the local authorities and with the country's economic and social orientation.

1.2.1.2   *Regulations*

These include all texts regulating the application of the law on archives. Such regulations may be adopted either by the public authority (in matters of organization) or by the directorate (in matters of the internal operation of archives services). They should be formulated in such a way that they can easily be kept up to date.

1.2.1.2.1 *Organization*

Staff (status, recruitment, training, competitive examinations, courses, etc.).

Superior council: composition and operation.

Archives repositories: operating conditions.

Transfer (general rules, time-limits, handing-over procedures, etc.).

Elimination (supervision by the archives service, lists and schedules of documents to be eliminated, etc.).

Access (closure period, access restrictions and limitations, issue of authenticated copies, photocopies, microfilms, reproduction, etc.).

Government departments (special reports on particular problems).

Non-public archives (archives of towns and parishes, hospitals, etc.).

1.2.1.2.2 *Operation*

Structure and organization of the repository.

Organization and operation of the service-room, rules governing access, removal, reproduction, etc.

Security measures.

1.2.2   THE STRUCTURE OF THE NATIONAL ARCHIVES SYSTEM

From the outset there must be a will to solve the problem of the country's archives as a whole and, consequently, a complete system must be planned. Subsequently, the initial project will undoubtedly be altered in the light of what proves practicable.

When we speak of a national archives system, we are thinking of the totality of archive holdings within the national territory, namely: archive groups from government departments, the responsibility for which devolves directly on the public archives; archive groups from private institutions or individuals, over which various rights of control may be exercised.

It is for this reason that, above all in countries which will have to set up a national system, care should be taken so far as possible to adhere to traditional structures, but at the same time to endeavour to innovate in a realistic manner and to create an integrated network, the development of which can be planned.

Planning the network of a national archives system is a complex matter, as it is necessary to take into account (a) the centralized or decentralized form of the structure of the State; (b) the degree of autonomy enjoyed by the local, district, ethnic and other authorities; (c) the extent to which the central authority has power to intervene in local affairs; (d) the social situation of the country (forms of individual property, forms of socialist economy, the State's power of intervention in economic undertakings and religious activities).

Generally speaking, more than three-fifths of the countries in the world have a simple archival structure, concerning which one may ask what its real administrative status is and what are its functions: does it take the form of: an archives department of the government's secretariat-general or cabinet office, a government archives service? A service responsible for the preservation of 'historic archives', more or less linked with a research institute? A directorate wholly or partially responsible for the archives of government departments?

Such are the questions which arise with regard to the parent body and the authority of the directorate of archives.

It is desirable, as has already been said, for the supervising (i.e. parent) authority to be a governmental institution with sufficiently wide-ranging interministerial powers to be able to exercise effective control over government departments as a whole.

The superior archives council will act as a counter-balance to this authority. In a federal system, it will be a meeting-point for the representatives of the different archives institutions in the country, will draw up the legislation and plans and, above all, will co-ordinate the country's policy with regard to archives. In a unitary system it will be an advisory body, and will co-operate with the directorate (it will be composed of representatives of government offices, users and professionals).

The archives directorate is an administrative department having set functions and, within certain limits, autonomy of management. Its competence will vary in scope according to the structure of the State. It will either deal with the central/federal state archives alone; or in other cases it will have broader authority. Generally speaking, it is desirable that the country's archives network be attached to the central directorate, at least from the technical point of view. This means that the directorate has the right to inspect repositories and check the standard of staff qualifications.

The existence of an archives inspectorate should make it possible to monitor records management standards in offices and the operation of repositories directly or indirectly subordinate to the directorate. This right of inspection should be universally recognized. In a federal State it will, under the auspices of the superior archives council, be able to facilitate the co-ordination and concordance of the activities and procedures of each federated State.

These different organs of direction and supervision operate in different ways at the four levels of archives which constitute the basic elements of a country's archives network: archives of national interest; archives of regional interest; archives of local (district or parish) interest; other archives, public or private.

Archives of national interest: a State archives directorate (national archives); one or more central national repositories; and one or more branch repositories in various places and/or dealing with archives holdings of different dates for the preservation of State documents in perpetuity; one or more intermediate repositories, and/or autonomous branches, for the management of records in the intermediate (or 'second') stage (departmental records); archives (departmental records) services, established in the ministries, and more or less autonomous; archives, often autonomous, belonging to major national institutions (institutes, academies, foundations and donor bodies, universities, etc.).

These last two, even when they are autonomous, may collaborate with the archives directorate and be placed under the latter's professional technical control.

Archives of regional interest: a directorate serving as the administrative centre of the network at this level (federated State, province, region, *département*); a regional repository (serving to preserve the archives of government departments functioning in the region); sometimes one or more branch repositories, specialized or not, which may or may not serve as intermediate repositories; sometimes autonomous repositories for certain government offices.

Archives of local (district or parish) interest, often more or less merged with those of regional interest (may also be placed under national or state management): a municipal repository; one or more branch repositories, which may or may not be specialized and may or may not serve as intermediate repositories.

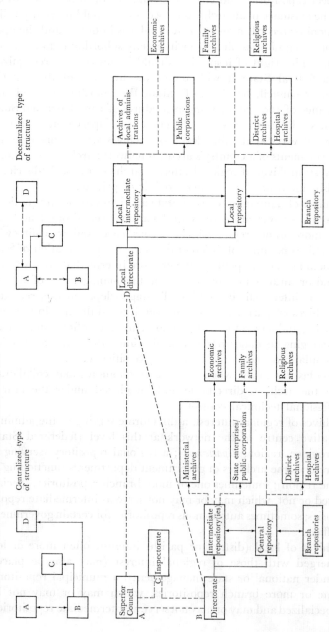

Fig. 1. Model structures for a national archives network

At each level the problems which arise are problems of size. The larger the services are, the more complex their tasks will be, and the more diversified they will be. The links between the different parts of the service will be more or less strong according to the situation.

Other archives, public or private: in this category can be grouped different institutions which may vary with the economic and social context of the country: (a) archives of nationalized undertakings and State corporations or companies. Generally speaking, it is desirable that the laws establishing the latter should state that their archives are public, as these organizations play an important role in the application of governmental economic policy. It is recommended that they take on staff either seconded from and/or trained at the national archives to manage their archives services; (b) archives of other institutions of public interest; (c) private archives: the State should extend its supervision to economic archives (firms), religious archives, archives of associations, political parties and trade unions, and family archives. In so far as they concern the history of the country and may be considered to form part of the national heritage, they should be listed and protected without their natural owners having to give up any of their rights over them. But those who own them ought not to be able to dispose of them (by destruction, dispersal, sale or export) without the authorization of the national archives. In certain cases the archives may purchase them or acquire them as a deposit or as a gift. At the very least the archives will propose that they be classified and listed for the purpose of microfilming.

I.2.3   FINANCING

A national archives service is a public service financed, for the main part, from the national budget. Two types of expenditure are incurred by archives services: ordinary expenditure, covered by the annual operating budgets of government departments, and extraordinary expenditure on equipment or development, covered by the plan. The need for archives services to use modern management techniques, especially in the matter of accounting, cannot be overstressed. Here, indifference and ignorance are often the rule.

Analytical accounting and the calculation of the amortization of materials and of the cost/benefit of activities should be part of normal practice.

1.2.3.1   *The archives budget*

The archives budget covers both operating costs and minor investment expenditure. Once extraordinary funds for archives development and equipment have been received, an increase in the budget for the new activities and the new requirements will have to be obtained from the parent authority.

Budgetary expenditure covers the operating costs of the service and expenditure on its activities.

1.2.3.1.1 *Operating costs*

These are sometimes called irreducible expenses, as they are unavoidable and are not liable to any great variation from one year to the next. They consist of: staff expenditure, upkeep and operating costs of buildings and equipment, internal expenses, taxes and dues of various kinds.

Staff expenditure. Expenditure on salaries represents the largest part of the budget, between three-fifths and four-fifths of the total. It comprises the salaries of the different categories of staff, including allowances, bonuses, overtime, etc., and also any contracts for expert services and for special and temporary work.

It will sometimes be possible to have outside help, from ministries in the case of staff for intermediate repositories and from local authorities in the case of local repositories, and to take advantage of the aid of voluntary workers, or use prisoners for instance.

In the developing countries, there is, as a rule, a proportionally larger staff than in the developed countries, but as their salaries are lower they account for a smaller proportion of the budget (three-fifths).

Upkeep and operating costs of buildings and equipment. Building expenses are of two kinds: maintenance and restoration of public buildings assigned for the use of the archives service and rental of buildings to cope with the growth of archives. Apart from maintenance proper, upkeep includes air conditioning, heating, water, electricity, cleaning, goods-lifts, painting, parks and gardens, enclosures, sheltered areas, etc.

It is also advisable to have the maintenance of the complex machines used in the workshops done under contract.

This expenditure may be wholly or partially covered by various other general budgets (for public buildings, etc.) depending on administrative circumstances. The proportion of the budget allocated to it may therefore vary considerably (2 to 30 per cent).

Taxes and dues. The archives will often have to pay certain dues or taxes, to local authorities in particular.

Internal expenses. Internal expenses (emergency repairs, simple electrical repairs, service vehicles, uniforms, etc.) cover minor day-to-day expenses, which may, however, add up to a considerable sum (5 to 10 per cent).

1.2.3.1.2 *Expenses relating to archives work*[1]

Office supplies. These include all the expenses incurred by the archives considered as a government department. They will vary a great deal in accordance with the country's administrative organization. In certain cases they may be wholly or partially covered by other budgets (central supply store, for instance); this is why the proportion of these expenses may vary between 1 and 30 per cent.

Staff. Staff expenses arise in the execution of archives work proper (they are generally coupled with salary expenses); they include travelling and training expenses.

Allowance must be made in the archives budget for travelling expenses as follows: inspection of local services, visits by local officers to the directorate, participation in regional work conferences and in national and international congresses, intercommunication between a repository and its branches, inspection of archives of administrative offices (departmental records), etc. This item, which is generally small, could be increased if various forms of aid were available.

Pre- and in-service training expenses have become a necessity today. This portion of staff expenses will increase fairly quickly in the future with the foreseeable spread of career-long training. In certain cases, a part of these expenses may be provided for in

---

1. The percentages mentioned in this section are calculated solely on the basis of expenditure relating to archives work. The reason for this is that it was difficult to obtain meaningful figures by considering the budget as a whole; operating costs (section 1.2.3.1.1) account for too large and above all too variable a part.

other budgets (e.g. of a Department of Education or a Civil Service Department).

Material for the upkeep of the archives. In the upkeep of the archives, everything depends on the initial choice made with regard to means of preservation: the use of full jacket boxes, folders, straps, string, etc. A small sum is usually set aside for this item, which is important with regard to the preservation of documents; it should be much higher if documents are to be kept in satisfactory condition.

Conveyance and transfer of documents. Depending on circumstances, expenses for the conveyance and transfer of archive holdings are borne to a greater or lesser extent by the archives service.

The problem of the transmission of documents to other repositories demands some attention today, and the growth of this pratice sometimes constitutes a heavy burden for the archives services, not to mention the dangers to which the documents are exposed. Perhaps it should be restricted by means of appropriate rules (establishment of a quota, the quality and importance of the research concerned, etc.).

Acquisitions. This includes both the acquisition of documents by purchase and the acquisition of reference works.

Even if one is of the opinion that archives services should be concerned with papers of public interest only, there exist private papers belonging to men in public life, to give only one example, which the archives should try to acquire. The archives should be granted an allocation in order to fill gaps in the national archives when papers come up for sale, or in order to acquire microfilms corresponding to gaps. Moreover, allowance will have to be made in the legislation for certain exceptional contingencies, and special exchequer credits and subventions from private foundations or associations will have to be provided for.

Then again, the setting up of a library unit is a necessity if one is to keep up to date with advances in historical work (books and reviews) and acquire reference works, publications of texts, etc., relating to the archives preserved. Lastly, it will be necessary to have access to the main works and periodicals relating to the archival field and to be able to obtain the technical publications that the workshops require. An adequate sum should be provided for this, so that the archives staff can keep on steadily adding to its knowledge.

Operation of workshop. Expenditure on this will to a large extent be dependent on the part these workshops play in each archives service, for it is this which determines expenditure on supplies and materials (the purchase of sundries and 'expendables' should often be included). Similarly, the relative sum allocated to each workshop will depend on the specific requirements of each repository. In view of the present-day needs for preservation, along with the development of modern techniques, these expenses can be expected to increase rapidly, and may constitute as much as 30 per cent of expenditure on archives work.

Publications and exhibitions. Part of the work produced in a national archives service should be published since its purpose is to facilitate research. Such work comprises: reports on archives work (mentioning the state of progress in sorting operations, new finding aids and research tools, new accessions); lists and inventories relating to archive groups open to inspection; guide to source materials or research in specific subject fields; publication of important texts; tables and indexes for certain categories of documents and lists; professional and technical reviews and bulletins.

If the service possesses offset printing equipment, a large part of these publications may be undertaken by the archives service itself. However, funds should always be provided for printing work that has to be carried out elsewhere.

Similarly, there should be an annual allocation for activities aimed at the general public: the running of an educational service, temporary exhibitions, etc.

Computer applications. Finally, today, steps should be taken to obtain funds enabling archives services, like everyone else, to have access to the new facilities provided by computer technology. To deprive archives of this possibility would be like condemning them to death. Computerization is undoubtedly the only way in which the future needs of intermediate archives work and historical research can be met.

1.2.3.1.3   *Equipment and buildings*

There are two kinds of expenditure: first of all, an annual allocation needs to be obtained for the purpose of acquiring new items required (office furniture, shelving, machines for the workshops, vehicles, etc.). These annual allocations provide the means of obtaining replacements for old stock. But if there is no amortization plan they are often insufficient, so that expensive repair work must be carried out and out-of-date and unsuitable equipment must continue to be used.

Second, and above all, there are the expenses arising out of the construction of buildings. Such construction work involves large sums of money and calls for special allocations by the government (general construction budget for public buildings, decree authorizing the implementation of a long-term programme, etc.) and in certain cases allocations by local authorities. It is to be noted that capital investment of this kind must be detached in the plan since it is closely linked to its implementation.

But apart from the archives budget there may be other means of financing.

1.2.3.2 *Other resources*

As we have just seen, archives services may be partially financed from other budgets and may even have their own extra-budgetary resources.

1.2.3.2.1 *Extra-budgetary resources*
There are several types of resources, differing according to the country; they are: registration fee for searchers (rarely); certified copies of various documents and certificates for legal purposes, for which a charge may be made; subvention for scholarly research, or for research undertaken officially for the administration, for university institutes and private research workers; sale of rights of reproduction (copyright) of documents cited in publications; sale of archives publications (books, microfilms, microfiches); charges for entrance to exhibitions, sale of catalogues, etc.; rental for microfilms loaned.

The sums obtained in this way are generally paid into the treasury. It is to be hoped that at least some of this money will be returned to the archives and be added to their budgetary allocation, rather than being deducted from it (as is sometimes the case), since the operating budget of the service is intended to cover its own needs and not those of other parties or bodies.

1.2.3.2.2 *Budgets of other departments*
We have already referred to these above; particular mention should be made of those of the education department and of whichever

civil service department is responsible for training grants and grants for courses, i.e. ministries, in connexion with intermediate archive operations; local authorities, in connexion with local repositories.

1.2.3.2.3 *Subventions from various bodies*
These bodies include public corporations and private companies, associations or individuals providing aid in the form of foundations, grants, gifts of equipment, assistance for publications, etc.

It is always advisable to encourage voluntary aid, particularly by establishing societies such as 'Friends of the Archives'.

1.2.3.2.4 *International aid (Unesco, multilateral or bilateral)*
International aid in the form of the services of experts, scholarships for training and gifts of machines. Requests for such aid should be fully substantiated.

1.2.3.2.5 *Joint operations*
In the event of joint operations with other institutions (for instance national museums and libraries) financing will be jointly ensured by the parties concerned.

The plan will therefore have to be drawn up with the participation of all the departments concerned: one of the chief functions of the superior archives council will be to plan operations so that the goals aimed at are commensurate with the funds that beneficiaries are really prepared to provide.

1.2.4   STAFF

The problem of staff is of crucial importance: unless the staff is skilled and sufficiently large, projects, funds and decisions will all be to no avail. The vitality of a service depends upon the people who work in it.

The plan should make provision for the recruitment and training of staff in accordance with the anticipated development of archives services. This training plan will set forth for each category of staff: (a) the number of staff to be trained, according to a definite time-table; (b) the establishments to be made responsible for the training, and/or the courses which will be organized for the training of each category.

It is extremely difficult to establish standards for the recruitment of the different categories. The number of staff has to be calculated in terms of the work to be carried out and the material and human potential of the country; this means that the number of staff desirable will not necessarily be the same for every country, even if the same amount of work is to be done.

Two factors are also to be considered in drawing up the recruitment plan: the availability of manpower on the labour market and its level of qualification; if the staff is too small, the savings made will be illusory, for an archives service which is hampered through lack of manpower will be unable to perform its function.

Archives development policy is bound up with staff policy. The latter should have three goals, which should be taken into account in any regulations concerning the archives staff. They are:

Recruiting and training skilled staff. The specific character of the archivist's skills should be emphasized, and it should be borne in mind that these skills represent an exceptional combination of intellectual and technical abilities.

Arranging for the staff to have their proper place in the government service, in accordance with their qualifications. This will be a touchstone of the government's real intention to recruit hard-working staff who will remain in the service and to promote an archives policy. The situation and career prospects offered should be such as to attract capable candidates. Otherwise, staff members will leave the archives service and enter other departments or the private sector.

Arranging for internal advancement at every level. As archives services can be expected to grow, it is important that staff be given the chance of promotion to a higher grade. All those who so desire and who have the necessary abilities should be able, by their efforts, to improve their qualifications, their intellectual capacity, their income and their social situation. This is an important aspect of individual dignity and freedom today.

Only a few years ago, the staff of an archives service was composed essentially of two quite distinct categories. On the one hand there were the attendants and storemen, who were responsible for material tasks, and on the other there were the university-trained archivists, who carried out archives and administrative work and also material tasks. Staffs were accordingly small.

The growth of archives today and the increasingly varied nature of the work to be carried out have resulted in the emergence of specialized staff in an intermediate category:

Archivist-technicians (non-university trained) for certain aspects of archives work and, nowadays, computer technicians.

Administrative staff for the day-to-day management of the service.

Technical staff and workmen required for the workshops for restoration and binding and microfilm and photography operations which have been recently established and are being developed.

Staff are nowadays divided into two major groups, with different tasks: (a) a group composed of persons responsible for carrying out traditional archives work; (b) a group of officials of various categories whose work is concerned with the day-to-day management of the archives service, a performance of its role as an administrative department.

The first group may be sub-divided into three categories according to the different types and different levels of work which they have to carry out. Thus:

Graduate professional staff (university level), responsible for the management of the repositories and the organization of the services. They are responsible for the reception, weeding and sorting of documents and for lists and publications. They are also responsible for the training and supervision of their colleagues. Steps should be taken to ensure that the instruments of research enable them to obtain university qualifications in order to gain recognition for the intellectual character of this work.

Intermediate or subprofessional staff (secondary school level), responsible for archives work (preparation and execution of transfers, weeding, sorting, classification and analysis) under the direction of the professional archivists.

Storeroom staff, attendants and guards (trained in the archives service itself).

Generally speaking, it is reckoned that this group represents 60 per cent of staff numbers. The internal distribution of such staff varies considerably with the nature of the work and the level of training and qualifications required of each of these categories by the legislation in force in each country.

Training conditions vary very much from one country to another as do the administrative situations which result from them. Steps should be taken to lay down common standards for all countries.

The second group comprises staff employed in the workshops attached to the service and staff employed in the administration:

The workshop staff are specialized workers—binders, restorers, photographers, microfilmers, etc.

Staff employed in the administration include, office staff (secretaries, accountants, typists) and maintenance staff (caretakers, casual labourers, workmen). Lastly, arrangements should always be made for a person to be in charge of the upkeep and day-to-day repairs of archives equipment.

The way in which these different activities are distributed will vary considerably and will depend on decisions as to policy, the needs which are seen to exist and the resources obtained for each particular workshop.

I.2.5   ARCHIVES BUILDINGS
         AND EQUIPMENT

Once the principle of archives services has been agreed to, the government must accept the consequences, that is to say, it must work out a modern solution to the problem of archives by: the construction of suitable and functional buildings and the acquisition and application of new techniques.

The following points should, however, be considered: the equipment plan is the other crucial part of the archives development plan; it will therefore be necessary in fact to co-ordinate the training and recruitment plan with the equipment plan as far as possible; this equipment plan will obviously be affected considerably by the dimensions of the archives problem to be resolved, local conditions, etc.; most countries have had little experience of constructing and fitting out archives buildings; in such cases, those responsible for archives will always find it useful to obtain information from colleagues who have dealt with these problems for a long time.

This construction plan should cover the following: new buildings or the conversion of existing buildings, including fitting them out for use as archive repositories and, if need be, intermediate repositories; the fitting out of premises to be used for archives in administrative departments, the cost of which will naturally be borne by the departments concerned; in some cases, the establishment of workshops to be used jointly with other institutions.

Three points seem particularly worthy of attention: the constituent elements of an archives building and the necessary equipment; the material conditions for the preservation of documents (a major problem in tropical countries); the use of new techniques in the archives service (the management and destruction of papers is the major problem of the developed countries).

1.2.5.1   *The constituent elements of an archives building*

We give here a list of the main units to be included in the building plan (for details see Appendixes 4 and 5).

Administrative unit. Office of the director or chief officer, secretariat, typing room, offices of assistants.

Reception and processing unit. Room for taking delivery of transfers, room for the fumigation of documents (indispensable in tropical climates) and for the removal of dust, room for sorting and classifying, room for documents to be destroyed.

Storage unit. Storage (stack) areas set beside each other, separated from each other in order to provide better protection for the documents. Such an arrangement makes it possible for the building to be extended as requirements increase (see below).

Technical unit. Comprises all the workshops: restoration (Appendix 6), binding (Appendix 7), microfilm (Appendix 8), photography (Appendix 9), instant copying (Appendix 10), data processing. These workshops are fitted with all the special equipment needed for the preservation, safety and proper use of documents. For various reasons (climate, frequency of use of documents, etc.) these workshops are indispensable in all countries nowadays.

Reference (searchroom) unit. Entrance hall, reading room equipped with all the available tools for searching; possibly special apparatus for the reading of microfilm, use of tape-recorder or typewriter; where appropriate, an administrative documentation room containing adequate supplies of official publications, yearbooks and lists, and an exhibition and conference room.

Miscellaneous. Cloakrooms and washrooms, central air-conditioning unit, storeroom for supplies, garage, etc.

All these units will be housed in one or more buildings, but will be linked in such a way as to form a functional whole.

It is obvious that the architectural form chosen for such a project will depend on factors such as the size of the site, the lie of the land, its position in the town, building conditions, etc.

1.2.5.2   *The storage unit*

The preservation of documents is the primary task of the archives service. Moreover, it is the major problem in tropical countries, where a continuous struggle has to be waged to ensure the 'survival' of documents. The problems with which the storage unit has to deal are therefore complex ones.

A particular type of construction is necessary because of the volume and weight of archives and the fact that they are continually being added to. The standards applicable to archives buildings are well known. Likewise, allowance must be made for the different shapes and sizes of the documents, so as to provide exactly the conditions required for their preservation.

But the most important of all the factors which need to be observed in constructing the storage unit, is that of the climate and especially the microclimate (sun, heat, humidity and pollution of the air). Air conditioning may seem to be the solution to all these problems, but the safety of the documents must not depend on this alone; on the one hand, breakdowns are always possible, and on the other permanent air conditioning entails extremely high running costs. For this reason the whole building should be planned so as to create a favourable microclimate: the building should be suitably designed and positioned (in relation to the sun and wind), constructed on piles or embedded in the earth, with appropriately positioned doors and windows; waterproof and isothermic materials or devices, filtering glass, etc., should be used.

Documents are just as likely to suffer from significant variations in conditions as from conditions that are harmful in themselves. It is therefore important to create as stable an environment as possible.

For paper, the conditions required are: a temperature of 18–25° C and a relative humidity of 45 to 55 per cent. For films the same conditions apply (20° C and relative humidity of 50 per cent). In addition, provision must be made for air circulation and a continuous supply of fresh air in the storerooms and, where necessary, for the cleanliness of the air (absence of dust—which is liable to soil the documents, and may be harmful or toxic—microbes and mildew).

Appropriate arrangements will therefore have to be made according to the climate. In cold countries, heating is required; humidification also will probably be necessary in order to avoid the destruction of cellulose matter (papers, films, etc.) through too dry an atmosphere. In temperate countries, climatic conditions are generally favourable (apart from seasonal variations). An air-filtering system will nevertheless be desirable to combat industrial and urban atmospheric pollution. In tropical countries, the problem is more complicated; some areas are dry others humid.

In dry regions it will be necessary, according to circumstances, to provide humidifiers during the dry season and to use either portable dehumidifiers or silica gel (adequate to achieve a relative humidity lower than 70 per cent) during the rainy season. In order to avoid excessive variations in the temperature, air conditioning could be used during certain seasons and/or at certain times of the day.

But it is the humid regions which present the most problems. Besides the disadvantages of heat there are those arising from a prevailing high humidity, which is likely to cause the disintegration of paper and especially the proliferation of mildew and insects. Permanent air conditioning is, however, so costly that a distinction should be drawn between intermediate repositories and permanent repositories.

The intermediate repositories will house documents that are to be destroyed after varying periods (at least 90 per cent of the total). Air conditioning will not be necessary, but dehumidifiers could be used (especially in a building of the traditional type).

Documents which are to be preserved indefinitely will be kept in the archive repositories. Air conditioning will therefore be necessary, but the cost of this should be kept to a strict minimum (to lower the cost even further, hand-operated compact mobile shelving could be used in order to reduce the volume of air to be conditioned).

1.2.5.3   *The use of new automation (computer) techniques*

Two major problems already confront archives services and will become even more acute, especially in the most advanced countries. These problems are: the control of transfer operations and the management of intermediate repositories (records centres); the control of information and the development of research. We must take steps at once to find a solution to these problems.

The general trend of contemporary civilization is such that government departments are producing more and more documents. Consequently, archives services are bound to receive more and more transfers from departments (corresponding each year to kilometres of shelving and hundreds of thousands of individual items).

However, as only a small proportion of these transfers are to be preserved indefinitely, it will be necessary, at the same time, to embark on thousands of operations for the destruction of documents not worth keeping. What complicates these relatively simple operations is the fact that such documents become ripe for destruction within shorter or longer periods of time, depending on their nature.

It seems clear that only appropriate computerized techniques, not unlike those used for stock control, are capable of mastering this enormous mass of papers which must be available for use on request, but which are expensive to preserve when they no longer serve any purpose.

Computerized control over documents as soon as they are transferred to an intermediate repository can be easily achieved if the transfer schedule is drawn up in what is in fact the traditional form: reference number of each item (transfer code), description of contents or keywords, destruction date, conditions of access, location in the storerooms (stacks). Any simple item, once defined in this way, can be managed by a computer. According to the instructions received, it will or will not produce the document for inspection in response to a particular request, will establish its destruction schedule or its transfer docket for archival accessing when the time comes, etc. Similarly, contacts with each administrative department can be programmed in accordance with the appropriate timetable. Lastly, it will be possible to devise schemes for classifying material which is to be kept permanently and, when conditions governing access have been fulfilled, to arrange for the classes of documents concerned to be entered automatically in computer memories, card-indexes, indexes, tables, etc.

To say that we have entered the information era is commonplace today. We must be able to retrieve information speedily, if it is to be really useful, and the search must be exhaustive if the information is to be complete. More than ever, archives services have a role to play here, and they will be all the better equipped to play it with the help of computerized systems which will enable them to review large quantities of documents in a short space of time. What is more, such a system makes it possible to replace the make-shift system regulating the length of time that must elapse before documents are made accessible to the public by a more flexible system, adapted (on the basis of schedules to be determined) to each category of documents and in some cases the status of the person making the request. In this way, general or individual catalogues and lists can be issued regularly, and searches will be punctually and immediately carried out.

No doubt the most urgent and most important task for archives services today is to prepare for the introduction of these techniques; and research on archival methodology should be chiefly centred on this field.

The financial problems entailed should not constitute a barrier to the need for modernization; with it, one is sure of obtaining documents, and both time and money are saved, which more than justifies any sacrifices made.

In order to constitute, co-ordinate and put into effect these very different elements, all of which are necessary if a modern archives service is to be achieved, a planning method is necessary.

2 Machinery for formulating a national archives plan and procedures for its implementation

In this second chapter, we shall consider how the basic infrastructure should be set up and used to the best advantage, in other words how some of the problems facing the community can be tackled at both the structural and the functional level. In this way we shall discern logical and chronological order for the procedures that have to be set in motion and brought to a successful conclusion. To begin with, however, careful consideration has to be given to the machinery by which the plan is formulated. The decision to formulate a plan is not taken by the national archives, but once that decision has been taken, the national archives become responsible for its application.

2.1 The machinery of plan formulation

It is worth repeating that any form of planning is a complex and difficult undertaking because it involves using the present situation as a basis for a realistic approach to a future situation, which does not yet exist.

The two basic aspects of archives planning are: (a) the formulation of development plans for the national infrastructures required for the archives; (b) the concomitant programming of the activities of national archives services.

The first item to be considered is the point of departure. In practice, the preparation of national archives plans involves dealing with one of a number of situations which may differ significantly as far as the organization and administrative status of the service is concerned. In Africa, for instance, the point of departure for the organization and development of the plan often consists of an old accumulation of archives preserved more or less haphazardly, such as official papers from the office of the governor of the territory during the colonial period. Hence the execution of the plan is based on this initial nucleus and, above all, on the goodwill of the parent department responsible, and the extent to which it can really exercise its powers. The interdepartmental character of archives activities should be stressed as an argument in favour of the super- visory (parent) authority being the department likely to enjoy most influence within the government, such as the cabinet office or the prime minister's office.

For archives, however neglected they may be, are to be found everywhere, in all government departments and administrative centres. What is lacking is an appropriate organization for the preservation of archives at the national level.

In most cases, governments have long ago issued regulations for the preservation of departmental archives, and have even appointed staff for the purpose. But present-day political and/or economic development has been such that it has not always been possible to see that the development of archives kept pace with it, or even to maintain the standard reached, with the result that regulations have fallen into abeyance and premises have been unattended and become untidy, infested with vermin and dirty. Transfers to the archives have been discontinued, and in some cases vandalism and looting have occurred. Any semblance of organization has virtually disappeared.

In other instances, an archives service may actually exist and have a proper organizational structure, but it has run down, and is making no impact. The accommodation may be overcrowded with documents and unsuited to their purpose, the staff not properly qualified, and regulations unapplied or inapplicable owing to the lack of means. The service has remained at the embryonic stage and cannot keep pace with the growth of the administration.

Lastly, there are countries where proper archives services exist, but need to be further developed. In such instances, laws and regulations have been promulgated and are applied, there is an adequate number of trained personnel, the premises are suitable, and transfers and consultations are part of the daily routine. However, these conventionally operated repositories need to be transformed into modern archives services; in other words, they must be fitted out with the latest equipment, have highly qualified staff, and employ the most efficient methods if they are to cope with the tasks facing archives today and those of the future.

No attempt has been made in the following pages to examine each problem in turn under the three main headings suggested above—that would have made the study too prolix and complicated. Instead, the problems involved are tackled at their most elementary level, on the principle that those who can grasp more complex ideas can also grasp the simpler ones.

2.1.1   RELATIONSHIP TO THE PLANNING
OF INSTITUTIONS OPERATING
IN APPARENTLY
ALLIED PROFESSIONAL FIELDS

This subject calls for three preliminary observations:

The problem is primarily one of the size of the service and the volume of work involved. In cases where the archives are voluminous, there should be material facilities and personnel available to form a complete technical unit, although these may be only just adequate to meet requirements. The real problem arises with small archives, where there is a risk of specialized and expensive staff and equipment not being used to the full.

What should be the nature of the relationship between such institutions? Appearances can be misleading. Archives, libraries, museums and documentation centres may have a good many points of cultural interest in common, but that should not blind us to the fact that they are fundamentally different in nature and purpose. While libraries are concerned with intellectual life and museums with civilization and taste, and documentation centres are usually geared to immediate and clearly defined tangible objectives, archives have a function to fulfil in the working of society. That is why there can be no question of integration, or of competition either. Instead, there should be co-operation on common problems, so that limited resources can be pooled in such a way that all concerned, provided they derive benefit from such co-operation, can solve their own specific problems. In Japan, for example, archives and libraries have so far been run jointly as a single institution, but the current thinking is towards splitting them into two separate entities.

It follows that areas of common interest will be confined to sectors that are suitable from the technical standpoint or because of considerations of efficiency or size. In other words, co-operation is more likely to be of value in small countries with limited resources and above all at the local level.

The main areas involved are: training of personnel; sharing of certain technical facilities; sharing of work connected with legal deposit; extra-mural activities such as the organization of exhibitions, etc.

Personnel training is the first area in which co-operation can be contemplated. Irrespective of whether a national or regional training school is to be opened, it is advisable to set up only one establishment, with specialized sections. This will make for savings in both investment and administrative costs and for increased efficiency in terms of actual training, because it will be easier to recruit highly qualified teaching staff and to organize joint courses for all sections as well as specialized classes. Furthermore, it is always possible for students who may prove to have taken the wrong course to change to another.

A parallel training scheme would also make it possible to harmonize career structures and professional codes.

There is likewise scope for co-operation in the technical field. This does not apply to actual preservation, where the proposition becomes impracticable owing to the different natures and requirements of the objects preserved in archives, libraries, documentation centres and museums; but it does apply to the activities carried out in technical workshops, such as restoration, bookbinding, microfilming, photography, reprography and multicopying.

The restoration of documents is an important aspect of archives preservation, and very sophisticated techniques requiring great skill are used for unique documents, the use of such techniques being justified precisely because they are unique. The needs of libraries are different: a simple repair job is often adequate, except in the case of a very rare or very ancient book, or, more often, books showing signs of wear and tear are simply replaced. With a few exceptions, such as national libraries, the function of such establishments is to use books rather than to preserve them. This is even more true of documentation centres, which assemble documentation for clearly defined purposes dictated by current events.

Although bookbinding is not one of the main tasks in archives services, care should be devoted to it, as the volumes to be bound are most often unique, whereas bookbinding in libraries is usually done in order to extend the time during which books can be used intensively; it is utilitarian in character. The problem scarcely arises in documentation centres.

Microfilming is an area where there are many more features in common, although the trend is towards filming archives documents on 35-mm reels, whereas books and articles are reproduced on microfiches. This subject is still very much open to debate, and the outcome depends to a not inconsiderable extent on the quality of the films produced and the equipment used. There is no doubt that microfiches will eventually come to be used in archives.

Documentation centres are heavier consumers of photography than they are producers, and this also applies to microfilm. Libraries have little occasion to use photographic records, but archives have to rely on them to a greater extent, especially when they are called upon to play a part in preserving the country's heritage of monuments.

By contrast, reprography is universally used, whether for direct copying purposes such as reproducing documents or books, for copying articles, statistics, official texts and so on, or for the duplication of indexes, catalogues, information or liaison bulletins, readers' cards or sundry working documents. However, a very wide variety of reprographic equipment is available, at very varied prices, and it is open to question whether several items of equipment, each adapted to a specific requirement, would not be more effective than a single shared installation which, although highly perfected, may prove more unwieldy and slower in the long run. Here again, there is no hard and fast rule, and everything will depend on the local situation.

Data processing by computer may prove to be a very fertile area for co-operation, firstly out of sheer necessity, because the costs involved are so high that several users generally have to combine to share the burden, and secondly because the capacity and scope offered by data processing systems are such that they have to be assigned tasks of sufficient magnitude to justify the capital outlay. This seems to be the right answer to the problem posed by union catalogues for reference data banks, whether these are specialized or not.

In any event, it is always a good thing for these different institutions not only to be aware of each other's existence but also to make a point of co-operating by sharing joint exhibition halls, holding joint conferences and so on.

The fact is that these services are expected to fulfil functions that are often very closely related, although the means they use are quite different. While the pooling of technical facilities may, in theory, do some good, a much more reliable way of ensuring swifter progress for all the institutions concerned would be for them to undertake joint research, compare experiences, compile union catalogues and indexes and apportion areas of responsibility in their policies for securing new acquisitions and building up their collections.

The problem of the legal-deposit system may be taken as an illustration of this assertion. Every country has a legal deposit system applying to the entire graphic arts output within its territory. Depending on the circumstances, the archives, libraries or some other government department are responsible for legal deposit. Such deposit covers all or part of the printed material produced, including books and periodicals as well as maps, posters and pamphlets, records, films and so on, but virtually none of the printed material produced by government departments is covered.

It might be possible to draft legislation stipulating that all graphic arts productions must be deposited and that works must be allocated thus: libraries would receive creative works and works of imagination or research, while archives would enjoy the right of legal deposit of government publications, including all publications, whether official or not, issued by public or private institutions or individuals in the performance of their functions—in short, those documents of which, by definition, archives are constituted. Obviously, a jointly-administered central organization would be needed to prevent anything from slipping through the net.

In conclusion, it can be said that the kind of co-operation we are thinking of would be more functional than structural. The advisability of structural co-operation depends on factors of size and volume of work. All these institutions, however, have a part to play in providing information, albeit in different ways.

2.1.2   POSSIBLE ARRANGEMENTS—
          DEFINITION OF STEP-BY-STEP OBJECTIVES

In drawing up a plan that is capable of being implemented, due regard has to be paid to the existing situation in the archives service and to the political, administrative and economic context. The idea is to carry out an indicative planning exercise, in other words to evolve a system gathering all the relevant factors into a coherent whole and laying down a programme for future development that can be said to be natural and organic. The system must be global, and all parts of it must be integrated, but it must also be flexible enough for those who wish to apply it to be able to adapt it to their own situation.

The complexity of planning arises out of two of its fundamental characteristics:

First, the fact has to be acknowledged that there is no such thing as perfect organization. While the service is growing, it will be perpetually subject to reorganization. The teams and the allocation of tasks decided upon at a given time will have to be constantly reviewed, so that they are capable of coping with the situation at all times. Reorganization, therefore, is not a feature or a stage of the plan, it is an integral part of its implementation.

Second, several quite distinct activities, all of which are directed towards the same objectives and have repercussions upon each other, have to be co-ordinated. These activities fall into two main categories: internal action relating to structural organization, i.e. the setting up of the necessary means of action; external action relating to tasks and functions, i.e. the application of these means in order to attain the objectives.

Chief among these are the following: (a) determination of the purposes of the archives service and definition of the objectives that are dictated by such purposes; (b) definition of possible objectives; (c) drawing-up of a schedule of operations in order of priority; (d) calculation of the capital investment required in the light of the resources known to be available; (e) identification of budgetary resources, which frequently come from several sources; (f) training of officials responsible for implementing the plan; (g) drafting of special laws and regulations; (h) systematic and constant study of the archive problems arising from the production of public papers at all levels of government service; (i) programming of classification and inventorying activities.

2.1.3   CONDITIONS GOVERNING THE PREPARATION
         AND IMPLEMENTATION OF THE PLAN

2.1.3.1   *The need for a resolute and decisive approach*

No progress can be made unless the desire for progress exists; and
the desire will only appear when a country that does not possess a
modern archives system becomes conscious of the need for one, faces
up to the problem and decides to solve it. This initial act of will is of
prime importance, especially if the supervising (parent) authority
is the head of state or if the initiative comes from the ministry of
finance, for example.

International organizations such as Unesco and the International
Council on Archives can play an important role in creating a
climate of awareness and even in promoting the decision-making
process by taking action within their terms of reference, for example
by dispatching missions to different regions of the world to examine
the situation and assess the problems raised by the lack of archives.

The role of the universities must also be mentioned. Their institutes and centres for research on historical, legal, economic and
other subjects can alert public opinion to the importance of archives,
and may also be able to take effective action through ministries of
education. Similarly, the ministry of foreign affairs can stress the
advantages the country would derive from attracting foreign
research workers rather than discouraging them. It would be a
mistake to disregard this form of international influence.

Once the need for an archives policy has been realized, it may
prove useful to take action in favour of the archives service as part
of a more far-reaching operation which would help to attain its
objectives, such as the launching of a development plan or an
administrative reform programme.

While governments are often favourably disposed to the idea of
having an archives service, it is important to ensure that their
goodwill does not result in the service becoming simply a historical
research institute. The priority that governments accord to archives
in their development plans should be a useful pointer and should
make it possible to gauge their real intentions. This should be one
of the main criteria governing external aid grants, for example for
pilot projects, as well as one of the terms of the unwritten contract
between a given country and any international organization.

2.1.3.2   *The body responsible for planning*
           and the work of the official in charge of the project

Once the decision to proceed has been taken at the top level, a high-ranking official, such as the secretary of the cabinet office, should be made responsible for the setting up of the national archives. His mission will be of a threefold nature:

He will have to recruit the future animator (driving force) of the archives project and make arrangements for him to be trained without delay (in the country and abroad). The choice of the future animator is crucial for the success of the undertaking will depend on his enthusiasm and ability.

He will have to set up a committee, composed of senior officials from the principal ministries, to arouse interest in the problem of archives. This committee should be established quite quickly, and can form a fairly powerful pressure group acting on public departments and government. It will have a contribution to make when the plan is being drafted.

He will have to draft the outline plan. The decision having been taken to modernize the archives service, it is important to programme the modernization process in terms of both time and space.

The official responsible for setting up the archives service should then draw up a preliminary draft of the plan, the procedure being of a type suggested below. This preliminary draft should be presented to the committee for consideration and comment. The draft can then be put in its definitive form and referred to the ministry of planning for inclusion in the national development plan. Further improvements or changes may well have to be made at this stage.

As action is rarely taken if it is not provided for in the national development plan, and then with great difficulty, the plan should be carefully studied with a view to getting as much benefit from it as possible. On the other hand, there is a greater chance of winning acceptance for a particular point of view if the development plan is at the preparatory stage.

If a proper forecast is to be produced, however, some facts and figures have to be collected, and the authority in charge will need to organize and carry out a preliminary survey for that purpose.

2.1.4   GENERAL SURVEY
         (DURATION: APPROXIMATELY
         ONE YEAR)

The plan has to be designed to cater for established and foreseeable requirements, and those requirements have accordingly to be determined. Once they are known, they can be used as a basis for calculating the size of the buildings that will have to be put up or to be assigned to the archives service, the number of personnel to be recruited, the size of the workshops to be fitted out and so on.

The preliminary survey should be of a general nature. It should cover all government offices throughout the country. The decision to conduct the survey should therefore be taken at the highest level, so that no department can argue that it has no need to reply. The survey should cover all levels of the administration. If necessary, the official responsible for setting up the archives service can seek advice from a team composed of officers from a number of different departments and who have had considerable experience in the organization and methods branch of administration. The official government yearbook should be taken as the basic document for selecting the people to whom the survey should be sent. The bureau or department can be considered as the basic administrative cell[1] and, as such, has its own set of archives. Hence the survey should reach that level.

The first over-all survey should take the form of a very general written questionnaire designed to provide information for an initial assessment of the following: (a) the state of preservation of the archives and the conditions of storage (premises and personnel); (b) the quantity of documents kept in the service (in terms of the number of linear metres of shelving filled and the number of files); (c) the volume and nature of the documents that may be eliminated at once or transferred to the national archives.

Any survey involves an element of chance, especially when it is conducted by circular letter, as it must necessarily be in this case. That is why it is short. Care should be taken to overlook as few

---

1. The administrative cell is the smallest administrative unit. It has an identity in the form of a set of initials, and its title will often indicate its position in the hierarchy and its functions. It also has an autonomous existence and certain resources, including a budgetary appropriation.

departments as possible when the list of addresses is being drawn up, and hierarchical protocol should be observed to the maximum extent.

In addition, a press and radio campaign should be launched—an 'archives week' might be organized, for example—to explain why the survey is being conducted and how the questionnaire should be completed. Information and briefing sessions could also be organized in each ministry. If more substantial resources are available, it will be advisable to set up survey teams composed of students who have been given prior training in the archives service. Further replies can be obtained if these teams are sent out with a more detailed questionnaire, like the example given in Appendix 11, and are equipped with tape-recorders.

Depending on what means are used to conduct the survey, it is possible to limit rigorously the number of unresponsive departments and to guard against vague or uninformative answers which will serve no purpose. The response to the questionnaire will show that there are conscientious officials and, above all, keen civil servants at all levels who take an interest in archives. At a later stage, contact should be made with these people, with a view to establishing the links that can be so useful when different tasks have to be performed by the archives service and the government.

No matter how incomplete the answers may be, they will at least constitute a sample from which an over-all picture can be built up, the situation assessed and the magnitude of the problem estimated, by providing data on the following: the immediate and short-term archive requirements of government offices; the volume of documentation which will have to be transferred as quickly as possible to save it from destruction and ensure its permanent preservation; the annuel increase per department and the over-all increase (in linear metres or feet); the annual document output of each department; the percentage of documents that can be eliminated from each department and the over-all quantity (in linear metres or feet); the number of transfers expected and the volume of material the archives service will have to deal with every year.

Once these estimates have been made, the long-term plan can be drafted in outline.

2.1.5   THE PLANS

In actual fact, any archives plan will be composed of three separate plans, varying in their degree of precision: the long-term plan, the medium-term plan and the short-term plan.

2.1.5.1   *The long-term plan*
            (preparation and selection of indicative plans
            for a period of ten to fifteen years)

This is an indicative plan which can be amended in the course of implementation in accordance with the requirements of the moment. It should be submitted for consideration to the advisory committee and, after the supervising authority has given its assent, it should be finalized in collaboration with the ministry of planning. This plan must be evaluated in terms of the capital investment required and the running costs, if it is to have any meaning.

The long-term plan is a forecaster's tool. It should consist of sections dealing with the following: organization of the national archives system, with an account based on the results of the survey, of the complete network it is intended to establish; laws that will have to be promulgated and subsequently amended as the plan is implemented; regulations that will be needed to ensure application of the laws and the attainment of the objectives laid down; personnel requirements, with a programme of recruitment and training for all categories and for the complete system of national and subordinate archives; setting-up of registries for current records in national and local government departments; construction, reconstruction or structural redesigning of buildings; fitting-out of premises; removal of documents to intermediate repositories, elimination of unwanted documents, transfers to repositories; disinfection and restoration programme; microfilming programme; classification and inventorying programme; programme for the automation of archives documentation, the control of accessions, for the implementing of records management and disposal procedures including intermediate storage, and for the archives service in general; archives research and publication programme; collection of copies of source material from other countries; budgetary requirements for each further stage.

2.1.5.2   *The medium-term plan*
          (duration: three to six years
          depending on the period covered
          by the national development plan)

This plan must be worked out in advance, as a period varying from three years to at least one year before the development plan commences is needed to complete the procedures for including any particular activity.

This plan is much more detailed than the long-term plan; it should be based on the national development plan and form an integral part of it. The section headings are the same as for the long-term plan. The capital investment and operating budgets needed to attain the objectives laid down are indicated. The importance attached to archives as a national priority will be reflected in the financial outlay the authorities are prepared to make for archives.

2.1.5.3   *Short-term plan (duration: up to two years)*

This plan is a year's programme of work for the directorate of archives. The archives receive an annual allocation to implement the plan, the aim being to use this sum to attain the objectives as far as possible.

Very often, however, the sums anticipated are not made available owing to some change in the economic or political situation. Allocation of funds may be affected by a drop in income as compared with forecasts, while political decisions may result in the archives being relegated to a lower position in the list of priorities. The funds made available will depend on the determination and resourcefulness of the supervising parent authority.

When the archives plan has been completed, it must be printed and widely distributed in the government departments. It may be described in articles in the administrative journals published for all government departments. It should not be kept secret.

The basic document for implementation purposes is the medium-term plan.

2.2 Implementation of the plan

It is quite impossible to give a golden rule or magic formula for the implementation of the plan. The actual situations encountered differ too much for any single time-schedule to apply to all of them. What we suggest is a probable chronological sequence that is divided into phases or stages. A given stage is completed when a new structure activity or objective takes shape.

A stage is also a functional unit which can be executed in a period of time that will depend on prevailing circumstances. We consider it unrealistic to try to fit these activities into the restricted compass of the precise timing characteristic of the medium and short-term plans. It will also be noted that the first stages are concerned with activities that could be said to be of an internal or traditional character, whereas the subsequent stages open out on to external activities that are typical of modern archives services.

Such planning implies an order of priorities, which will be the same for all countries regardless of their level of development, and applies to two sets of tasks: functional tasks and, following on from them, structural tasks.

The functional tasks are as follows: salvage of archives in jeopardy; preservation of historical documents; records management; classification, inventorying and opening to inspection of documents.

Complementary priorities in the structural sector include the following: establishment of the national archives as an administrative entity; consolidation and development of existing machinery; beginning of document restoration work; preparatory work for drafting legislation, recruiting personnel, erecting buildings and installing equipment; establishment of working relations with the most important departments of central government and introduction of procedures for the management of current files; setting up of structures for intermediate repositories and finding premises for them; development of service to users; extension of the network to central and local government departments.

In such planning by objectives, the timing of the stages also allows for the continuation of activities that have already been begun and for the preparation of subsequent stages. The short-term objectives are combined to form broader medium-term objectives.

2.2.1 DEVELOPMENT OF EXISTING MACHINERY (AVERAGE DURATION: THREE YEARS)

2.2.1.1 *The establishment of the national archives*

The establishment—or more often the re-establishment—of the national archives marks the real start of practical action, in as much as, with it, the preparatory phase is superseded by the operational phase.

Preparations for this phase require a number of measures to be taken more or less simultaneously: the recruitment and training of the archives animator, who will be responsible for organizing the service. It is advisable to select a person with considerable drive, who is new to the profession. Ideally, he ought to be able to alternate between studying and spending periods working in archives, so as to become familiar with the work and size up the problems he will have to face.

During this running-in period, it may be considered advisable to ask for the assistance of one or more foreign experts to help with the survey, the training of the animator and similar tasks.

It will be for the official in charge of the reorganization of the national archives to request such assistance if he considers it advisable.

The expert can offer him the benefit of his experience and assist him in preparing and carrying out the first stages of the plan. Dual control is good training and also limits the risk of errors. Moreover, in the initial stages, it can help allay any feelings of despondency and solitude which may threaten to overwhelm the official responsible for the project.

When the national archives are established, the existing archives service and repository will usually be placed under the control of the new institution. This first component will be the means by which the service will begin to function.

2.2.1.2 *Reorganization and development of the national archives*

The national archives themselves constitute the first sector in which action must be taken. The aim in this next phase is to strengthen the existing structure. The service has to be radically changed and reorganized in quite a short period, and the next stage has to be prepared for.

The internal reorganization phase is a crucial one; in it, an instrument which has fallen into disuse has to be rehabilitated and continuity must be restored in the chain linking infrastructures to objectives. New means, however limited, will be used to lift the existing institutions out of the rut. In these circumstances, outside help can make all the difference, and the means of action available should be identified, given a new lease of life and exploited to the full.

As far as personnel is concerned, an endeavour should be made to dispense with the services of all incompetent or unnecessary employees and to engage competent officials to make up the full establishment. Staff training can then be considered. It will often be found that the best policy is to replace some the current staff, especially the older ones and those who are unwilling to be retrained or likely to resist any changes that would upset their routine.

Posts might well be found for them in sections dealing with government departments, since their length of service and wide range of acquaintances should make such contacts easy for them, when surveys and document transfers are being carried out.

A list of all the premises used by the service should be drawn up and advantage should be taken of the circumstances to obtain additional or more suitable premises. Any necessary repairs or conversion operations, for example providing drainage and an electricity supply, should be carried out. The premises should be cleaned out and made secure by fitting locks, disinfecting the documents and installing air conditioning, so that the best possible use can be made of them as storage stacks, offices or workshops.

A comprehensive list of equipment should also be drawn up, and any items which are obsolete or falling to pieces with age should be removed and replaced or repaired, depending on requirements.

The relevant legislation should not be overlooked in this survey—a list should be drawn up of all texts (laws, decrees, regulations, instructions and so on) pertaining to the archives and the preservation of documents in offices. All these should be examined, and compliance with any legislation still valid should be insisted on.

All these new openings will require a full-scale reorganization of the service; if it is set in order, it will be reflected in the manner in which the archives' traditional functions of preserving and providing access to documents are performed.

After the documents have been checked in, they should be treated with insecticide and moved to proper storage. At the same time, all material, including official and administrative publications and journals should be reclassified and listed, even if this work is only done in a summary manner in the first instance. This will provide an opportunity to review and check the entire archives classification system. The principle of arrangement of items according to source should be applied and, if necessary, a classification system can be introduced. If such a system already exists, it can be simplified, since its purpose is to assist the archivist in carrying out the arrangement. It should not become restrictive or over-theoretical.

Documents that are to be opened to inspection can thus be consulted by the public as they are processed.

After being reorganized and rehabilitated, the archives will become a new instrument capable of further development.

2.2.1.3 *Resumption of traditional tasks*

At the same time, with a view to providing the new means of action, an effort should be made to collect scattered historical documents, which the general survey has shown to be in very serious danger of destruction. This rescue operation should be started at the place where it is most urgent and/or most easy to carry out (for example, in the capital city).

The procedure should be as follows: the total number of such documents should first be evaluated by categories and then estimates should be made of the resources needed in respect of personnel (to carry out preparation for transfer, listing and rearrangement tasks), accommodation and equipment (for the processing and storage of the documents), credits for financing all these requirements and, finally, administrative regulations (to define the procedures relative to the transfer of such documents).

In the light of the information so gathered, an operational plan should be drawn up for priority transfers. Disinfection equipment and a restoration and bookbinding workshop will then become essential if the rescue operation is to be a success. It is at this stage that the greatest effort will have to be made because the oldest documents will be collected from premises that are not suitable for their preservation. While this plan is being carried out, action must be taken concurrently in order to prepare and fit up the new accommodation, procure equipment, increase the credits for capital expenditure and operating expenditure, draft the relevant decrees and administrative instructions.

After starting with the existing resources, the rescue operations can be carried on with enlarged facilities. In the case of historical documents, the aim is to co-ordinate the following operations: transfer, the neutralizing of destructive agents (insects, acidity, etc.), restoration, classification and listing, so as to lose as little time as possible and ensure the permanent preservation of these old documents while allowing them to be produced immediately at the request of research workers.

2.2.1.4   *Preparation and creation*
of the new general means
of action provided for in the plan

It is not enough, however, to take immediate concrete action in one sector only and to confine our efforts to rescue operations. Once the most urgent needs have been attended to, preparations have to be made to create the large-scale means of action provided for in the plan and designed to ensure that the national archives will function properly. The first step in this direction is to create an advisory body with increased powers, if necessary by converting the committee into a superior archives council, whose guidance will be essential throughout this stage.

At the same time, it will be expedient to take advantage of the reorganization of the national archives and the transfer of the oldest collections to resume the campaign to alert the public which was first started when the general survey was launched. Every opportunity should be taken to make the national archives better known through talks and lectures and even to create a more general movement of interest and sympathy through the media of the press, radio and television (as in the case of the pilot project in the Ivory Coast). This may help to stop the untoward destruction of documents in government departments.

Regulations will also have to be drafted for the recruitment and management of all categories of personnel, taking due account of the situation prevailing in the labour market. Such personnel will become stable and qualified only if they are properly integrated into the civil service. This is a necessary condition for the continuation of archives development.

The drafting of a law on archives might also begin to be considered so as to provide a firm foundation for current action and prepare the ground for later developments. Thus, while the traditional activities are still going on, this will be the most important stage in the building up of the new national archives service.

The possibility should be explored of fitting out existing premises or converting buildings at reasonable cost. It has to be ascertained whether such measures can be considered satisfactory in the long term, or whether they would be merely a stopgap offering no adequate solution to the storage problem.

In fact, the new archives will really begin to take shape when a functional building is erected for the central repository. Work must therefore be started on the necessary studies. The competent authorities (the ministries concerned with public buildings and works) should be contacted with a view to finding a sufficiently large and well-situated site. The preparation of a building project, the search for sources of finance and the integration of the project into the general development plan (involving contacts with the ministries of finance and planning), should all be undertaken simultaneously.

During the preparatory period, the chosen organizer will have been trained and have given proof of his ability and can thus either be appointed Director of National Archives or be put in charge of the service under the direct supervision of the high-ranking official responsible for the archives project.

The execution of the first medium-term plan will thus have been a time of reorganization involving the intensive development of the component units of the archives service. If an expert has been consulted, his assistance can now be dispensed with, for the archives have acquired the main assets they need for success. However, it is worth while to arrange for the expert to come back some time later. His second visit will afford an opportunity to review the situation afresh and with the benefit of a specialist's opinion. He will also be able to give advice based on experience. As he will be freer to do so without fear or favour, his remarks are more likely to be heeded. Lastly, in so doing he can help to revive the enthusiasm and drive of the early stages which may tend to flag with the passage of time, once the aim of the first plan has been fulfilled.

2.2.2   INTRODUCTION OF NEW FUNCTIONS
         (FIVE YEARS AT LEAST)

2.2.2.1   *Initial action in central government departments*
           with priority requirements

It must be remembered that during this period the traditional tasks will be pursued and that work will likewise continue on the planning of future projects and the running in of the new microfilm service.

At this stage, the archives objective should be to develop action directed towards government departments in order to prepare long-term plans for records management and the provision of intermediate repositories (*préarchivage*).[1] What will be of immediate importance is to keep the administrative authorities interested in the problem, not by asking them, as in the past, to participate in a survey, nor by taking their old documents off their hands, but rather by offering them a new service. Having been reorganized, the archives service will possess virtually exhaustive documentation covering two areas; the first being public administration, and the second the human and social sciences. The time will have come to make more of this material available to public authorities and to set up an administrative documentation centre which, in addition to providing the usual archives services, finding aids, official publications and collections of press cuttings, will bring together information about every aspect of the life of the country and hold it, not in the form of documentary files, but in that of works of reference, card cabinets and indexes. Since the archives service will be functioning as a real administrative inquiry bureau, it will even be possible, at this point, to consider publishing a monthly

1. See p. 292.

information bulletin to be distributed to all government offices. This will be an additional and permanent link with the public authorities. Such a link will be particularly useful because of the increasing tendency of government departments to set up their own documentation centres, a factor which will make it necessary to ensure that these centres are not created independently of the archives service, but under the latter's supervision fulfilling the role of correspondent. It will also be necessary to continue encouraging the goodwill and zeal of individual officials. An archivist should be made responsible for visiting them to brief them on developments, offer advice on the preservation, storage and classification of documents (see Appendix 11), and carry out more systematic and precise surveys. As the archives service extends its network of relations, it will become better equipped to perform its proper functions. (This method has given excellent results in East Africa, where it has been used by a Unesco expert.)

Such preparatory work will make it possible for the government departments concerned to resume transfers of papers in the content of which they have a special interest—public and private property, land concessions, agriculture, forestry concessions in particular, drought and meteorological phenomena, public works, files on current works and completed buildings, development projects, public health, documents on epidemics, endemic diseases and campaigns to combat them.

This in itself will ensure that the collection of historical source material will make progress.

At the same time, the first centres for the management of current files will be opened in the most favourably disposed government offices. In taking this additional step, archivists will be placing a new service at the disposal of the administrative authorities, making their work easier and paving the way for the future enrichment of their archives collections by enabling the most significant items to be selected from documentary material at the source.

Meanwhile, a number of documents containing the regulations drafted at an earlier stage will have been published, decisions will have been taken and means provided. These will then have to be introduced into the archives circuit.

2.2.2.2   *The use of the new means*
           of action developed
           by the archives service

With regard to the staffing problem, the new means of action are
the publication of the regulations governing the employment of the
different categories of archives personnel. When they come into
force it will be necessary to work out the measures to implement
them; this means determining the conditions for the integration
of the different categories of personnel, and preparing the rules
and programmes for the competitive examinations on which
the initial recruitment or in-service promotion of each category
depends.

Training courses should also be organized, either on the spot
(short elementary courses of variable duration) for staff in executive
categories or in the ministries for officials in charge of current
records management centres. In addition, lectures on the functions
and methodology of an archives service could be given to students
at schools of public administration.

Scholarships should also be provided to provide for the training
at a regional or national training school of supervisory (intermediate grade) personnel, and university graduates should be
selected for appointment, after appropriate training, to posts on
the director's staff.

The archives organization structure should be worked out, indi-
cating the number of staff in each category to be recruited each
year. A timetable should be drawn up for the steps to be taken in
organizing and holding competitive examinations, awarding scholarships, organizing training courses and so on, to ensure that
qualified personnel is available at the right time. A distinctive
feature of this stage of growth in regard to personnel requirements
is rapid development of the middle-level categories.

As far as equipment is concerned, the establishment of a complete
workshop unit should be organized, possibly in conjunction with the
library and the documentation services (see p. 270 et seq.).

However, the main question to be considered under this head
relates to the development of document storage capacity. Discussions on the construction project for an archives building should
therefore be pursued with the ministry concerned. A request for
funds should be submitted to enable the architect's brief and the

FIG. 2. Stages in the growth
of an archives service—theoretical organization chart

First stage

Service in its infancy (employing two to six people). Situation static, traditional tasks being commonly carried out by the same people.

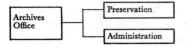

Second stage

Service partly organized, but activities still very limited (employing six to twelve people). Incipient task-sharing and specialization of staff.

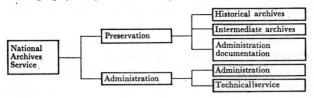

Third stage

Typical organization of a modern archives service embracing all activities (to be developed in varying degrees depending on local needs). The size of the service and the diversification of activities, lead to task-sharing and ever-increasing specialization at all levels.

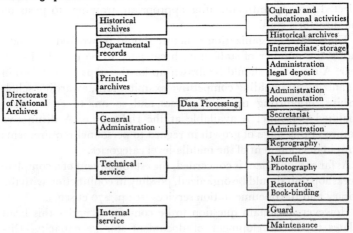

plans of the building to be prepared, at the same time as the necessary steps are taken to have the construction project included in the law defining the long-term programme. At this point, the archivists will have to indicate not only their personal desiderata, but also the material requirements and constraints of the archives service.

A special appropriation of funds will obviously be necessary for the construction of the archives building and it may be possible, as a last resort, to consider financing the project by means of a foreign loan repayable over several years. The actual work could be completed quite quickly (within one and a half years).

In order to guard against unpleasant surprises, it will be advisable to follow the progress made on the building site step by step and to be ready, when the time comes, to give precise instructions regarding the finishing work and the special fittings required, especially for the workshops. Without interfering in the architect's or building contractor's work, archivists can give advice, make suggestions and express preferences. In this context, it should be possible to obtain a good idea of what is needed and to avoid mistakes by benefiting from the experience of neighbouring archivists and by making a critical study of plans after the premises for which they were prepared have come into service.

Furthermore, at about this juncture, the promulgation of the new archives law will have to be followed up without delay by the publication of the implementary regulations (decrees and administrative instructions). As these will have been drafted at the same time as the law, on the lines considered necessary at that time, the legislative provisions and the regulations will be fully concordant.

In the meantime, the arrangements for the removal of the archives should be made several months in advance if the operation is to be carried out smoothly. Taking advantage of the general check-in, the removal operation should provide an opportunity for rearranging the holdings and, speaking more generally, for reorganizing the service. Once the removal has been completed, every effort should be made to hold on to all or part of the premises formerly occupied by the archives, as they are likely to be a useful means of obtaining the next objective, namely, the establishment of an intermediate repository policy.

2.2.2.3   *Preparations for* préarchivage[1]
*and for permanent co-operation
with government departments*

This preparatory phase will be a further period of consolidation. The rescue work undertaken at the very beginning of the archives operation will have been completed by the time this stage is reached. The classification of the greater part of the collection of historical material and the appropriate finding aids that will have been provided as the transfers were being carried out will make the archives service the principal centre for research and historical documentation in the country. As a result of the increasing number of research workers and of applications for permission to consult documents both on the spot and outside, it will be necessary, in order to guard against the risk of documents wearing out too quickly and even of being destroyed, while making it easier to produce them on request, to microfilm them for security, and even for searchroom (reference) use. One can then go on to develop the system of substituting microfilm copies for documents that have to be withdrawn from circulation.

Among old documents transferred from government offices, the archives service may find that it has rescued material concerning legislative provisions and regulations to add to the collection of the administrative documentation centre. This centre will gradually grow into an important service and its work will become widely known through a monthly information bulletin. This section of the national archives may also be led to collaborate more and more closely with the department responsible for the official gazette, by acting as the repository of its records, assisting with the preparation of indexes or even assuming editorial responsibilities. Likewise, the archives service may undertake the management of the government documentation centre, which, moreover, is often merged with its own administrative documentation centre; and indeed it is desirable, in the interests of the efficiency of all administrative documentation centres, for them to come under the archives service.

---

1. This French word has no equivalent in the English language. It embraces the whole field of the management and storage of non-current records until their disposal either by destruction or transfer to the archives.

At this point, it will at last be possible to begin to consider the introduction of automatic documentation techniques with a view to increasing the efficiency of the traditional finding aids used in archives, this being the prelude to the more thorough use of computerized data processing on a larger scale.

While pursuing these two lines of action, it will be necessary to continue to ensure a normal rate of increase in material facilities (equipment), manpower (personnel recruitment and training), the drafting of regulations (in implementation of the archives law) and financial resources (budgeting). It will also be essential to prepare for the next stage, at which the archives network will be extended both in space and time.

The studies and contacts should be undertaken which are the essential preliminaries to the establishment of the first local repository. Since the old archives will have been saved, the aim will now be to tackle the preservation of contemporary documents.

Similarly, the archives service should actively explore possibilities for converting vacated premises or finding inexpensive storage space, depending on whether one or more intermediate repositories (records centres) are contemplated (directing the search towards former administrative, commercial, industrial, or military buildings, etc.).

Meanwhile, the development of the centres responsible for the management of current files in ministries should be promoted in two ways. First, officials delegated by ministries or individual services will be given theoretical and practical training at the national archives or in a government department. Second, consultant archivists will be called in by government departments to help with the establishment and organization of new centres, and they will continue to give regular assistance especially when their advice is needed to solve problems arising on specific points (in connexion with conversion work, transfers of documents and so on).

Wherever possible, elimination and transfer schedules should be drawn up for all categories of documents.

When these conditions have been met and when the accumulation of papers in government offices makes it necessary, the first intermediate storage buildings can be equipped, thus enabling the transfer of documents to become the general practice. This will mean that government offices will be relieved of the burden of retaining documents that are no longer of immediate value, while the archives service will avoid the danger of becoming choked up with records to be kept only for a certain length of time.

As regards local repositories, the country's administrative structure may have made it possible in some instances to provide for their establishment by drawing on the resources of local rather than national budgets. As a general rule, if the repositories are of some importance, the State will often play an active part by giving financial support and providing the supervisory personnel, who will be seconded or appointed, as appropriate, by the national archives.

This further operation will usually be conducted in the country's second largest city and will be all the easier to carry out if an archives office formerly existed there.

2.2.2.4 *Establishment of* préarchivage

This seems to be the right time to introduce a records management and intermediate storage system, for several reasons. In the first place, most of the old documents of historical interest will have been brought together in the national archives; in the second place, the organization of administrative archives (departmental records) in all government departments will be well under way. When the time comes, the disposal schedules show which worthless papers can be destroyed with the consent of the archives service and which documents have to be transferred periodically to the national archives for permanent preservation. But in point of fact, these documents, although not negligible in quantity, only account for a small fraction of departmental records. The vast majority (80 per cent) comprises files that have been closed (after a certain number of years, varying from department to department and from country to country); the authorities still need to consult them occasionally, but virtually all are destined to be destroyed sooner or later. Consequently, after the archives service has ensured that the country's heritage of historical documents will be safeguarded, it will still have a second mission to fulfil: this is to organize the management of these files on up-to-date lines. This great accumulation of documents, although of little value, has to be kept and in such a way as to be readily accessible. The problem amounts to this; how to ensure, at the lowest possible cost, that documents are reviewed, listed, transferred, packed for storage, and ultimately eliminated or, in the case of those which are to be kept indefinitely, transferred to the historical archives.

It is difficult to co-ordinate all these complex operations owing to the diversity of the documents involved, their unequal value and the fact that the value of each document changes with the passage of time. These problems are similar to those encountered in the control of stocks or spare parts and there can be no doubt that, in the years to come, computerized techniques will offer a solution to a problem that is so difficult to master today.

What the archives service must do at the present stage is to draw attention to the various factors involved and ensure that the cost of keeping the papers is always proportionate to the services they are expected to render.

As regards the transfer problem, the cost of the entire operation, from the point at which documents are removed from registries up to that at which they are housed by the intermediate records centre under their final storage conditions, is not very high; it is equivalent to the cost of one year's preservation in the intermediate records centres. If the operation is well organized, and perhaps simplified, the cost can be reduced by two-thirds.

But what are the criteria for deciding whether such an operation is expedient or not?

The first criterion is quantitative and takes account of the economic and financial implications of the intermediate storage system. One way of determining whether the operation is worth while is to analyse the cost (in real terms) of keeping departmental records. In calculating this cost, no allowance has been made for the possible use of the system of substituting microfilm copies for regional documents, since this solution gives rise to a number of different problems.

A comparison of costs for the same quantity of documents can be made (see Table 14 on the following page).

The savings made on rental value and operating costs must not be swallowed up by the cost of dispatching documents for reference outside the records centre: the sum of A must be greater than the sum of B (total A > total B). The transfer of files to a records centre (intermediate repository) will only be an economic proposition for holdings that are seldom consulted.

However, this quantitative evaluation must be measured against

TABLE 14

A. In the administrative service (government department)	B. In the intermediate records centre
Rental value of the office space occupied	Rental value of the storage space occupied (ten times less)
Maintenance, administrative expenses and possibly air conditioning	Maintenance and administrative expenses (save in exceptional circumstances, no air conditioning —hence ten times less)
Furniture (seven-year depreciation)	Shelving (twenty-five-year depreciation, ten times less)
Management and handling (pay for administration personnel, including social-security contributions, etc.)	Management and handling (pay for stack attendants, including social-security contributions, etc.)
Production for consultation on the spot	Production for consultation outside the centre, involving travel (cost of transfer by van service and half a day of travel time).

means of a qualitative criterion of convenience, based on considerations not easily expressed in terms of figures. Two situations may arise:

The files are properly arranged and efficiently managed in the registries, in which case the intermediate storage system is unnecessarily time-consuming (because of the distance factor) and rather inconvenient in the case of files that have to be consulted frequently; it is only justified is total B $\leqslant \frac{2}{3}$ total A.

The files are in disorder, and then the lack of organized archives generates: functional disorders (administrative procedures are obstructed); material hindrances to the work of the service; loss of time in looking for documents (the time spent by administrative personnel); a heavier work-load owing to the need to reconstitute lost files.

An intermediate storage system which will minimize these costly shortcomings is justified if total B $\leqslant$ total A.

In the light of the above criteria, we can trace a pattern of operations through the three stages in the life of archives, and this suggests how the endless flow of papers could be brought under

Fig. 3. Pattern of integrated *préarchivage*

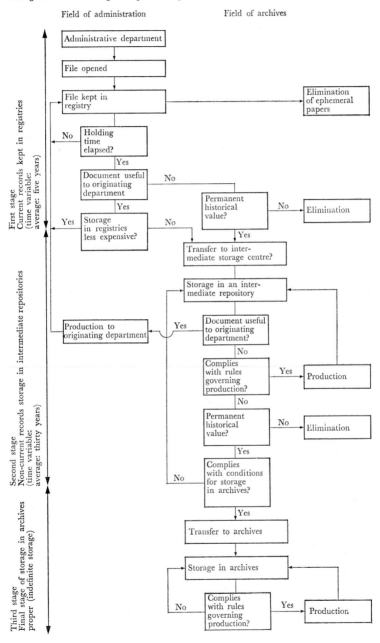

Field of administration Field of archives

First stage
Current records kept in registries
(time variable: average: five years)

Second stage
Non-current records storage in intermediate repositories
(time variable: average: thirty years)

Third stage
Final stage of storage in archives proper (indefinite storage)

Administrative department

File opened

File kept in registry → Elimination of ephemeral papers

No — Holding time elapsed? — Yes

Document useful to originating department — No

Yes

Storage in registries less expensive? — No

Yes

Permanent historical value? — No → Elimination

Yes

Transfer to intermediate storage centre?

Storage in an intermediate repository

Production to originating department ← Yes — Document useful to originating department?

No

Complies with rules governing production? — Yes → Production

No

Permanent historical value? — No → Elimination

Yes

Complies with conditions for storage in archives? — No

Yes

Transfer to archives

Storage in archives

Complies with rules governing production? — No / Yes → Production control. The solution consists in using a simulation method to show all aspects of the system (Fig. 3). This gives an over-all picture of the way in which the intermediate storage organization works. It should also be stressed that the process illustrated on the chart shows that trained archivists are soon found to be essential and hence it is quite clear that archivists should be in charge of intermediate repositories.

There is one last, commonsense argument in favour of this intermediate storage system. This is that government departments should be relieved of the burden of the management of their own files, which is not their principal function (and all too often they neglect it for that very reason). Instead, this task should be entrusted to the people who have made it their profession, namely, the archivists.

2.2.3   SETTING-UP
OF THE STATE ARCHIVES SYSTEM
(DURATION: AT LEAST FIVE YEARS)

The more remote they are from the present, the more objectives become blurred and prove difficult not so much to visualize as to programme satisfactorily. For the final objective, that of completing the national archives system, remains quite clear and can be achieved by extending the network of archives and the range of archive activities.

2.2.3.1   *Extension of the network*

The objective, at this next stage, should be to extend records management and intermediate storage systems (*préarchivage*) to all government departments. This will entail keeping up to date the card index of areas of competence, transferring all non-current documents at the stage of intermediate storage (the second stage), constantly updating the disposal schedules and transferring archives selected for permanent preservation to the historical documents repository.

The expenditure involved in operating a *préarchivage* system should be carefully evaluated: (a) if the system has been introduced because the government has become aware of the importance of the problem, it will provide the archives service with all the resources, including funds, that it needs if it is to bear the entire financial burden itself; (b) if the system has been introduced as a result of a long campaign of persuasion, the operating costs will be shared among user departments, in proportion to the amount of shelving occupied; (c) however, if *préarchivage* is only a facility that is offered, a sort of reception centre, then each department will use its own personnel, methods and procedures, and the archives will only administer the centre as premises equipped for the purpose.

The second objective should be to extend the network of local repositories to all the basic territorial subdivisions such as states, provinces and regions, since these local repositories will provide a *préarchivage* service. They should be financed, at least in part, from local budgets.

Control over semi-public archives should likewise be extended. The national archives should always be consulted when disposal schedules are being drawn up, and the documents should be transferred to them after longer periods of time, depending on the circumstances in each case.

Inquiries should be made about the papers of industrial and commercial enterprises which might be of value in relation to economic and social history, and arrangements agreed for the deposit by the former of their documents in the archives. The latter should also offer advice as to which documents can be destroyed and which ought to be kept. The presentation to, or deposit in, public archives of private papers, which are the product of the lives and activities of individuals, families, associations or societies, should be encouraged. Microfilming of these documents for the sake of safety can always be proposed.

By building up its holdings in this way, the archives service will be able to extend the range of documents which can be opened to inspection.

2.2.3.2 *Extension of the arrangements for allowing access*

Workshop activities should increase as further expert technicians are recruited and new equipment is purchased. This growth, especially in restoration and microfilming activities, will be needed to meet the demand for documents to be made available for inspection in the archives themselves or for consultation outside.

At the same time, the period of thirty years which normally has to elapse before documents may generally be opened to inspection should be reduced wherever possible, and the various finding aids should be kept complete and up to date.

The conventional approach to provide access facilities should be supplemented by more zealous efforts, of a social and educational character, to make the resources of the archives known to everybody interested in history. Various means can be used, including:

An archives museum for the permanent display of documents, its purpose being to resurrect and portray the country's history. Particular care must be devoted to ensuring the proper conservation of the documents exhibited in such a museum.

Temporary exhibitions, lectures, press and radio articles and television programmes which can be organized periodically for the general public.

An education service whose function it is to encourage visits to the museum and temporary exhibitions and to publish annotated material for the use of pupils in secondary schools.

Moreover, university teachers and historians ought not to be forgotten. If the local scientific and cultural environment is favourable, a historical society should be formed and, when possible, a professional journal published. Steps should also be taken to see that an introductory course on archives and archives science, given by professional archivists, is included in the university training of historians in all disciplines.

Searches for source materials which may be held in other countries should lead to the formulation of policies for exchanging microfilms with other archive repositories.

Within the limits of the resources available to them, archives services can contribute to the collection and preservation of oral source materials. They should also enlighten the authorities and public opinion as to the importance of safeguarding old buildings and historical sites in the context of the protection of historical monuments and the environment.

Lastly, in order to ensure that the professional standards of archivists are constantly improved, national and/or regional professional associations should be formed to facilitate exchanges of information, study problems to be discussed at congresses, lay down standards, prepare detailed studies on common problems and circulate archives documentation among their numbers.

The continual adaptation of archives services to the problems of growth they will have to face and, above all, the permanent search for new objectives and new resources in the service of the community will ensure the effectiveness of a dynamic plan.

2.2.4   EVALUATION AND CONTINUING REVIEW

Implementation of the plan should be constantly subjected to scrutiny by the Superior Archives Council, whose working document should be the service's annual report on its activities. On the basis of the results achieved each year in executing the annual plans, it will be possible to supervise the implementation of the plan and to allocate the remaining objectives among the subsequent annual plans so as to comply with the guidelines of the medium-term plan.

This continuous working-over of the plan is necessary to allow for new contingencies—urgent needs, opportunities or difficulties—which will necessitate a change in the order of priorities laid down when the plan was drafted. Recruitment, investment, the setting up of services, etc., will necessarily be affected. For example, the quantity of documents produced for government departments and academic research workers may prove very different in both volume and substance from the original estimates.

The annual report should therefore contain a complete set of statistics on the basis of which the true growth of the different activities can be measured and a decision reached as to whether the objectives have been attained or not, or whether they have been exceeded. From an analysis of these results, new trends can be identified, time limits can be put forward or backward, policies can be adjusted and, above all, new objectives can be selected in the light of new exigencies and new prospects.

The return on investment in the development of archives services should also be evaluated on the basis of calculable data, such as the saving made by the government as a result of the introduction of records management and intermediate storage, searches conducted for the government or private individuals, furnishing of information and so on. A management accounting system should be systematically used to measure the utility of such investments and their rate of amortization.

However, the contribution which archives make to the development of a country is not only a matter of increasing administrative efficiency and improving the quality of the information available to the decision-making organs of the State. Account has also to be taken of the invaluable contribution which archives make to the quality of life of the nation and of the international community at large. Here lies the importance of archival development, which unquestionably helps to promote cultural wealth and civilization. This is why we must preserve the evidence of each country's past which is the common property of all mankind.

Appendixes

I   Note concerning a superior archives council or commission, or advisory committee on archives

Aim. To enlist the participation of producers and users of archives in the framing of archival policy.

Membership. It shall comprise:

Qualified representatives of the administration
From the chief ministerial departments
(Finance, planning, civil service, education, home affairs, justice, public works, foreign affairs, defence, etc.).
From the regional authorities (commissioners, prefects, etc.).
From the universities (faculties of arts and law) and academic research institutes.

Professional archives staff
The head of the administration responsible (parent department).
The secretary-general of the government (secretary to the cabinet).
The director of the national archives.
The directors of federated State archives services, in the federal States (in order to ensure better over-all co-ordination of archival policy).
Representatives of autonomous State archives repositories, who are not subject to the jurisdiction of the State Archives Central Directorate (repositories of ministerial departments).
One or several representatives, elected or delegated by staff associations, from various categories of staff (central and local archives, professional and sub-professional personnel).

Various members
Of parliament.
Of the supreme court.
Of State enterprises.
Of chambers of commerce.
Of the major religious bodies of the country.

Functions. The Superior Archives Council is an advisory body presided over by the secretary-general of the government (secretary of the cabinet) or by the minister of the parent department responsible. Its functions are:

To be consulted on all projects of a legislative character relating to the archives or to the fields of activity which they cover.

To participate in the preparation of archival regulations.

To co-ordinate the country's archival policy.

To give its opinion concerning the establishment or modification of the archives network.

To give advice on procedures with regard to transfer, destruction and consultation.

To ensure the adequate distribution of staff and the application of staff regulations.

To comment on the annual report on the operating of the national archives service.

To determine priorities when the archives plan is being drawn up.

To propose objectives to be financed by the government and to be attained by the archives, and to monitor their implementation.

Functioning. The council shall meet every six months or once a year.

A standing committee, meeting more frequently, shall be empowered to take emergency measures. The chairman of this committee shall be the parent authority or the secretary-general of the government (secretary of the cabinet), and the secretary, the director of the national archives.

The operating principles and the terms of reference of the council shall be determined by law, whilst the texts regulating the application of the law shall set forth the (changing) details of its membership and its functioning.

2 Outline model law on archives[1]

Article 1. Definition of the public archives. They are the property of the State and are inalienable and imprescriptible. They include documents of every form and nature originating from the State authorities, organs and offices as well as those originating from public corporations and economic industrial enterprises belonging to the State or under its control.

Article 2. The responsible archives authority. As the archives have an inter-ministerial mission, they should be placed under an authority situated at the highest level of the State (president of the republic, offices of the prime minister or secretariat-general (cabinet office) of the government).

Article 3. The Archives Directorate-General. Organization and jurisdiction. The directorate-general shall be the organ of the State for all matters relating to archives. The director-general shall be appointed by the council of ministers.

Article 4. Definition of the following concepts: current departmental records, *préarchivage*,[2] transfer to the archives.

Article 5. The different categories of public archives repositories under the control of the directorate-general: central State archives, intermediate repositories for departmental records, territorial archives (archives of territorial subdivisions: provinces, regions, *départements*, etc.).

Article 6. The Superior Archives Council, responsible for determining archival policy and for planning in this field. Membership of the Superior Council: chairman, secretariat-general, *ex-officio* members and appointed members.

PART II. PROVISIONS RELATING TO STAFF

Article 7. Definition of categories of staff: professional staff, executive staff and sub-professional staff.

---

1. This outline was drawn up by the working group on 'Archives and co-operation' set up by the Minister of Cultural Affairs at the Archives Directorate of France (report of June 1972), with whose authorization it is reproduced here.
2. See page 292.

Article 8. Professional qualifications and procedures for recruitment, appointment and promotion: to be specified in the appropriate regulations.

Article 9. Rules of procedure concerning current records preserved in government departments: approval of these rules by the archives directorate-general and supervision of their application.

Article 10. Destruction of departmental records which need no longer be kept, formal approval by the archives directorate-general.

Article 11. Transfer of documents to intermediate records centres (repositories): time-limits for transfer, possible exceptions in the case of documents of a confidential nature.

Article 12. Transfer of documents to the central State archives.

Article 13. Procedure for transfers referred to in Articles 11 and 12. Special regulations should be established separately for each ministry.

Article 14. Disposal of documents which are ripe for destruction in the intermediate or central archives repositories. Formal approval by the originating department.

Article 15. Government departments preserve the right to consult freely the documents transferred by them in pursuance of Articles 11 and 12.

Article 16. Compulsory deposit in the central archives of two copies of all publications originating from public offices and bodies.

Article 17. All the provisions contained in Articles 9 to 15 apply, with the necessary adaptations, to the territorial archives. In the absence of a territorial archives service, the director-general of the archives shall exercise jurisdiction as defined above over the archives of public offices operating within the territorial area.

Article 18. The archives directorate-general shall be responsible for the material preservation and integrity of documents transferred to the central State archives and to the territorial archives.

Article 19. The archives directorate-general shall be responsible for sorting, classifying and listing documents preserved in the central State archives and in the territorial archives.

Article 20. The archives directorate-general shall be responsible for collecting and preserving copies of documents relating to the history of the country and preserved abroad.

Article 21. Standards as to physical preservation. Obligation to have premises specially set apart for the preservation of documents. Security regulations. Protection against the elements, accidental damage and biological agents.

Article 22. Documents, according to their nature, shall be open to consultation by the public on the expiry of a variable closure period.

Article 23. These specific periods shall be defined by the Superior Archives Council and shall come into effect when approval has been jointly signified by the minister in charge of the archives and the minister responsible for the department from which the documents originate.

Article 24. Exceptional cases of non-applicability, with the authorization of the originating department and on the proposal of the director-general of the archives.

PART VI. NON-PUBLIC ARCHIVES

Article 25. Definition of archives in this category: archives of notaries, economic bodies, cultural institutions and associations and organizations of every nature.

Article 26. Measures for the protection of these archives.

Article 27. The central archives and the territorial archives of the State shall be empowered to accept non-public archives on deposit or as a gift.

PART VII. PENAL PROVISIONS

Article 28. Penalties for infringements of the following provisions: alienation or destruction of public archives (Art. 1); improper destruction of documents in government departments (Art. 10); improper destruction of documents in repositories under the jurisdiction of the archives directorate-general (Art. 14); non-deposit of official publications in the central archives (Art. 16); violation of security regulations (Art. 21); improper communication or divulgation of documents in repositories under the jurisdiction of the archives directorate-general (Art. 24).

3 Standards for the recruitment of the different categories of staff for a typical national repository

If what is really required is to provide a country with a workable archives system, the following figures may be put forward as guidance. But obviously, for a much larger organization, the standards might be quite different.

Supervisory and/or directive staff

1 director or organizer (assistant director), then as the service expands:
1 person in charge of historical archives.
1 person in charge of records management and intermediate archives (*préarchivage*).
1 person in charge of printed archives and administrative documentation.
1 person in charge of general administration.
1 person in charge of each local repository.
1 person for each ministry or for each group of ministries, according to requirements, in charge of *préarchivage* and the supervision of current records management.

Executive staff

1 for each kilometre of documents.

Repository staff (attendants, storemen)

1 for each kilometre of documents, i.e. 1 for every executive officer.
3 for each kilometre of documents in intermediate records centres (*préarchivage*).
3 for each kilometre in local repositories.
Temporary staff may be hired for major and urgent work (removals, transfer operations, etc.).

Technical staff

2 restorer-binders and two photoprinters-photographers are the strict minimum.
The binding workshop, especially if it functions as a pool (i.e. common service), may comprise from 20 to 30 persons.

Likewise the restoration workshop (there is often an enormous amount of work to be done).

The photographic and microfilm service may function effectively with a staff of 3 (if the corresponding equipment exists). Here, too, everything depends on requirements.

At all events, a foreman will be necessary for a maximum of 12 persons. Beyond this figure, work will have to be divided up progressively as the service develops.

General and maintenance staff

At the very least there will have to be a secretary to the director, an accountant, a shorthand typist, a driver, a caretaker, a person in charge of internal services, plus, at least, one secretary for each departmental head.

Standards for the construction of a typical national archives repository

(capacity of 9,000 linear metres or the equivalent in linear feet)[1]

Administrative unit (100 m²)

Office of the director (30 m²).
Secretariat (15 m²).
Typing (15 m²).
Offices for professional assistants: minimum of two (20 m² each).

Unit for reception and processing (110 m²)

Room for taking delivery of transfers (20 m²).
Room for fumigation, desinfection and removal of dust (20 m²) suitably equipped.
Room for sorting, arrangement and classification of transfers (50 m²).
Room for documents scheduled for destruction (20 m²) provided with a system for the destruction of paper and means of external transport (vans) and internal transport (trolleys).

Storage unit (1,300 m² of standard shelving)

Six storage units or stack areas (about 200 m², i.e. 1,500 linear metres each) provided with fire-proof doors.
One stockroom (20 m²).
Special rooms for the preservation of maps and plans, microfilms and photographs, magnetic tapes and other machine-readable documents (80 m²).
Stairs and a goods-lift where necessary (i.e. if there is more than one floor).
It is recommended that provision be made for storage accommodation capable of meeting anticipated requirements for ten years to come.

Technical unit (100 m²)

The figures shown are those for workshops each employing only two workers; this is why they have been grouped together in units of two.

1. The following figures are to be converted, where necessary, into square feet.

Restoration-binding (30 m²). Where there are more than two workers it will be necessary to divide the two activities up, and even, where there is a larger number of staff, set up separate workshops for each.

Microfilming-photography; the same remarks apply. The size of the workshops is often dependent on the work assigned to them.

Photographic studio (20 m²).

Developing room (20 m²).

Instant copy room (30 m²).

Reference services (searchroom) (260 m²)

Entrance hall (30 m²) and information office.

Reading room for twenty readers (100 m²).

Special sound-proofed or darkened areas for viewing audio-visual archives (20 m²).

Administrative documentation room (30 m²).

Exhibition and conference room (80 m²) connected to the reading room and for use by the educational service.

Possibly, a permanent museum.

Miscellaneous (150 m²)

Cloakrooms and washrooms (30 m²).

Welfare service (30 m²).

Air-conditioning unit (30 m²).

Storeroom for supplies (30 m²).

Garage and car park (30 m²).

Housing

Possible accommodation for the director and the caretaker.

A small apartment for visiting colleagues.

5   List of miscellaneous archives equipment

Shelving

Preferably this should be of metal and the shelves should be adjustable. This shelving (shelves and uprights) should, after being specially treated, be given a coating of enamel paint in order that it may stand up to wear and use and be protected effectively against rust.

It should be erected in the storage (stack) rooms in the form of double-sided shelving, in rooms 2.2 m high with lanes measuring 0.65 m and 1 m (to permit circulation), there being six shelves (1 m × 0.40 m) between each pair of uprights.

In the case of compact mobile shelving, it will be wise to choose a simple and sturdy system: double-sided shelving, set on manually operated roller-tracks, whilst ensuring suitable air circulation.

Storage cabinets for plans, maps and posters

Vertical cabinets with the maps suspended seem preferable to horizontal ones; the documents are easier to handle and to locate; there is no danger of them becoming crumpled or rolling up and they are not exposed to abrasion. But the documents must first of all be perfectly flattened, attached to a cardboard strip and, where necessary, reinforced.

Vertical filing cabinets

On rollers for transfer schedules, location lists of official and periodical publications.

Sliding drawers for card indexes

For indexes on cards, for microfilms and microcards, photographs and postcards.

Material for packing and handling operations

Storage boxes, folders and protective covers, straps, labels, etc.
Trolleys for moving documents.
Shredding machine.

Furniture for searchrooms and offices

Reading room, room for sorting and classifying documents: large tables
(3.60 m × 1.50 m × 0.76 m high).
Offices.
Chairs and armchairs.
Cupboards and vertical filing cabinets.
Typewriters and adding machines.
Tape-recorder.

Display material

Adjustable panels.
Spot-lights.
Mural and horizontal display cases (1 m × 0.60 m × 0.20 m) on tabular metal
tube stands.
Material for audio-visual montage.

Equipment for conservation

Recording thermometers and hygrometers.
Dehumidifiers, humidifiers.
Industrial vacuum cleaner.
A fumigating chamber for the disinfection of documents.
Fire extinguishers (powder) for the storage (stack) rooms.
Fire extinguishers (foam) for the workshops.

6   Standards for the equipping
and operating
of a typical bindery

EQUIPMENT

Major items

Universal binder.
Standing press (60 cm × 50 cm).
Hand cutter for boards (cutting length 80 cm or 110 cm).
Hand guillotine (cutting length a minimum of 45 cm).
Possibly, hand cutter for paper.
Binding table with a large top (2.50 m × 1.60 m approximately).
Rack for the flat storage of boxes and papers.
Stools with adjustable backs.

Minor requirements

Sewing frame, slitting saw, scissors, dividers, glue and paste brushes, square with
and without wooden stock, bone and boxwood folders, backing hammer, rulers
with graduated straight edges, polishing iron, boxwood band-stick, large beating
stone, large-size cutting and backing boards, dowels, finishing tools, zinc plate,
knives for cutting and paring, etc.

OPERATIONS

Supplies

Binding calls for a wide range of fairly awkward and cumbersome articles, a stock
of which should be established when the workshop is being set up:
Boards of varying thickness.
Muslin, linen thread and string, paste and glue.
Coarse linen (jute cloth or register), head-band.
Different types of papers (cover paper, end-paper, marbled in different colours,
    of different strengths).

Maintenance

Maintenance of the machines is comparatively simple.

7 Standards for the equipping and operating of a typical medium restoration workshop

To a large extent the equipment is the same as for the bindery; in addition the following must be provided:

Major items

Special table for restoration work.
Glass-topped table for lamination by the Indian process.
Possibly a laminating machine (cold process).
Document dryer.
Tables and chairs according to requirements.
Tape-edging machine for maps.
Foam fire extinguisher.

Minor requirements

Scales, enamelled bucket, scalpels, dusting brushes, sheets of glass (glass-plate), solvent-proof brushes, three pyrex bottles (30 l), bottle of carbon dioxide (CO_2), reinforced valve for nitrogen from the bottle of CO_2, etc.

Services

For fumigation and disinfection (either a vacuum fumigating, or small hermetically sealed chamber).
For deacidification: two work-sinks for immersion (80 cm × 55 cm × 20 cm), draining boards (at least 65 cm × 55 cm), filtered running water.

OPERATIONS

Supplies: glue, rag paper and chiffon in various sizes, Japanese tissue, a wide range of cellulose acetate, technical acetone, technical quicklime in pieces, precipitate of pure calcium carbonate, absorbent cotton wool, fairly thick blotting paper, etc.

8 Standards for the equipping and operating of a typical microfilm workshop

Major items

Still camera, it should be in a fixed position, it should use 35-mm film and be able
 to photograph old registers, maps, newspapers (minimum size 50 cm × 60 cm).
A voltage rectifier and possibly a transformer should be laid on.
Automatic developer (a water-filter will always be necessary).
A continuous microfilm processor for positive or negative silver film.
In tropical countries this process should be chosen rather than diazo duplication
 that uses film which is more difficult to procure, more sensitive to heat and
 which does not last as long as photographic film.
Table for checking of microfilms (viewing apparatus and splice).
Cabinet for storage of spools.
Microfilm reader: electrostatic reader-printer.
Tables and chairs as necessary.

Minor requirements

Buckets and washing facilities, vessels made of opaque plastic (for the sake of
 durability).
Sheets of glass (plate glass), winding reels, etc.

Services

Electrical points with earth connections.
Supply and drainage of water (flow, pressure and temperature should be adapted
 to the equipment).

OPERATIONS

Maintenance

It is absolutely necessary that specialist servicing arrangements (through a maintenance contract) should be made to ensure emergency repairs. Likewise, a stock of spare parts for the different machines (at least light-bulbs, fuse-wire, etc.) should be assembled, bearing in mind local delays in obtaining replacement parts.

Supplies

Film (preferably film sufficiently sensitive to be able to photograph even very dark paper should be chosen).

Developing solution and fixing solution (if production is small, these solutions should be obtained in made-up form).

9 Standards for the equipping and operating of a typical photographic workshop

EQUIPMENT

Major items

Still camera: standard photographic camera.
Manual developing tank.
Enlarger: a medium-sized appliance (6 cm × 9 cm, maximum size) should be
used with sets of condensers and lenses.
Sodium-vapour lamp.
Masking frame.
Timer.
Plastic bowls of different sizes.
Rotary drier glazer.
Tables and chairs as necessary.
Sliding drawers for storage of negatives and photographic prints.

Minor requirements

Plastic buckets and vessels for washing, funnel, scissors, cloths, rubber gloves,
squeegee rollers, rust-proof pliers, etc.

Services

Dark room with screens and sealed windows.
Electrical points with earth connexions.
Large plastic basins with adequate supply of water.

OPERATIONS

Maintenance

May be ensured by the local supplier and/or a contract in conjunction with the
microfilm service.

Supplies

Whatever is most easily obtainable locally should be used: film, paper, products.

10   Standards for the equipping
      and operating of a typical
      instant copy unit

EQUIPMENT

Major items

Instant copy: electrocopying machine (electrostatic photocopy).
Multicopy: electric typewriter with carbon film, with variable characters or
mechanical justification for the composing of texts or the direct typing of
offset plates; vacuum printing frame for offset plates; offset duplicator on table
(equipped with an additional inking block); collator; jogging machine; thermo
binder (American binding); spine binder; stapler.

Services

A sink with filtered water.
Electric power current (high voltage) and large number of power points.

OPERATIONS

Maintenance and supplies

No special difficulties particularly if locally obtainable materials are used, as these
are very common processes.

Specimen of a survey
     questionnaire intended
     for government departments

In order that archival development may be satisfactorily planned, it is necessary for a wide-ranging survey to be organized at the level of all public offices producing archives, in order to obtain all relevant information, arrange for transfers, regulate the destruction of documents and institute records management procedure (*préarchivage*).

If a coherent record management and disposal policy is to be implemented, especially in the initial phase, a perfect knowledge of each institution is called for, and this is all the more difficult to acquire in that this is a field which so far has received relatively little attention. It is absolutely necessary for the administrative and structural organization charts to be created for each department and for each functional unit. This is an exacting task and one which is made all the more difficult by the fact that often important structural reforms come about as a result of an unpublished decree, a circular, or simply a memorandum, which it is very difficult to trace. Once office notices have been assembled, it will be far less difficult to organize and to keep up to date a systematic record of organizational structures.

The way in which this survey is carried out will vary a great deal from country to country owing to administrative realities (rules and traditions) and also material and human resources.

The example that we give below constitutes a way of proceeding which seems to us to combine flexibility with efficiency. The survey is conducted in two stages:
The archives parent authority writes to the head of each ministerial department
   to remind the latter of the purpose (laid down by the law) of the archives service
   and to request his approval and his assistance in having a short written
   questionnaire distributed among all the sections and offices of the ministry. This
   short questionnaire is accompanied by a brief and tactfully worded note
   describing the national archives and the services which the latter can provide.
After this first contact has been made and when the results of the questionnaire
   have been received, survey staff will be able to be sent into the offices armed
   with a second and far more specific and detailed questionnaire, the results of
   which will be of use in putting the final touches to a records management and
   disposal policy (*préarchivage*) and in the drawing up of the plan.

Questionnaire no. 1
(to be circulated among heads
of departments and branch offices
in the ministry)

Name of the department:
1. Are you at the present time in a position to ensure the preservation of your departmental records (do you have adequate premises and staff)?
2. If not, would you like to make transfers to the national archives and at what intervals?
3. Do you make an administrative deposit of your printed or duplicated documents? If so, to whom?
4. What quantity of documents do you preserve (number of files, metres of shelving occupied and/or volume)?
5. What is your annual production of records (number of files created and metres of shelving they occupy)?

Questionnaire no. 2
(survey for the organization of records and archives in public departments)

This questionnaire should be filled out by divisions, departments and branches in each administration. Replies should be as detailed as possible. In order to obtain an exact assessment of your ministry's requirements with regard to archives, specific information must be provided in the first part concerning your department, its present organization and its history.

1. *Organization of the department*

1.1 Name
1.2 Initials or abbreviation by which known
1.3 Address
1.4 Date of creation and reference to the legislative texts and/or regulations creating and organizing the department
1.5 Functions: give references or attach the texts defining them
1.6 Names and abbreviated titles of predecessor departments (dates of reforms and references to the texts making mention of these changes). Former functions if applicable.
1.7 Administrative authority to which the department is attached
    Ministry
    Directorate
1.8 Services coming under it (external services in particular)
1.9 Organization chart (copy to be attached)
1.10 Name of the head of the department (director, deputy director, branch head), previous post, seniority in present post
1.11 Name of his predecessor, present post
1.12 Number of staff and distribution by categories

2. *Nature of the documents preserved*

2.1 Documents created and preserved in originals by the department
    Studies
    Personal files, accounts, etc.

2.2 Documents created and preserved in the form of copies with the original sent elsewhere
Outgoing letters
Reports

2.3 Documents received in the course of administrative transactions and preserved incoming letters

2.4 Documents received and dispatched for information only

2.5 Year of origin of oldest documents

2.6 State of preservation (good or bad)

3. *Quantity of record holdings*

Approximate quantity of documents in the department at the present time (in linear metres of shelving)

3.1 Files and other assemblies of papers (containers, box-files, bundles)

3.2 Registers
Printed documents
Special categories of documents (give number)
  Total
Maps and plans
Photographic documents
Films
Card indexes
Listings
Others

4. *Annual rate of accrual (in linear metres of shelving)*

4.1 Files and other assemblies of papers (containers, box-files, bundles)

4.2 Registers

4.3 Printed documents

4.4 Special categories of documents
Maps and plans
Photographic documents
Films
Card indexes
Listings
Others

4.5 Equipment for document reproduction (photocopy, roneo, offset) and for destruction (shredding machine)

5. *Physical conditions of preservation*

Accommodation and services

5.1 Places where the documents are stored

5.2 Conditions of preservation
Temperature of the premises and relative humidity

Ventilation
Air conditioning
5.3 Protection against:
Fire
Theft
Light
Insects and rodents
Furniture (storage capacity in linear metres)
5.4 Filing cabinets
5.5 Metal (or wooden) cupboards
5.6 Shelving
Metal
Wood
5.7 Special items of furniture
5.8 No furniture

6. *Organization of current records*

6.1 Does a records service exist for the department?
6.2 Name and position in the hierarchy (cf. organization chart) of the officer responsible for records (departmental record offices)
6.3 Type of registry system used to control documents (a copy of the classification system may be attached)
6.4 Number of years on average after which the documents are no longer of current interest
6.5 Are any procedures operated for destruction of documents?
6.6 System used for the review and weeding of documents (a copy of the disposal schedules (with destruction periods) may be attached)

7. *Organization of the national archives*

7.1 Does the department wish to delegate one of its own staff to the national archives to be responsible for its own documents?
7.2 Approximate quantity (in linear metres of shelving) of documents which could be transferred immediately to the archives
Files and other assemblies of paper (bundles, boxes, jacket-files)
Registers
Printed documents
Total
Miscellaneous documents requiring special conditions of preservation
7.3 State of arrangement of the documents which could be transferred (percentage and quantity):
Classified and with lists provided
Classified, but without finding aids
Unarranged

Bibliography

Archivum (international journal on archives published under the auspices of Unesco and the International Council on Archives)[1] of which:

Archives legislation. I: Europe. Part I: Germany-Iceland, vol. XVII, 1967. 268 p.

Archives legislation. I: Europe. Part II: Italy-Yugoslavia, vol. XIX, 1969. 258 p.

Archives legislation. II: Africa, Asia, vol. XX, 1970. 243 p.

Archives legislation. III: America, Oceania, vol. XXI, 1971. 239 p.

ASSOCIATION DES ARCHIVISTES FRANÇAIS. *Manuel d'archivistique, théorie et pratique des archives publiques en France.* Paris, SEVPEN, 1970. 805 p.

BAUTIER, R.-H. Principes de législation et de réglementation des archives. *Manuel d'archivistique tropicale*, p. 33-58.

CARBONE, Salvatore; GUÈZE, Raoul. *Draft model archival law: description and text.* Paris, Unesco, 1971. 243 p. (Studies and research, 1.)

DAVIES, John. *A study of the basic standards and methods in preservation and restoration workshops applicable to developing countries.* Paris, Unesco/ICA, 1973. 83 p. (Mimeo.)

DUBOSCQ, Guy; MABBS, A. W. *Les dépôts de préarchivage/Records centres.* Paris, Unesco/ICA, 1973. 194 p. (Mimeo.)

DUCHEIN, Michel. *Les bâtiments et équipements d'archives.* Paris, ICA/Unesco, 1960. 312 p.

EVANS, Frank B. *Automation and archives in the United States.* n.d., 21 p. (Mimeo.)

GONDES, Victor. *Reader for Archives and Records Center Building, the Society of American Archivists.* 1970. 127 p.

JØRGENSEN, Dr Harald. *Rapport sur le coût des services d'archives présenté devant la XIVᵉ Conférence Internationale de la Table Ronde des Archives (1973).* 94 p.

KECSKEMETI, Charles. *Archives, développement et souveraineté nationale (1971).* 20 p. (Mimeo.)

LEISINGER, Albert H. *A study of the basic standards for equipping, maintaining, and*

---

1. With the exception of *Archivum* no mention will be made of the various regional or national professional journals in which we found a large number of articles which were of great assistance to us both at the level of formulation and information.

operating a reprographic laboratory in archives of developing countries. Paris, Unesco/ICA. 1973. 120 p. (Mimeo.)

PEROTIN, Yves. L'administration et les 'trois âges' des archives. *Seine et Paris,* no. 20, October 1961. (This joint work contains several specialized chapters particularly on the preservation of documents.)

Recommendations of the Seventh International Congress on Archives, Moscow, 21–25 August 1972. 14 p. (Mimeo.) (See also the different reports submitted to this congress, which have been published.)

SCHELLENBERG, Th. Programme pour l'établissement d'un service d'archives publiques. *Manuel d'archivistique tropicale.* p. 9–15.

——. *Modern archives, principles and techniques.* 2nd ed. Chicago, Ill., The University of Chicago Press, 1957.

VALETTE, Jean. *Le rôle des archives dans l'administration et dans la politique de planification dans les pays en voie de développement.* Paris, Unesco, 1972. 79 p. (Mimeo.)

VERHOEVEN, F. R. J. *The role of archives in the public administration and the national planning policy of developing countries with particular reference to South-East Asia.* Paris, Unesco, 1972. 73 p. (Mimeo.)